WHOSE *is this* SONG?

BALKAN NATIONALISM, GREECE AND SHARED CULTURE

EDITED BY
ELENI ELEFTERIAS KOSTAKIDIS

This book is copyrighted. All Rights Reserved. No part of this publication may be reproduced, stored in a retrieval system, or transmitted, in any form or in any means — by electronic, mechanical, photocopying, recording or otherwise apart from any fair dealing for the purpose of private study, research, criticism or review, as permitted under the *Copyright Act 1968*, — without prior written permission. Enquiries should be made to the publisher.

© Eleni Elefterias 2024

PO Box 513 Ashfield NSW 2131
elenielefterias.com.au
eleni@elenielefterias.com.au
hellenictheorem@gmail.com

First published 2024 by Hellenic Theorem Publishers.

The moral right of each author has been asserted.

Every effort has been made to trace and acknowledge copyright material in this publication. The authors and publisher would welcome information from copyright holders who could not be traced.

Copy Editing by Alfred Vincent.

Layout Design by Marina Thiveos.

ISBN: 978-0-6468199-4-5 (Paperback)

Dedicated to the memory of my parents
Eleftheria (nee Amanatidis) and Vasilios Kostakidis
who left the Balkans to migrate to Australia
and who 'threw a black rock behind them' never to return.

Contents

Dedication

Acknowledgements... 1

Foreword
Mary Kostakidis 3

Part One – On the Film and the Tune 5

1. Introduction: Exploring Balkan Cultural Topography Through Documentary Film
   Eleni Elefterias Kostakidis 7

2. *Whose Is This Song?* Nationalism And Identity Through The Lens Of Adela Peeva
   Eleni Elefterias Kostakidis 13

3. From A Distant Place: The Ownership And Uses Of A Melody
   Alfred Vincent 35

4. Patriarchy And Nationalism In Adela Peeva's *Whose Is This Song?*
   George Michelakakis 61

Part Two – The Balkans 69

5. Four Views Of The Balkans From Down Under
   Marian Țuțui 71

6. The Visual Heritage Of The Manakia Brothers In The Balkan Countries
   Marian Țuțui 77

7. The Balkans In Europe: And The Curse Of Too Much History
   Helen Vatsikopoulos 89

8. Greek Music And Its Formal Complexities
   Vrasidas Karalis 107

9. The Mediterranean World, Identity And Migration: Some Ancient And Modern Examples
   Nicholas Doumanis 123

10. The Balkans: Europe's Periphery
   Michael Karadjis 137

11. Fortress Europe
    Jorge Sotirios 165

12. Balkans So Close Yet So Far
    Costa Vertsayias... 181

13. Absorbing Greece: Its Historic Impact On The Balkans And Near Neighbours
    Billy Cotsis 193

14. Afterword: The Inspiration For This Book
    Eleni Elefterias Kostakidis.. 207

15. The Balkans: Reference Notes
    Alfred Vincent.. 211

Acknowledgements

I would like to acknowledge the help of Dr Alfred Vincent in the production of this book. His insights, suggestions, expertise and willingness to spend many hours on editing have been invaluable.

I am deeply indebted to the director of the documentary film *Whose Is This Song?*, Adela Peeva, and thank her for allowing me to use the cover of her DVD as my book cover and to include photos taken directly from her film.

I am sincerely grateful to Professor Vrasidas Karalis for always believing in me and encouraging my writing; to my sister Mary Kostakidis and brother-in-law Professor Ian Wilcox for their constant moral and financial support and their kind encouragement; to Harry Fandakis of AHEPA Chapter Chiron for his support and to AHEPA NSW for funding some of the production costs; to the committee of the *La Boîte Performance Space* for their support and also for funding part of the production costs; to Dr Helen Vatsikopoulos for all her encouragement and guidance; and finally to my family who have supported and helped me throughout the publishing process.

Eleni Elefterias Kostakidis

Foreword

The Balkan region with its fascinating historical and geopolitical intricacies and shifting borders is a cauldron of contested ownership of culture.

Nowhere else is the apparent strong relationship between culture and identity so categorically challenged at every level, and with it, the notion of cultural ownership so vital to the traditional prism through which groups are defined and differentiated. And yet it is the commonality that is captivating – with perhaps its most enchanting manifestation in music and song, the topic that lends the book its title.

We need to recognise and celebrate this commonality. The study of this phenomenon is vital – it may indeed contribute to the development of an alternative way to look at our fellow human beings, an antidote to pernicious nationalism.

Australia is home to many migrants from the Balkans. Though many were glad to leave behind the political and social upheaval and the internecine hatred, the connection with this enchanting place persists for generations.

It will be no surprise to many who know her that this book has been put together by Eleni Elefterias Kostakidis. Music continues to be the passion of my sister's life. She is treasured by students for her inspiration and warmth and by many in the broader community for her contribution to the enrichment of cultural life, providing an ongoing opportunity for musicians and writers across cultures to come together over many years.

My hope is that the book will inspire you to navigate the Balkans in all their complexity.

Mary Kostakidis

PART ONE

On the Film and the Tune

ELENI ELEFTERIAS KOSTAKIDIS

Introduction: Exploring Balkan Cultural Topography Through Documentary Film

Mother: Do birds know about borders?
Child: No.
Mother: How come you know?
Child: Because I'm human.
(from the film *Mother Europe* by Petra Seliškar)

This book arose out of my interest in the Balkans after readings suggested to me by my supervisor, Professor Vrasidas Karalis, Chair of Modern Greek and Byzantine Studies at the University of Sydney.

The focus was to be on documentary films on the Balkans, and in my search I came across many fascinating documentaries, such as *The Majority Starts Here* by Lode Desmet, *Mother Europe (Mama Evropa)* by Petra Seliškar, and *Twice a Stranger* by Andreas Apostolidis and Yuri Averof. These and many other films present a view of the Balkans as an area of communities which in the past had lived closely together, sharing aspects of their culture such as music, songs, dances and folktales, but which were now divided by nationalism and religious differences. These divisions, together with the creation and occasional re-drawing of national borders, all added to problems of identity and led to governance issues in the often very fragile modern states. All these films advocate strongly for peace and co-operation between communities, and each one is a beacon of hope projecting a voice of reason in the region.

But the film that inspired me most, probably because of my music background, was *Whose Is This song?* by Adela Peeva. I knew the tune in question, having heard the Greek version many times. The fact that a tune could cause so much discord was a small glimpse into much larger issues of nationalism, borders, democracy and human rights. It was as if a wound had been opened and underneath there lurked the gangrene of hatred and racism, where even the smallest of things, such as a tune or a dance, could incite violence. I was intrigued and decided to use this documentary as the focus of a thesis on the Balkans. The title of this book refers specifically to Adela Peeva's film.

Books on the Balkans by Australian writers have mainly focused on the World Wars and the role of Australian forces. Not much has been written by Australian writers on the Balkan communities themselves, particularly in the aftermath of the break-up of Yugoslavia. This is surprising, since Australia is home to so many communities from the region. Hence I decided to compile this book by inviting historians and other writers to offer a variety of points of view on Balkan topics.

Countless tunes have travelled the length and breadth of the Balkans, especially under the Ottoman Empire, and have been assimilated into the musical heritage of different ethnic groups. Even today, many songs with Turkish versions are popular in Greece: "Kalenin bedenleri" / "Σήκω χόρεψε, κουκλί μου", "Darıldın mı gülüm bana" / "Χαρικλάκι", "Zeytinyağlı yiyemem" / "Γιατί θες να φύγεις", and "Bekledim de gelmedin" / "Περιμένω μα δεν ήλθες" are just a few examples. The song featured in Peeva's film has one of these shared tunes with a particularly wide distribution over the Balkans.

Many of the instruments used in Greek folk music have counterparts in other Balkan cultures: the bagpipes, the pear-shaped fiddles (such as the *lyra, lijerica,* and *gadulka*), the violin, the long-necked lutes (including *bouzouki, bağlama, cura, tamburica* and many more), the hammered zither (*sandouri*), the shawm (*zournas, zurla*) and the more recently introduced clarinet. The musics of Bulgaria, North Macedonia, Serbia, Romania and parts of northern Greece often feature brass instruments like the horn and the trumpet, used prominently in the work of Bosnian composer Goran Bregović.

I wanted to create a work that would include some basic information about the Balkan area together with an in-depth discussion of Peeva's documentary. The contributors are all people I have had the good fortune to meet personally (or, in one case, online) in my career; they are mainly of Greek heritage, from Australia, together with one from Romania. They are all experts in their fields, and have taught and/or published on history, film studies, music and other aspects of Balkan culture. Their views are not uniform and are not necessarily those of myself as compiler and editor. On the contrary, I have tried to include a variety of different approaches. Each author is responsible for their own statements and for the accuracy of the information they provide.

Geographically, the Balkan peninsula is the area of southeastern Europe that can be roughly marked off by a line from around the northwest corner of the Black Sea to the northeast corner of the Adriatic. The word "Balkan" is believed to derive from Turkish *balkan,* denoting a chain of wooded mountains. The area received its name from the Balkan Range, which runs from the Serbian-Bulgarian border eastward through central Bulgaria to the Black Sea.

In terms of political communities, the Balkan region is usually thought of as including the states of Albania, Bosnia and Herzegovina, Bulgaria, Croatia, Greece, Kosovo, Montenegro, North Macedonia, Romania, Serbia, Slovenia and the European part of Turkey. Of these. the largely Albanian-speaking Kosovo, formerly part of Serbia, has not gained universal recognition as a sovereign state. Hungary has sometimes been included in the Balkans, but really belongs more to Central Europe, despite sharing some historical experiences with its southern neighbours. Although both Slovenia and Croatia are often regarded as Balkan countries, partly because of their incorporation into former Yugoslavia, their people tend to identify more with central Europe. Romania is not, mostly, within the geographical area we have described, but it is useful to include it with the Balkan states because of its largely shared history.

Most of these countries were once part of the multinational Ottoman Empire; some northern areas, in particular Croatia, were linked to the Hungarian kingdom, later the Austria-Hungarian Empire. Earlier still, most areas were either an integral part of the Byzantine Empire, or were at least strongly influenced by Byzantium in religion, culture and governance.

The formation of the modern nation-states can be dated back to the First and Second Serbian Uprisings of 1804 and 1815, which led to the recognition by the Ottomans of Serbia as an autonomous vassal state. Serbia became formally independent in 1878 and in 1918 was merged into the Kingdom of Serbs, Croats and Slovenes, later renamed

Left to right: Solon Lekkas, Lesvos, 1946-2022, singer and stoneworker; Omer Pobrić, 1945-2021, the "accordian wizard", Sarajevo; Tereza Kreshova Cingit, Albania, 1949-

Yugoslavia. Montenegro, mountainous and remote, had been largely autonomous, ruled by its its prince-bishops under Ottoman sovereignty; it became a principality in 1860, a kingdom from 1910, and was united with Serbia in 1918, hence becoming eventually part of Yugoslavia.

Meanwhile, the Greek Revolution of 1821 led to internationally recognized independence in 1830. Subsequently Greece acquired further territories with Greek populations: the Ionian Islands in 1864, formerly Ottoman Thessaly in 1881, southern Epirus and Greek Macedonia in 1912, Western Thrace in 1920 and the Dodecanese in 1947.

Romania was created by the merging of the Ottoman vassal states of Wallachia and Moldavia in 1862 and gained formal independence from the Ottoman Empire in 1878. Bulgaria became a principality under Ottoman sovereignty in 1879 and gained full independence in 1908. Albania was finally established as an independent state in 1913.

The formation of national states out of larger entities has continued dramatically in recent years with the break-up of the Federal Republic of Yugoslavia, starting in 1991, when the individual states began to establish their independence. Kosovo, formerly an autonomous region within Yugoslavia, is still not universally recognized, as we have mentioned.

As a result of this history the term "Balkanization" came to be used for the process of fragmentation of a large political entity into smaller independent units. It has come at the cost of bitter territorial

The Balkans

disputes, war and sometimes ethnic cleansing. The fact is that in past centuries few Balkan regions had homogenous populations. Almost everywhere there was a mixture of religions, languages and cultures. The absurdity of insisting on rigid ethnic labels for people in these fluid societies is illustrated by the Manakia brothers, famous as pioneer Balkan filmmakers.

Despite its conflicted and often tragic history, the Balkan area is actually a rich, complex mosaic of languages, cultures and religions, a creative melting-pot which has much to offer now and in the future. If this book helps to foster understanding and appreciation of its diverse heritages, it will have served a useful purpose.

Our hope is that this book will provide valuable insight for the general reader about the Balkans and the situation there. It could also be a good introduction to the area for students of Balkan politics, society, music, cinema or general culture. We would like it to be a chronicle of the Balkan peoples' substantial commonalities, a tribute to their rich and varied cultures, and a testament to the aspiration of harmony for the region and its peoples.

Eleni Elefterias Kostakidis

Whose Is This Song? Nationalism And Identity Through The Lens Of Adela Peeva

A search for truth

"The unexamined life is not worth living" (Socrates)

The film *Whose Is This Song* portrays the Balkans as a palimpsest of overlapping cultural layers and explores the imagined cultural and ethnic stereotypes of those communities through a well-known shared tune. It is a documentary about a popular melody that is common throughout the Balkan region, but which is the cause of much dissension and is the incitement for the events portrayed in the film. Many have commented on, or tried to trace the archetype of, the song "Üsküdara gider iken" ("On the way to Üsküdar", the Turkish version) or "Από ξένο τόπο" ("From a foreign land", a Greek version). As Adela Peeva says in the film, she is on a quest for "the discovery and communication of truth".[1] This paper is mostly concerned with the "documentary voice" created by the director through the scenery she selects to show and the subjects she chooses to interview.[2] How she uses her camera lens, and its focus on the background, not only adds to the mystery of the film, but more importantly helps to focus on the greater issues of cultural similarity and perceived diversity, of nationalism and identity within the Balkans.

---

[1] Gail Pearce, Cahal McLaughlin (eds.), *Truth or Dare, Art and Documentary*, Bristol: Intellect, 2007.
[2] Trish Fitzgibbons, Pat Laughren, Donald Williamson (eds.), *Australian Documentary, History, Practices and Genres*, Cambridge: Cambridge University Press, 2011, p. 16. On documentary film in general see also: Carl Rollyson, *Documentary Film*, Expanded edition, New York: iUniverse, Bloomington, 2010.

Adela Peeva is a Bulgarian documentary film-maker who has been involved in the making of over thirty international films.[3] Her documentary *Whose Is This Song?* is considered an international work as it was part of a project developed within the European Documentary Network, including workshops in Thessaloniki, Greece and Dubrovnik, Croatia, with funding by various European sponsors. The film stresses the importance of the geographical context in a region that shares a cultural and historical past. Some of the films by Adela Peeva made in the period before 1989 were banned by the communist authorities.[4] Peeva's films *Whose Is This Song?* and *Divorce Albanian Style* are till now the only Bulgarian films, in the whole history of Bulgarian cinema, nominated by the European Film Academy for European Film Award for Best Documentary (Prix Arte).

Whose Is This song? begins with a dramatic reconstruction in a "performative mode", where the filmmaker herself is sitting at a table with friends enjoying a meal in the Turkish city of Istanbul. Peeva as narrator describes how the conversation that night gave her an idea for the documentary. The presence and positioning of the camera lens, accompanied by the narration, creates initially a kind of "direct cinema" style,[5] but as the story unfolds the film reverts to the tradition of "cinéma vérité", in a more interactive and even a "reality" mode.[6] The participants in this first scene behave as if there is no camera. The camera itself does not focus on any person in the beginning. It frames the action and stays still at one end of the table. In fact, it is as if the camera itself is an appendage of the table or even another guest. The style is akin to a feature film rather than a documentary. The voice-over, Peeva's own voice, begins to narrate, as if retelling a story, remembering an event in the past tense, replaying the scene, directing the audience, but it is also like an exposé that both the viewer and the narrator share. This narration sets the autobiographical tone of the film.

---

[3] Adela Peeva has been working as a director for TV stations in former Yugoslavia and in the Studio for Documentary Films and the Studio for Feature Films in Sofia. She has been a teacher of Documentary Film and a juror in a number of Film Festivals. See her biography at https://adelamedia.net/adela-peeva.php, accessed 5.9.23

[4] These include her films *Mothers,* which received the Silver Rhyton prize at the National Non-fiction Film Festival, and *In the Name of Sport,* which was awarded the Critics' Prize at the same festival.

[5] Fitzgibbons et al. (as in note 2), p.5.

[6] This "promotes communicative exchange between filmmakers and participants through, for instance, techniques such as interview, talking heads and testimony" (Fitzgibbon et al., p. 6).

Left: *Whose Is This Song* (DVD cover artwork). Right: Adela Peeva

The scene is set for the style of "cinéma vérité" in Balkan documentary film for which Adela Peeva is well known. The film is autobiographical for Peeva, as it involves the director herself in the pursuit of a childhood memory of a song with which she identifies. The director not only directs the film, she acts in it, she is the narrator, she is the interviewer and her reactions are documented as the reactions of the "other", whether it be another "missing" ethnic group, the audience or the viewer. "Cinéma verité" or "observational cinema" works well in this form of documentary as it combines improvization with the use of the camera to unveil hidden truths; but it can also provoke a reaction from the subjects being interviewed, which in turn exposes the "imagined" of their perceived reality.

When the camera position changes to scan across three members of the orchestra, it is as if the camera is invisible. A close-up of the female vocalist, singing "Üsküdar'a gider iken", one of the Turkish versions of this song, a love song (the other being a military march), ignites the argument at the table where our director sits with her multi-ethnic friends. Through the frame of a door, a third camera peers in at the director, who is speaking to the guests at her table, adding to the realism factor of the "cinéma vérité"; the main characters, oblivious to the existence of the camera, argue among themselves as they each claim the song originates in their own country. Suddenly, the camera imposes on the party, giving us a close-up of one man's face, and Adela speaking to another male at the table as they try and argue their case; in Adela's words: "Then we started a fierce fight: Whose is this song?" The fight was in fact not "fierce" but merely rather animated, entertaining and even funny, as Adela herself seems to be quite theatrical.

Again, the camera focusses on the orchestra and the singer. The band consists of two violinists, an *oud* (*outi*) player and a *kanoun* (*kanonaki*) player, a percussionist playing *toumbeleki* (a goblet drum) and the vocalist, the only female. In front of the musicians and on the stage is a very big and old-looking wooden chest, covered in books, and an old wooden music stand that the violinists and the singer seem to be reading their score from. It is very appropriate for the whole theme of this film as the wooden chest can be seen as a keeper of the culture, a treasure chest that has travelled and ended up here in Istanbul surrounded by people of various backgrounds. A Pandora's Box full of the rich and colourful Ottoman culture, bringing with it both the wonders and the woes of the area. Even the wall in the background, with its broken and missing plaster, and the many small frames hanging on it, gives a feeling of the war-torn history of the past and adds to the song's significance. The scenery and the atmosphere of this tavern make sense, adding to the mystery of the song. The "documentary voice" is introduced and lives in the scenery, the atmosphere and the music of this typical Turkish, but also very much cosmopolitan, restaurant.

Suddenly, the camera is out of the restaurant and in front of Adela as she walks uphill through a narrow picturesque street in Istanbul. She visits a CD shop and asks for the recorded version of this song. From this scene on, she employs a type of reality cinema where it seems as if she is randomly talking to people on the street. As a documentary filmmaker she has succeeded in incorporating her research on the topic, seemingly coming by chance upon interesting characters to interview. The people she speaks to are used to express not only the "documentary's voice" but also the "director's voice", uncovering the issue of belonging. The sense of belonging to one culture and therefore rejecting the "other" is a theme her film is trying to develop through this song. As one review attests, the film explicitly reveals how a popular musical piece can become associated with any given national imaginary (for example Albanian, Bulgarian, Greek, or

Turkish). It comes as no surprise that the characters categorically refuse to accept that representatives of a foreign, though neighbouring, community could sing the same melody and love it as they do. By a bitter irony, instead of dividing them, the song binds together these national territories like a thin red thread, uniting collective memories and personal stories. Above all, however, according to this reviewer, it shows "the typical Balkan predisposition to stubborn negativism".[7]

The film has been advertised as a "funny, dramatic and tragicomic search for the truth about a song" that has been claimed by the various peoples mentioned as their unique heritage. It is, in fact, an exposé of the character of the people of the Balkans, especially at the time it was filmed in 2003, so soon after the Bosnian-Serbian conflict. "In the Balkans, the issue of the search for roots is raised because of collective forgetfulness."[8] The elements common through Ottoman cultural influences are thrust aside in the search for unique national identities; common elements in the culture of the Balkan region are ignored or rejected. Cultural aspects considered good are considered the heritage of the "one chosen culture" and the "collective memory" is discarded. This issue of identity, or lack of it, is one of the main causes of struggles in the area. According to the DVD's cover, it is a "film showing with a sense of humour some of the typical features of the character of the peoples of the Balkans, as for example their habit of appropriating all that is good and denying the others the right to possess the same qualities, the same songs, the same customs, the same temperament".[9] The first man Peeva interviews in Turkey insists the song is Turkish. "No!" he says, "It is not Arabic, Greek? No! It is Turkish!" Another says it is a symbol of being Turkish and as Turkish as "shish kebab and Turkish delight". And so the film continues as Adela travels to search for the "truth" from Turkey to Greece and then to Albania, North Macedonia, Bosnia, Serbia and Bulgaria. Adela approaches the Balkans as a type of shared "historically connected, cultural space", something that almost all the people she interviews are ignorant of.[10] They are not

---

[7] Gergana Doncheva, National Academy for Theater and Film Art (NATFA), Sofia, Bulgaria. From https://www.kinokultura.com/specials/5/song.shtml, accessed 5.9.23.
[8] Petia Slavova, "Adela Peeva, Bulgaria. *Whose Is This Song?*" in Matthieu Darras and Maria Palacios Cruz, (eds.), *Balkan Identities, Balkan Cinemas,* NISI MASA, European Network of Young Cinema, 2008, p. 36.
[9] *Whose is this Song?* DVD Cover.
[10] Margit Rohringer, "Case Study I: 'The Balkans' Cultural Historical Context or the

interested in the "uncomfortable facts, which refuse to be fitted in", and which, as Maria Todorova says, "we find ourselves ignoring or distorting so that they do not disturb these established assumptions".[11]

Film is the perfect medium for expressing political situations, historical perspectives and national pride; how other or different nationalities appear or do not appear is paramount. The presence and treatment of the "other" in these films expresses the society portrayed. The perception is that in order to claim an identity a culture must differ from the culture of the "other". Therefore, differences are magnified and even sometimes manufactured. In this documentary, Adela Peeva is aware of the "other" and brings it to the attention, through this beautiful melody, of all those she interviews; however. their reactions confirm the divisions between the cultures in the Balkans. She tries to counter this omission of the "other" in her documentary by suggesting to each ethnic group that maybe this song originated elsewhere; however, the need to feel a part of a privileged identity makes the people distance themselves from the rest. Her camera captures this raw reality and questions it. It is the documentary voice, her "voice", an autobiographical gaze at the many troubled "imagined communities" that make up the Balkans.

In Serbia, a Roma community claims the song was sung by a famous Gypsy singer, Koštana. Adela finds and speaks to a couple who say they are Koštana's grandchildren; the camera focuses on their wrinkly faces and toothless smiles; their sincerity. Here her film reverts to an old, highly sexualized, film portraying the very attractive Koštana singing the melody, a different version still, in a musical-theatrical production. Later, she comes across a Roma parade celebrating St George's Day where they play a version of the song in a lively brass band style. The loud music, happiness and joy of the Roma parade is then juxtaposed with the absolute silence and severity of a young Serbian priest. He appears in his study, surrounded by books, giving the impression that he is well-educated and "civilized" in comparison to the Roma enjoying themselves out on the street. He questions why the "Gypsies" should celebrate St George's Day at all. Further

---

Question *Whose Is This Song?*" in her *Documents on the Balkans – History, Memory, Identity. Representations of Historical Discourses in the Balkan Documentary Film*, Newcastle (UK): Cambridge Scholars Publishing, 2009, p.85. See also the introduction by Saša Vojković to her edited volume, *Re-imagining the Balkans* (= *New Review of Film and Television Studies*, 6.1 [2008], pp.1-4).

[11] Maria Todorova, *Imagining the Balkans,* Oxford: Oxford University Press, 1997.

evidence of the non-homogeneity in the Serbian nation is when the priest blames the well-known Serbian composer Goran Bregović and the internationally acclaimed filmmaker Emir Kusturica for the popularization of such "Gypsy" music and even refers to the "gypsification" of Serbian music, the term being derogatory and outright racist.

In the later twentieth century, nationalism once again prevailed in the area, with the many ethnic groups vying for independence and sovereignty. When the government of the Yugoslav federated republic of Bosnia-Herzegovina declared its independence from Yugoslavia in 1992, war broke out and over the next several years, "Bosnian Serb forces, with the backing of the Serb-dominated Yugoslav army, targeted both Bosniak (Bosnian Muslim) and Croatian civilians for atrocious crimes resulting in the deaths of some 100,000 people" by 1995.[12] Peeva's documentary does not focus directly on these issues, though the background scenery speaks for itself with the shattered and torn buildings in Bosnia and Albania. Her goal is to expose the many problems and differences between these nationalities; the tragedy and the comedy of it all. She exposes the ridiculousness of the situation, that they are willing to fight over a song.

Adela Peeva uses the same tragic-comic mode in her film *Divorce Albanian Style,* with its light-hearted title but very serious topic, about the separations enforced on Albanians married to women from the Soviet Union, after a political falling-out, by the Albanian government in 1961. "Since the fall of Soviet-styled socialism there has been an explosion of discourses about nationalism and nostalgia. Many critics have pointed out that nostalgia signifies a longing (algia) to 'return' home (nostos). The construction of a homeland, driven by longing, in turn can conveniently be used as a means of legitimizing the 'emerging' nation-state after the age of (Ottoman, Russian, Austro-Hungarian) empire and the Old World order."[13] The nationalism of the people interviewed is evident and representative of the various cultures in the Balkan area. Their inability to recognise the familiar, the shared memory, leads them to such preposterous claims regarding this song. "This 'return' to the nation-state, however", as Benedict Anderson and Stathis Gourgouris argue, "is more a product of imagination and dreams than an historical fact, since it involves more the recent past (and even present) than

---

[12] https://www.history.com/topics/1990s/bosnian-genocide , accessed 5.9.23.
[13] Kriss Ravetto-Biagioli, "Reframing Europe's Double Border", in Anikó Imre (ed.), *East European Cinemas,* New York and London: Routledge, 2005, p.182.

recollecting a more distant past."[14] In reality there can be no "return" to an imagined past, only the nostalgia for a medieval feudal kingdom.

Through the "documentary voice" Peeva has succeeded in breaking through the barriers which separate one ethnic group from the other, simply by acknowledging the existence of what they share. Through the use of the melody, she shows how foolish nationalism is and how much all these people have in common. It is, however, how the people interviewed view the "other" that stands out in the film. The way they view themselves as "special" and the song as their property, their community's unique heritage, exposes the identity they have created and the nationalism that is forever re-shaping their collective memory.

Re-inventing a cultural and national identity of belonging

"Man is an animal suspended in webs of significance he himself has spun" (Clifford Geertz)[15]

The Balkan region has had two crucial historical legacies. One is "the millennium of Byzantium with its profound political, legal, religious and cultural impact. The other is the half millennium of Ottoman rule that gave the peninsula its name and established the longest period of political unity it had experienced."[16]

Though there is no precise definition of where the Balkans start and where they end, the Balkan Peninsula is a geographical and cultural region of Southeast Europe of some 490,000 km^2.[17] Once part of the Ottoman Empire, from the early nineteenth century most of the Balkan area has progressively split up into smaller states, each fighting for independence, sovereignty and a national identity. This balkanization continued in the area after WWI and again during the breakup of Yugoslavia in the 1990s.

"Ottoman rule is considered to have been a major interruption in the development of the Balkan countries as part of Europe, and is conceptualized

---

[14] Ravetto-Biagioli, ibid., p. 182.
[15] Clifford ,Geertz, *The Interpretation of Cultures,* London: Fontana Press/HarperCollins, 1993, p.5
[16] Todorova, *Imagining the Balkans*, p. 9.
[17] The Serbian filmmaker Dušan Makavejev is clearly bring facetious when he suggests that Asiatic Turkey, Austria and Hungary could all be included in the Balkans. Note the humorous title of his text: "Dans les Balkans, là où les rivières coulent au-dessus des ponts", *Positif,* no. 479, Jan. 2001, p. 42, and quoted in Darras and Palacios Cruz (eds.), *Balkan Identities, Balkan Cinema* (see above), p.15.

as a significant impediment to the fulfilment of these nations' European goals."[18] During the Ottoman period, which lasted roughly between 400 and 500 years, the whole area was a mixture of various ethnic groups who shared many aspects of the same culture. Later on, this shared culture and historic memory would be set aside in an attempt to grab as much territory as possible. Each ethnic group struggled to lay claim to various aspects of the culture as well and to preserve or maintain what they perceived to be their own unique heritage. The balkanization of the area was, therefore, based on the differences between one ethnic group and the "other". "All identities are constructed"[19] and this "territorial identity is a fundamental anchor of belonging."[20] Similarities were claimed as heritage or influences that had been somehow either borrowed or stolen. This rise in nationalism in the area accounts for much of the hostility between neighbouring states and so their focus has been on their "differences" rather than their "similarities". Therefore "what is called cultural identity is constantly compared to and at the limit conflated with 'national identity'."[21]

Religion has been another basis of dissention, as we see when Adela visits the Muslim sections of Albania, Bosnia and North Macedonia. "Religious practices and symbols" are "thought of as affirmations of cultural identity or of privileged anchoring points for *imputing* a cultural identity."[22] Each nation within the Balkans, despite its shared heritage, is far from a homogenous society. The Serbian priest who remarked about the "gypsification" of his culture and what he refers to as "the Balkan evil" is an example of this mentality of nationalism, which is encouraged by the State in an effort to keep the nation "pure" and strive to be more western European. The importance of "identity" that "is people's source of meaning and experience" is in itself not evil.[23] After all, it is natural for all humans to want to belong to a community. It is only when one's identity becomes nationalistic, when it is based on the non-existence of another person's right to the same identity, that it becomes outright dangerous. It becomes the source of evil evident in

---

[18] Dina Iordanova, *Cinema of Flames. Balkan Film, Culture and the Media,* London: Palgrave Macmillan 2009 (or British Film Institute, 2001), p. 36.

[19] Manuel Castells, *The Information Age. Economy, Society, and Culture,* Volume II: *The power of identity,* Second edition, Chichester: Wiley-Blackwell, 2010, p.7.

[20] Castells, as above, p. xxiii.

[21] Étienne Balibar, "Culture and Identiry", in John Rajchman (ed.), *The Identity in Question,* New York and London: Routledge, 1995, p. 177.

[22] Balibar, "Culture and Identiry", p.180.

[23] Castells, as above, p. 6.

"ethnic cleansing" during the breakup of Yugoslavia and elsewhere in the Balkans.

Culturally none of these countries want to be seen as being part of the Balkans and "the political situation, the historical background, the mixture of nationalities and the issue of national pride all make the position of the 'other' in the Balkans a particularly complex and interesting element of filmmaking."[24] The negative connotations of being Balkan are "a synonym of war and painful tragedy"[25] and of "exoticism, ambiguity and 'third-worldization'".[26]

In the Bosnian capital of Sarajevo, in the background, the lens captures the remnants of the war, which are evident, as many damaged buildings are still standing, with people still living in them, even though walls are missing and the buildings are open to the elements. There is no need for narration as the camera conveys its own story. The question "Whose song is this?" could just as well be "Whose story is this?" A story of the Balkans using this beautiful tune as the catalyst.

When, in Albania, Adela asks if the song could be Serbian, she is told: "Serbs have no traditions". The situation is the same in most of the other countries she travelled to. In Albania the camera shows scenes of children playing on the military bunkers, of which, as the narrator tells us, there are 750,000, built by the dictator Enver Hoxha to keep others out, a reminder of the long period of communist rule in the country and the lack of freedom. This is the raw face of the Balkans. It is in total opposition to the façade of a civilized western nation that the singer wants to portray when she says, "We are the most ancient of peoples", as if that is some claim to civilization. The fact that the Albanians may well have been in the area for 4,000 years and view themselves as descendants of the ancient Illyrians is used as a strong case for Albanian nationalism.[27] What has occurred since is forgotten. "In the Balkans the issue of the search for roots is raised because of collective forgetfulness."[28] As Peeva asks people on the street for their opinions

---

[24] Jasna Žmak, "Introduction: Claustrophobic Balkans", in *Balkan Identities, Balkan Cinema*, as above, p. 10.

[25] Maria Palacios Cruz, "Imagining the Balkans in Film", in *Balkan Identities, Balkan Cinema*, p. 15.

[26] Maria Palacios Cruz, as above, p. 18.

[27] http://www.balkaninsight.com/en/article/serbian-and-albanian-gcontrasting-history, accessed, 6.9.23.

[28] Slavova, as above, p. 36.

about the song, they fervently claim it as their own and scoff at suggestions it could also belong to any of their neighbouring countries. Here in Albania the song sounds like a classical song, accompanied by guitars and mandolins, a wonderful fusion of the country's Ottoman and Italian influences.

Balkan cultural identities are constructed around a perceived glorious historical past, a common language, folklore, music and dance. Culturally groups tend to be "self-defining in terms of their ability to articulate differences between self and other."[29] These are attributes that people are willing to die for in the belief that their cultural or ethnic group is somewhat superior or different from the "other". The achievement of this new, reconstructed identity and sense of belonging, as Balibar says, "is never a peaceful acquisition: it is claimed as a guarantee against a threat of annihilation that can be figured by 'another identity' (a foreign identity) or by an 'erasing of identities'".[30] Authenticity in music and identity are closely related as "it focuses a way of talking about music, a way of saying to outsiders and insiders alike 'this is what is really significant about this music, this is the music that makes us different from other peoples'."[31]

With the term "balkanization" coming to be perceived as "the tribal, the backward, the primitive, the barbarian" many nationalities want to distance themselves from it.[32] In fact, the term "Balkan" is a term of such contention in this area that Croatia and Slovenia have issued "documents explicitly stating their desire not to be referred as 'Balkan'" as they strive to be considered European.[33] The Balkans are always the "others". The fact that new intellectuals and filmmakers are now going back to the "orientalization"[34] of the Balkans in an effort to renew the cultural similarities once enjoyed by all in the Ottoman period is a much welcomed respite from the almost self-flagellation of the Eurocentrist Balkan martyr, who is trying to beat the devil (the Ottoman heritage) out of his system in an effort to identify with what is perceived as a more civilized and cultured Western Europe. This "re-imaging" of the

---

[29] Martin Stokes (ed.), *Ethnicity, Identity and Music. The Musical Construction of Place*, Oxford: Berg Publishing, 1994, p. 5.
[30] Balibar, as above, p. 186.
[31] Stokes, as above, p. 5.
[32] Todorova, *Imagining the Balkans*, p.1.
[33] Dina Iordanova, *Cinema of Flames*, Second Edition, London: Palgrave Macmillan, 2009, p. 34.
[34] Iordanova, as above, p. 56.

Balkans, whereby the Ottoman history is embraced, is one of the underlying issues in many of Peeva's documentary films and the "lens", or point of view, from which she views these issues.

One fact remains, "because of its proximity but also because of a period of some 500 years of occupation by the Ottoman Empire, much of the Balkan Peninsula has music clearly related to and often even definitely a part of the music of the Middle East."[35] This cultural diffusion in the area has led to many shared cultural activities, including in the fields of dance, music and traditional crafts. The "Üsküdar" song attests to this, as do a myriad of other tunes. Songs such as, for example, the Turkish and Greek "Smyrna" versions of "Fırtına" ("Στο'πα και στο ξαναλέω"), "Aman Doktor" ("Αμάν Ντοκτόρ"), "Izmir'in Kavaları" ("Ο Τζάκιτζης"), "Gözün aydın" ("Αρμενάκι"). There is even an Albanian equivalent of the famous Greek "Dance of Zalongo" ("Χορός του Ζαλόγγου"), the music of which has been attributed to various people as early as the 1800s. One of the earliest recordings I found was a version by Panos Glykofridis in 1926, based on a traditional 7/8 rhythm, with no lyricist listed.[36] This is an example of a song that eventually became entrenched in the national song repertoire taught in schools and therefore can no longer be associated with "folksong" as such.

The common themes of some Balkan folksongs go back much further, centuries in fact. An example is the Greek ballad "The Bridge of Arta" ("Το γιοφύρι της Άρτας"); in Serbia, a similar ballad is known as "The Building of Skadar" and in Romania as "Mesterul Manole" ("The Masterbuilder Manoli"). The common theme is human sacrifice of a woman, often the Master Builder's wife, in order for a structure to stand strong. This same theme is also present in the oral ballads of Albania and the other cultures of the Balkan Peninsula. Who knows where this notion of human sacrifice originated? The common narrative motifs in various versions of this song are all similar: the building that cannot be built, the demand for sacrifice of the wife of the Master Builder or some other prominent person, that person's vain attempt to avoid the sacrifice, the trick by which the victim is put in place. The idea of human sacrifice has been around from antiquity. We have only to remember the Homeric legend of Iphigenia, who was sacrificed by her father

---

[35] Bruno Nettl (ed.), Bruno Nettl, *Excursions in World Music*, Fifth Edition, Upper Saddle River (NJ): Prentice Hall, 2008, p. 61.

[36] https://vmrebetiko.gr/item/?id=5341 accessed 16/11/2023

Agamemnon so that the winds would come, and his ships could sail. More recently, the same themes are used in new musical works by the classical composers of the area, such as Manolis Kalomiris' opera *The Master Builder* (Ο Πρωτομάστορας, first performed in 1916), with a libretto based on Nikos Kazantzakis' play of the same name, which was, in turn, inspired by the ballad of "The Bridge of Arta". These poems, passed down from one generation to another in oral tradition, do not necessarily share an archetype, an original, that can be pinned down to one particular area. Their multiple variations were evolved over the centuries over large areas of Europe, the Middle East and Asia. These shared elements of culture are the beauty of cultural diffusion, though at the same time they are the nemesis of nationalists as they deconstruct all that nationalism stands for.

After the collapse of the Ottoman Empire and the constant re-invention of historical contexts the folk tunes took on a new function. They went from songs to be enjoyed at secular festivals such as harvest time and on religious occasions to songs expressing a national identity performed at nationalistic celebrations. In the process of nation building as homogenous ethnic nations of the Balkans, common folk tunes, like other cultural attributes, were appropriated and their new "pure" identity created. When nations are being torn apart and new nations are forming, the folksong takes on a new role in unifying the ethnic group by supporting the idea of a collective historical memory.

With the onset of recording the dissemination of the music changed from an aural-oral process to a fixed "learn it from the record note-for-note" approach, which meant the music and lyrics became stagnant. It also meant that those who first recorded a song claimed it as their own original work. This is the case with many of the *rembetika* songs recorded in America by Panayiotis Tountas in the 1920s and 30s, which many listeners assume he composed. Once folksongs are recorded and notated in songbooks they stop being folksongs, their function changes. "They became national songs learned from songbooks and taught in classes… and sung at concerts."[37] In other words they are claimed by a nation as being part of its cultural repertoire. They become identifiers of culture and ethnicity. They change from "melodies sung unaccompanied to choral settings with harmony, and from songs that existed in many variations to standardized versions."[38] Semiologically,

---

[37] Nettl, as above, p.19.
[38] Nettl, as above, p.19.

they take on a new meaning. From that moment on they have a different life to the creative process and fluidity they had before.

The function of a song in the construction of an identity is paramount as folksongs have always been important in the creation of cultural awareness. Sometimes this is used in a nationalistic way to help form an identity that is perceived to be unique.

A song's journey

"Only when all of us — all of us — recover our memory, will we be able, we and them, to stop being nationalists" (Xavier Rubert de Ventós)[39]

The peoples of the Balkan area shared many cultural characteristics, the transmission of music through the aural-oral tradition being one of them. As Nettl says, "Music is a cultural universal; it is not a universal language"[40]; therefore the idea that music is universal crossing borders and that it unites us all is a fallacy. What is true is that different cultures adapt a melody and create an entity that performs a function in that society or community. In this way a new identity is constructed and the melody is identified by one ethnic or cultural group as belonging to them. This can happen simultaneously in different parts of the world. In the Balkans, the same basic folk tunes, for which there was no written notation, have been adapted, stories or histories created surrounding their pre-existence or conception, and they then are used to form the identity of that ethnic group as they see themselves. The aural way that music is disseminated in such cultures, and the constant re-invention of tunes, was a natural process or phenomenon culminating in multiple authorships and variations of the same tune.

However, another influence on the folk tune is when "different cultures' musics are affected differently when they come into contact with other musical cultures"[41], as once these folk tunes travel to different nations they are almost certainly influenced by the various musical traditions and outside influences of that particular region. This occurs when different localities create different re-imaging of the music, thus simultaneously creating an entity that satisfies their cultural modes of expression. For example, in Albania, the song takes on a classical air, whereas in Turkey it is both a love song but also a military march celebrating the fall of Constantinople in 1453, where the German band

---

[39] Quoted in Castells (as above), p.30.
[40] Nettl, as above,. p.13.
[41] Nettl, as above, p.14.

style musical influence is apparent. Historically, German band music was very much a part of the Ottoman Empire as the Ottomans used German maestros to organize their military marching bands.

On mainland Greece it is known as "Από ξένο τόπο". However, Peeva does not travel to the Greek mainland, but instead to the Greek island of Mytilene. Of the Greek versions the most interesting was the one of the almost toothless Solon singing in a Greek taverna whose rendition of the Mytilenian song, "Έχασα μαντίλι μ' εκατό φλουριά" ("I lost a handkerchief with a hundred gold coins") was similar to that of a Turkish-style *amanes*, recalling the Ottoman influences on the island.

In North Macedonia (previously FYROM)[42]. the camera follows Adela to the house of a Dervish community leader, Baba Orel. Orel asks the director: "Let me dress up properly first" (meaning for the camera) before they interview him, but the camera is already rolling, documenting this reality. He claims it is a jihad song used for the islamization or rather the radicalization, of the people in Bosnia.

While travelling in the car the camera records Adela being accused of not being objective by her North Macedonian driver, as in his view she is only showing the culture of Muslims in his country. She does not cut this from the scene. It adds to the reality of her search for "truth" and "cinéma vérité" style. The culture is not homogenous. There are great differences of religion and even dialect in many of the countries in the film. The camera scans the ruins of an old dilapidated Orthodox Church. The suffering of these people is evident. The driver says that too much emphasis is placed on historical events in the Balkans. He doesn't care whether Alexander the Great was Macedonian or Bulgarian, "He waged wars, he lost, that's that!" The fact that he did not know that Alexander was never defeated in battle just highlights the fact that many of these people don't know their collective history at all. However, more important and very current is the young man's plea when referring to the whole Balkan area: "We are too preoccupied with history, that is our fault". In a way this young man, in need of a job in a crisis-riddled southeastern Europe, sums up the problems of his generation who are stuck in a time warp and used as pawns by various nationalistic governments. Hence he contributes to the expression of the "documentary voice" in the film. He sees history as being meaningless

---

[42] At the time of filming North Macedonia was known as the Former Yugoslav Republic of Macedonia.

to his survival. His remarks underline the use (or misuse) of history to justify the unjustifiable, the use of a mythologized past in order to validate a nationalism worth dying for.

At a Serbian dinner party, Peeva provocatively plays a Bosnian song with the same tune, which may not have been the best tactic since these countries were only recently out of a war with one another. "This is theft!" one of the guests exclaims. Whether she got the effect she expected or not, the party broke up with Peeva and her crew forcefully asked to leave. She seemed quite upset. This is the first instance when we see that there is a camera and that its presence is acknowledged, when she instructs the camera person to continue recording even though a skirmish is breaking out. She wants it all documented. All in all, it was a good outcome as it added to the "documentary voice" of the film and the context she wanted to explore.

The documentary ends in Bulgaria where the reaction is as bad as in Serbia. Even though Adela remembered it as a lyrical melody in a love song "A Clear Moon", it has been adopted as "the anthem of the Strandzha insurgents", as was mentioned in the documentary, for the liberation of the area. The gathering is to commemorate the liberation of Strandzha from the Ottomans which began in 1876. The men she speaks to threaten to stone or hang anyone who says it is not Bulgarian. The film ends when a fire takes hold in a field and the soldiers and others rush to try and put it out. The fire and "the way of editing the images is designed to foster a concentration of such patriotic elements".[43] The film's ending serves as an allegory for the situation in the Balkans; the fire represents the Balkans, everything is heated, hatred is burning people up, the ethnic cleansing, the divisions, the balkanization of an area, the patriotism and struggle for a national identity in an area that once shared a common past and still shares many common cultural elements but refuses to accept it, is powerful.

The nationalistic and sometimes dangerous aspects of Remembrance days are questioned. As Rohringer asks "Which function do such ceremonies have until today?" Many of the Greek Klephtic songs sung at these ceremonies are different versions of similar tunes in the Balkans sung by Greeks, Bulgarians, Serbians and Romanians. An example is the Vlach song "A Black Life we Black Klephtes Live"

---

[43] Quotations in this and the following two paragraphs are from Rohringer, as above, pp. 91-94.

("Μαύρη ζωή που κάνουμε εμείς οι μαύροι κλέφτες"), an ode to the difficult life lived up in the mountains by these rough freedom fighters during Ottoman times. The need for these, sometimes even small, ethnic groups of the Balkans to celebrate and keep alive sometimes manufactured notions of history and grandeur, within a framework of nationalistic self-importance, has become a dangerous and extremely volatile tradition. The use of folksongs in such commemorations and their function is also evident as the folksong now represents to them an anthem of their previous glory which they now aspire to regain.

"The fact that the Balkan peoples do not know about the existence of the same song in their neighbouring countries might result from such socially constructed processes of forgetting." Could this be unique to the Balkan region? Probably not. Rohringer refers to the "fencing off" of the different nations in the film, as they do not have any knowledge of a "collective memory" of the song. The film shows up "how 'different' memories about the song are constructed in the 'different' places". This poses many questions and the "director's voice" becomes a stimulant for understanding and change, which is why it has won a number of awards and been nominated for countless others.

Peeva has been successful in showing that part of human nature that is open to the brainwashing of nationalism and contrived history. Although music is "an art which transcends all borders"[44] and so is supposed to unite people, in this instance it is a catalyst for hatred. As she says in the film, "When I first started searching for the song I thought it would unite us… I never believed the sparks of hatred can be lit so easily".

The reception of the film is also interesting in that in many reviews it is branded as a "tragicomic depiction of the Balkan region."[45] A blogger, Sammish, writes: "It is so sad to know that old wounds never heal when it comes to ethnicities in the Balkans. Although Peeva's approach of going and interviewing common people instead of seeking academics and experts in music history is well taken, it falls short of getting an objective assessment of where this song originated. I guess this approach (common people interviews) is excellent in assessing the deep political differences and ethnocentric tendencies of the population."[46]

---

[44] Petia Slavova, as above, p. 36.
[45] Rohringer, p. 86. See also reviews at http://www.imdb.com/title/tt0387926/reviews?licb=0.5328082018531859. Accessed 6.9.23.
[46] https://globalvoicesonline.org/2009/01/20/balkans-whose-is-this-song/. Accessed 6.9.23.

A very important element that must also be considered is the language of the lyrics sung to this tune. One reason people feel so strongly about it is because of the language. The assumption is that if the lyrics are in Greek or Turkish or Serbian, therefore it must be an exclusively Greek or Turkish or Serbian song. They don't recognize that a melody from elsewhere can be assimilated into a culture. The fact that the song has a similar theme; a love song about a girl, in so many of the countries attests to its "translatability" in the area. It attests to the cultural diffusion and shared values of the people who lived in such close proximity for hundreds if not thousands of years.

One criticism of Peeva is that she has stereotyped the Balkan people and that her questioning technique and interviews tend to be directed at a westernized audience, as an audience considered to be more "civilized" compared to the "Balkan Madness".[47] The film is sometimes a shock for the more westernized audience, who see in it the hatred these people feel for each other as an unsolvable problem, whereas those of Balkan background can see the ridiculousness of it, the humour. "Both audiences, however, repeat stereotypical constructions of extremes and polarization."[48] Rohringer believes that the westerners take the film too seriously and regard the animosity between the cultures as extreme and worrying. It is also important to mention that this film was made soon after the war in the former Yugoslavia, so there would have been a lot of antipathy between the nations. The film actually won the OSCE Award for Human Rights and Diversity at the Dokufest Film Festival in Prizren, Kosovo in 2006; it was said that the "film educates people about tolerance and diversity".[49] It seems that the context in which the film is shown and the melody that is heard plays a major role in its favourable reception and the viewer's understanding of it.

So, who owns this song?

> "To arrive where we started and to know the place for the first time" (T. S. Eliot, "Ithaca")

In the documentary *Whose Is This Song?* Adela Peeva chose to interview what seemed more like random people she met or heard of along her travels rather than experts in ethnomusicology. Though she did speak with some artists, mostly musicians and singers, they were generally not

---

[47] Rohringer, p. 98.
[48] Rohringer, p. 86.
[49] Rohringer, p. 87, footnote.

experts in music nor academics of cultural studies. She purposely did not ask the question "Whose is this tune?" The "Whose is this Song?" question fails to resolve the confusion in the minds of most of Peeva's interviewees, who identify melody with song. It is more likely she chose to speak to typical people on the street since the experts would no doubt give "politically correct" answers to her questions. By choosing to interview lay people she unravelled the core of one of the greatest challenges that people of the Balkan area face, one of identity. This is what leads to nationalism, sectarianism, racism and the hatred that has ravaged the area for centuries. However, by doing so she also exposes the ridiculousness of it all and joins the many other documentary film makers of the Balkans, many who came along after Peeva, such as Petra Seliškar (*Mama Europa* – Slovenia, North Macedonia, Croatia), Lode Desmet (*The Majority Starts Here* – Bosnia, Montenegro, Serbia, North Macedonia), John Zaritsky (*Romeo and Juliet in Sarajevo* – Bosnia), Andreas Apostolidis and Yuri Averoff (*Twice a Stranger* – Greece, Turkey) to name a few. Adela's other films also continue this theme with award winning documentaries such as *The Unwanted, Born from the Ashes, I Dream of Mummers* and *The Mayor*. Her latest documentary film *Long Live Bulgaria* also deals with nationalism within her home country.

The "Üsküdar" song in *Whose Is This Song?* is well known in many other countries within and without the Balkan region. It has travelled all over the world, including Egypt and the Middle East (in Egypt it's known as "Ya Banat Iskandaria"), the USA (Eartha Kitt sang it in Turkish in the 1950s[50] and it has been performed by the jazz flautist Herby Mann) and it has even been performed in Japan (by electric guitarist Takeshi Terauchi). The only Balkan voice of dissension (and of reason) in the documentary, as far as the tune goes, is North Macedonian composer-musicologist Ilija Pejovski, who says: "It is not a Macedonian tune. There is no such beat in Macedonian folklore". He is the only one not to claim it for his own culture.

In versions of the tune, the 4/4 metre, played slowly or fast, is of course common in western music, but is partnered here with an eastern-sounding melody, giving it a very exotic sound. Considering all this controversy, it would be hilarious if it originated from a most unexpected northern European country such as Scotland, as is one view by a couple of Turkish bloggers.

---

[50] Under the title "Uska Dara": see http://en.wikipedia.org/wiki/Eartha_Kitt.

The empirical quest to find the song's origin comes to an end. This song, another fluid creation where there is no particular cultural ownership, belongs to all. It is "…a multiplicity of complex conceptual structures, many of the superimposed upon or knotted into one another…" After all, "culture is located in the minds and hearts of men."[51] If you identify with it, it belongs to you just as much as to anyone else who also identifies with it.

However, this film is not just about a song, this song, it is about hundreds of such shared cultural experiences that belong to all in the Balkans. It is about multiple origins and multiple interpretations that share commonalities with countries around the globe and, in this tune's case, even as far as Persia and India. It is a film about the similarities and the perceived differences. It is about "a society in constant fluidity and instability".[52]

For Adela Peeva it is an effort not necessarily to find the true origin of this song, but to show a truth about the Balkan region, one that no nationalistic state will accept. The documentary can only ever be a snapshot of the dominant perceptions of the Balkan peoples at a particular time. After all, "Can one divide human reality, as indeed human reality seems to be genuinely divided, into clearly different cultures, histories, traditions, societies, even races, and survive the consequences humanly?"[53] Adela leads us, directs our responses and fuels our outrage, while all the time allowing us to experience the "beauty and the beast" that is the Balkans. Peeva believes in the Balkan entity. This most beautiful tune may be viewed as divisive, but the documentary itself "stresses the existence of a collective memory".[54] Peeva's challenge to find a commonality through the common tune was fraught with difficulty, even though she chose a narrative that tried to build upon their relativity. The autobiographical tone of the "documentary voice" in this film adds to its truthfulness and its positivity encourages discourse and understanding between the various Balkan countries. Peeva is not afraid to question the mistakes of the past and portray ethnic issues in the Balkans and hence her

---

[51] Geertz, as above, pp. 10-11.
[52] Vrasidas Karalis, *A History of the Greek Cinema*, New York: Continuum, 2012, p. xx. Karalis refers here to Greece but it is pertinent to the whole of the Balkan area.
[53] Todorova, as above, p. 8.
[54] Rohringer, p. 88.

documentaries have consistently won documentary film awards in the Balkans and overseas.[55]

The film: details

Production: 2003

Length: 55/70 min

Formats: Betacam SP 35 mm. Film copy

Director: Adela Peeva

Producers: Slobodan Milovanovic, Paul Pauwels

Adela Media website:
http://adelamedia.net/movies/whose-is-this-song.php

---

[55] See Adela Media website http://adelamedia.net/movies/whose-is-this-song.php.

ALFRED VINCENT

From A Distant Place: The Ownership And Uses Of A Melody

What is a song?[1]

Adela Peeva's documentary *Whose Is This Song?* (2003) opens with a group of people from various southeast European countries sitting in an Istanbul tavern, where they hear the band play the famous Turkish song "Üsküdar'a gider iken" ("On the Way to Üsküdar").[2] The song seems familiar to them all, and each person claims that it is part of their own national culture.

But in what sense does this song "belong" to any nation or group? Is it really the same song in each country? What do we know about its history? Might the same "song" serve to unite peoples rather than dividing them?

Let's start by asking: what is this thing that we call a "song"? A song, in the full sense of the word, consists of music (melody) and lyrics

---

[1] I am grateful to Eleni Elefterias Kostakidis for introducing me to Peeva's film *Whose Is This Song?* Sincere thanks also to the many friends and colleagues who have provided information, corrections, or materials not available in Australia. They include: Rosemary Bancroft-Marcus, Judith Cohen, John Coombs, Markos Dragoumis, Nicolae Gheorghiţa, Themis Kallos, Eleni Kovaiou, Eirini Lydaki, Francesco Martinelli, Thanasis Moraitis, John Plemmenos, Manolis (Emmanuel) Seiragakis, and Zdenko Zlatar – with apologies to any who I may have inadvertently omitted. All internet and YouTube references in this chapter were checked in November 2023.

[2] Üsküdar is an urban area on the Asian side of the Bosphorus, opposite the historic centre of Istanbul. It is the Byzantine Skoutari(on) (Σκουτάριον or Σκούταρι), on the site of the ancient city of Chrysopolis. Until the opening of the first Bosphorus bridge in 1973, the only way to get there from the city centre was by boat.

(words, or quasi-words such as tra-la-la). These two elements are partly independent of each other. The words of a song can be changed or completely replaced by new lyrics, in the same or a different language, without changing the melody. But if we do attach completely different lyrics to an existing tune, then we have a new song, which may be performed in a different context and may have a different purpose or function to the original. To cite a Greek parallel, among the Cretan folksongs known as *rizitika* multiple sets of words share the same melodies.[3] The famous rebel song "Πότες θα κάμει ξεστεριά" ("When will the Skies be Clear") is sung to the same tune as the lyrical "Αυγή τς αυγής" ("At Break of Day"), about climbing a mountain to hear the falcon, the hawk and the partridge, but no one would think of referring to these as "the same" song.

Despite the word "song" in the film's title,[4] Adela Peeva is really following the traces of a melody, which is heard with various sets of words, in several languages. What we are hearing, then, is *not* the same song, but different songs sharing the same tune. (From now on we will refer to this tune simply as "the Melody" with capital M; we avoid terms such as "the Üsküdar'a melody" so as not to imply any assumptions about its national origins or history.) However, Peeva's film is not concerned with musical analysis or criticism. It focuses on exploring cultural nationalism – which it does to great effect. It suits her purpose to ignore the distinctions between "song", "melody", and "lyrics". Yet imprecise use of the term "song" can cause great confusion; in discussing the origins and dissemination of the words and the melody, we need to take these two elements separately.

But would it be true to say that what we are hearing is the same song in different *versions* or *variants*? This too would be incorrect and misleading. By "version" we would normally mean a song sharing the main features (melody and basic verbal content) of one or more others. By contrast, the words attached to the Melody differ dramatically in content, tone and function, and are not generally translations or adaptations of some original text. The main exception is a group of

---

[3] Mikhail Vlazakis (Βλαζάκης), *Ριζίτικα τραγούδια Κρήτης*, Chania: 1961, gives melodies in western notation, indicating which texts are sung to each. See also Stamatis Apostolakis *(Αποστολάκης)*, *Ριζίτικα. Τα δημοτικά τραγούδια της Κρήτης*, Athens: Gnosis, 1993, especially pp. 527-36.

[4] The word "pesen" in the film's Bulgarian title and narrative is the exact equivalent of "song".

From a Distant Place

Üsküdar'a Gider İken
Kâtibim

The Melody

songs which have similar lyrics in closely related Slavic languages, as well as sharing the same Melody. With these it may be appropriate to use the term "version"; they will be discussed later.

The distinctions between "song", "lyrics", and "melody" are recognized implicitly by some of the film's participants: the choirleader Mehmed in Sarajevo, the dervish Baba Erol, the musicologist Ilija Pejovski in North Macedonia, and the Serbs in Vranje, who claim that Bosnians "stole" their song and turned it into a war song by substituting new words.

The Melody and the songs set to it have been widely discussed, both before and after Peeva's film.[5] We will be referring frequently to a particularly valuable study by Donna Buchanan.[6] Music and lyrics, in the original and in English translation, can also be found in the *Poemas del Rio Wang* website.[7]

Buchanan discusses songs with the same Melody in Turkish (including a version by Eartha Kitt), Greek, Hebrew, Arabic, Serbian, Bosnian, Slavonic Macedonian, Bulgarian and Albanian, as well as instrumental versions by Jewish *klezmer* musicians, multilingual lyrics by a Sephardic songwriter, and a parody of "orientalizing" Balkan neo-folk by the Croatian group Vatrogasci (Firemen). Yet even Buchanan's rich study only touches the surface. By the early twentieth century the tune had become popular in many parts of the Balkans, and in time was taken as far afield as East Asia and the USA. In this essay, however, we will remain with Peeva in the southeast European area, with just brief glances at Asia Minor.

In the film, when participants claim that the song "belongs" to their own nation, they seem to imply exclusive ownership: that if its creators were from nation X, then members of nation X have a unique claim to "own" it and must defend it against rivals. Taking their statements, provisionally, on their own terms, what could be the basis for such a claim?

A traveling tune?

To be taken seriously, any claim about the origins and dissemination of the Melody would have to be based on compelling evidence. Vague references would not be sufficient; it would have to be documented by an actual musical score, or, in modern times, on a recording. An added

---

[5] See for example the discussion "Λίγα ακόμα για το 'Uskudar'" on the Ρεμπέτικο φόρουμ website (rembetiko.gr). Such discussions should be read critically; not all participants are well informed. On modern approaches to regional music studies, see for example Danka Lajić-Mihajlović and Jelena Jovanović, "Introduction: Music and Ethnomusicology – Encounters in the Balkans", in *Musical Practices in the Balkans: Ethnomusicological Perspectives,* ed. Dejan Despić et al., Belgrade: Serbian Academy of Sciences and Arts, 2012, pp. 14-27. On Balkan music in general see the comprehensive monograph by Jim Samson, *Music in the Balkans,* Boston: Brill, 2013.

[6] Donna A. Buchanan, "'Oh, Those Turks!' Music, Politics and Interculturality in the Balkans and Beyond", in *Balkan Popular Culture and the Ottoman Ecumene. Music, Image and Regional Political Discourse,* edited by Donna A. Buchanan, Lanham (Maryland): The Scarecrow Press, 2007, pp. 3-54. To save space, from here on references to Buchanan's study will consist simply of her name and a page number.

[7] riowang.blogspot.com (search for "Whose is this song?").

difficulty is that in the early modern Balkans and the rest of the Ottoman empire most secular music was composed, performed and transmitted without the use of written scores.

The earliest documented appearance of the Melody known to me is from 1850, several decades earlier than the oldest example cited by Buchanan. It was published in Bucharest, the present capital of Romania, in a collection of popular songs, *Spitalul amorului (The Hospital of Love)*, compiled by the famous church cantor, musician, poet and folklorist Anton Pann (c. 1794-1854).[8] Originally published in Byzantine notation, it was attached to the lyrics of the love song "D-ai ști, sufletelul meu" ("If you but knew, my little soul"). Anton Pann did not claim authorship of either the lyrics or the music of the songs in *Spitalul amorului*. He was an adapter, compiler and publisher rather than an original creator, and his sources for lyrics and/or melody could be Romanian, Turkish, Greek, Bulgarian or from some other Balkan ethnic group.

Anton Pann, songwriter,
Sliven 1790s – Bucharest 1854

Pann was a person ideally qualified to contribute to the Melody's travels. He was multilingual, mobile, and cosmopolitan within the Balkan world.[9] He was born Antonie Pandoleon Petrov or Petroveanu, in the Ottoman town of Sliven, in present-day Bulgaria, between 1794 and 1798. His mother, Tomaida, is thought to have been of Greek background. His father, who died when Antonie was young, was a metal worker of Romanian, Aromanian (Vlach) or Roma (Gypsy) heritage. As Sliven had a significant Turkish-speaking community, it was

---

[8] See the modern edition Anton Pann, *Spitalul amorului sau Cîntatorul dorului*, ed. Adina Kenereș, Bucharest: Compania, 2009, pp. 67-68 (melody in western notation) and 251 (in "Byzantine" notation). On Pann, see Ilia Dan, *Anton Pann*, Bucharest: Albatros, 1989. The melody is performed by the Anton Pann Ensemble and guests with Romanian, Turkish and Greek lyrics at https://youtu.be/ZxH-xj3oOsI.

[9] Luminița Munteanu, "Being *Homo Balkanicus* without Knowing it: The Case of Anton Pann", in *Turkey and Romania: A History of Collaboration and Partnership in the Balkans*, Istanbul: Union of Turkish World Municipalities and Istanbul University, 2016, pp. 123-138.

presumably there that Antonie acquired his knowledge of the language. In the Russo-Turkish War of 1806-12 he and his mother took refuge in Russian-occupied Kishinev, now Chişinău, capital of the present-day Republic of Moldova. In 1812 they made their way to Bucharest, then capital of the Ottoman vassal state of Wallachia. Like its sister-state Moldavia, Wallachia was administered by Greek princes or "hospodars" appointed by the Sultan from among the elite families known as Phanariots, from their base in the Phanari district of Constantinople/Istanbul. Wallachia was to be Antonie's home for the rest of his life.

In Kishinev Antonie had already begun to show his prodigious talent as a boy cantor in an Orthodox church. In Bucharest he became a student of the famous cantor and historian Dionysios Foteinos (1777-1821) and of another Greek teacher, Petros Efesios (Πέτρος Εφέσιος or Petre Efesiul, d. 1840). Antonie himself became a music teacher, and in 1845 published a handbook, *The Theoretical and Practical Basis of Church Music, or Musical Grammar*. He was also in demand as a singer and musician (*lăutar*) in the taverns of Bucharest and among the entourage of the Phanariot princes.

Petros Efesios was also a printer, and it was with him that Antonie learned his other principal trade. In 1843 Antonie acquired his own printery, which he used to publish his writings. His vast output included: Orthodox liturgical texts; a collection of stories about Nasreddin Hodja, adapted from Greek or Turkish; a selection of Turkish proverbs with Romanian explanations; a trilingual book of dialogues for language learners in Russian, Romanian and Turkish; and numerous songs and poems. Anton Pann, to use his pen name, was so addicted to writing poetry that he even wrote his will in verse. When the metropolitan bishop refused to accept it, Anton replaced it with a second will, in which he also included some verses, but wrote them out as prose to get the will validated.

In view of his practice of adapting existing material, we cannot assume that Pann was the Melody's composer. He may have found it in some unpublished, and perhaps now lost, manuscript collection of Phanariot, Romanian or Ottoman music; or he may have picked it up by ear from the unwritten popular music of his time.

Theories on the Melody's origin abound. One ascribes it to an eighteenth-century Armenian composer in the Ottoman Empire, Küçük Artin or Arutin.[10] However, to judge from published melodies by Artin,

---

[10] Francesco Martinelli on www.rootsworld.com/reviews/savall10.shtml. On Artin see

he was working in a different, more complex musical idiom, that of Ottoman "classical" music, about which more below.

An assertion that the Melody was created by the nineteenth-century Iraqi composer Mullah Osman al-Muselli, when Iraq was part of the Ottoman Empire, can hardly be assessed without a knowledge of Arabic and access to relevant sources. The claim is mentioned on the *Poemas del Rio Wang* blogsite, but does not have general support.

One attribution to a specific composer is a simple error. The original sleeve notes of the 2006 CD *An Ancient Muse* by the Canadian singer and arranger Loreena McKennitt name her as the composer of an instrumental version of the Jewish song "Sacred Shabbat" featuring our Melody. McKennitt has herself made clear that the piece should be described as "Traditional, arranged Loreena McKennitt".[11]

Many commentators mention the intriguing theory that the Melody was introduced to the Ottoman Empire by a Scottish military band during the Crimean War (1854-56).[12] It is a fact that in the war the Selimiye Barracks in Üsküdar were assigned to the British army and became a military hospital, served by Florence Nightingale and her nurses. However, despite her own Celtic heritage, Buchanan (p. 47) rejects the theory outright. In any case Anton Pann's publication proves that the Melody was known in the Balkans before this War. Any claim about authorship implying a date after 1850 is obviously not valid.

Although a search for the origin of the Melody has produced no clear results, evidence on its international *dissemination* and its adoption for a variety of functions can be a valuable contribution to cultural history. Here too, though, care is essential.

Buchanan (pp. 10-11) considers it a fact that the Melody featured in the famous comic operetta *Leblebeci Hor-Hor Ağa (Hor-Hor the Chickpea-Seller)*, completed in 1875 by the Armenian composer Dikran Choukhadzhian (also spelled Chukhajian), with a libretto in Turkish by Takvor Nalian.[13] The operetta toured in Smyrna and Athens in the 1880s

---

Eugenia Popescu-Judetz (ed.), *Tanburî Küçük Artin. A Musical Treatise of the Eighteenth Century*, Istanbul: Pan Yayıncılık, 2002. The edition includes a Roman-alphabet transcription and a commentary, but no translation.

[11] See McKennitt's commentary on this piece on loreenamckennitt.com, last accessed 3 November 2023.

[12] E.g. Merih Orel, *Greek Orthodox Music in Ottoman Istanbul: Nation and Community in the Era of Reform*, Indianapolis: Indiana University Press, 2015, pp. 28-29.

[13] On *Hor-Hor's* impact in Greece see Thodoros Chatzipantazis (Χατζηπανταζής),

and was translated into Greek and other languages. Its story of a rustic out of his depth in the city had a strong appeal to urban audiences, in combination with its mix of oriental-sounding melodies and western harmonies. *Hor-Hor* helped set in motion whole new genres of Greek musical theatre: the operetta and the *komeidyllion* (κωμειδύλλιον) or romantic musical comedy.[14] Without suggesting that the Melody was an original composition by Choukhadzhian, Buchanan claims that "the operetta boosted its [the Melody's] popularity up and down the Asia Minor coast, entering the vernacular tradition in a number of variants".

Hor-Hor's influence was indeed pervasive. When the Swiss ethnomusicologist Samuel Baud-Bovy was collecting traditional songs in the Dodecanese in the early twentieth century, he was frustrated to find that many of the songs the islanders liked to sing were not actually traditional folksongs, but pieces from the operetta.[15]

The *Hor-Hor* theory fits in well with the first documented appearance of the Melody in Greece, in 1888 (see below). But is it true that it featured in this operetta? The theatre historian Emmanouil (Manolis) Seiragakis, who has studied *Hor-Hor's* reception in Greece (see note 15), informed me that it is *not* to be found in an original score to which he had access. He noted that the lyrics of "Üsküdar'a gider iken", which he assumed would have been Choukhadzhian's source, do not fit easily into the operetta's plot. However, he pointed out that songs were removed and added in different productions of *Hor-Hor*, so a connection with the Melody cannot be ruled out. Choukhadzhian was one of several Armenian composers developing Turkish-language opera

---

"Εισαγωγή", in his *Το κωμειδύλλιο και η εποχή του*, vol. 1, Athens: Ermis, 1981, pp. 59-61 and see his index, p. 281. On the first performance of *Hor-Hor* in Faliro in 1883 see Theodoros Synadinos (Συναδινός), *Ιστορία της νεοελληνικής μουσικής 1824-1919*, Athens: 1919, pp. 224-31. Four songs from *Hor-Hor* were recorded in Constantinople in 1908-9 (?) by the Σμυρναίικη Εστουντιαντίνα; see Aristomenis Kalyviotis (Καλυβιώτης), *Σμύρνη. Η μουσική ζωή 1900-2000. Η διασκέδαση, τα μουσικά καταστήματα, οι ηχογραφήσεις δίσκων*, επιμέλεια Νίκος Διονυσόπουλος, Athens: Mousic Corner & Tinella, 2002, p. 195; five were recorded in Smyrna in 1912 by the Armenian singer Ovannes (ibid., p. 193).

[14] See Chatzipantazis, as above.

[15] Emmanouil Seiragakis (Σειραγάκης), "*Leblebidji Hor-Hor Agha*, a Glorious Ottoman Peddler", in *New Trends in Ottoman Studies, Papers Presented during the 20th CIÉPO Symposium, Rethymno 27 June – 1 July 2012*, editor-in-chief Marinos Sariyiannis, Rethymno: University of Crete, Department of History and Archaeology/Foundation for Research and Technology Hellas/Institute for Mediterranean Studies, 2014, pp. 812-825, on p. 820).

in the Ottoman empire, any one of whom could have incorporated the Melody in his work.[16]

In 1888 the doctor, cantor and all-round scholar Nikolaos Fardys found a version of the song "Από ξένο τόπο" ("From a foreign place", see next section) sung to "our" Melody on his native island of Samothrace (Buchanan, p. 11). This is apparently its earliest documented occurrence with Greek lyrics.

The Melody was recorded in 1902 with the lyrics of "Üsküdar'a gider iken" by a German doctor, archaeologist and ethnographer, Felix von Luschan, in the province of Gaziantep in Anatolia, 1,200 kilometres east of Istanbul. His informant was a twelve-year-old Armenian boy, Avedis, who had a remarkable repertoire of Turkish-language songs.[17] The Melody with the Turkish words was published in 1913 in a Russian anthology of world folksongs (Buchanan, pp. 6-7).

Why was the Melody adopted into so many different musical cultures? Part of the answer lies in its musical form. It uses a scale similar to that of the Ottoman *makam,* or mode, *nihavend,* which resembles a variant of the western minor mode. Similar scales can be heard in many parts of the world. It is a "catchy" tune, easy for people in different traditions to relate to and remember. It is also highly versatile; as we see in the film, it has been coupled with different words to form anything from a lyrical love song to a military march or a militant anthem. The first line was even used as the hour-striking tune of cuckoo-clocks (!), once very popular in Istanbul (Buchanan, p. 47).

The four musical lines or phrases follow the pattern AAB1B2: the second line is a repeat of the first, the third line is different, and the fourth is a variant of the third. In the first two lines the leap of a fifth from the tonic to the dominant, and the continued play of notes around the dominant, create a mild aesthetic tension, which is resolved at the end of the third and fourth lines by the notes clustering around the

---

[16] Mehmet Baltacan, "The Relationship between Turkish and Armenian Regarding the Ottoman Empire and Contributions of Armenian Artists to the Turkish Opera", *International Journal of Humanities and Social Sciences* (published by the World Academy of Science, Engineering and Technology), vol. 8 no. 5 (2014), pp. 1229–35.

[17] Dorit Klebe, "Das Überleben eines osmanisch-türkischen städtischen Liebesliedes seit einer frühen Dokumentation von 1902. Metamorphosen eines *makam*", in *Das 20. Jahrhundert im Spiegel seiner Lieder,* edited by Marianne Bröcker, *Schriften der Universitätsbibliothek Bamberg,* 12 (2004), pp. 85-116.

tonic. In addition to these four lines modern Greek versions of the Melody begin with a separate instrumental introduction.

The Melody belongs to the musical universe loosely referred to as "Ottoman music", an umbrella term encompassing different musical genres.[18] To generalize, its most basic division is between the "classical" or "art music" and "popular" music, the former being associated with the imperial and local courts, the urban élites and the dervish orders. Both forms are basically urban and can be distinguished from the rural folk music of the various regions of the sultans' empire. The Melody belongs to the "popular" category; the song "Üsküdar'a gider iken", with which it is associated in Türkiye, has been classed as an urban *türkü*, or folksong, rooted in urban popular culture and passed down in oral tradition.[19]

The term "Ottoman music" does not refer exclusively to works by ethnic Turks and/or in the Turkish language.[20] In the cities of the empire, many people were bilingual or multilingual, and many composers and performers came from non-Turkish groups – in particular Greeks, Jews and Armenians.[21] An illustrative case is that of Zakharia Khanendeh ("the Singer"), whose family came from what is now northern Greece and were involved in the fur trade.[22]

The multiethnic and multilingual character of the Ottoman musical world goes back a long way. Both Byzantine music and the prestigious musical traditions of the Arab and Persian worlds contributed to the melting-pot. Even religion was not a barrier to musical syncretism; Orthodox church composers assimilated features of eastern music, and their own music was used by Mevlevi dervishes.[23] It was not unusual for

---

[18] See Walter Dev Feldman, "Ottoman Music", in *Grove Music Online*, Oxford: Oxford University Press, 2001, at https://doi.org/10.1093/gmo/9781561592630.article.52169; Kurt Reinhard, Martin Stokes and Ursula Reinhard, "Turkey", as above, article.44912.

[19] Turkish writers may also refer to it as a *şarkı*, which in modern usage is simply a general term for "song". Historically it was a specific type of song, widely cultivated in the late nineteenth century.

[20] See, for example, Marinos Sarigiannis (Σαρηγιάννης), "Οι Φαναριώτες και η οθωμανική παράδοση: Επιδράσεις και στεγανά, 17ος-18ος αιώνας", in *Τουρκολογικά. Τιμητικός τόμος για τον Αναστάσιο Κ. Ιορδάνογλου*, Thessaloniki: Stamoulis, 2012, pp. 305-322.

[21] Christos Tsiamoulis (Τσιαμούλης) and Pavlos Erevnidis (Ερευνίδης), *Ρωμηοί συνθέτες της Πόλης (17ος – 20ος αι.)*, Athens: Domos, 1998, includes an anthology of works by Constantinopolitan Greek composers transcribed into western notation. A selection is performed on the 1987 LP *Bosphorus* by the group of that name.

[22] See *Zakharia Khanendeh. Ζαχαρίας ο Χανεντές*, επιμέλεια – edited by Kyriakos Kalaitzides, Thessaloniki: Εν Χορδαίς, 2005.

[23] See, for example, John Plemmenos, *Ottoman Minority Musics. The Case of 18th-century*

composers such as Zakharia Khanendeh to combine working in ecclesiastical and secular genres.

Another instructive case is that of Dimitrie Cantemir (Καντεμίρης, Kantemiroğlu, 1673-1723), a Moldavian noble who ruled briefly as hospedar in 1693 and 1710-11. A true polymath, Cantemir's interests ranged from history and geography to philosophy and music. He attended the Orthodox Patriarchal Academy in Constantinople, and studied Ottoman music with the Greek composer *tanburî* Angeli and with Kemani Ahmed, a Greek convert to Islam. Cantemir himself had both Greek and Turkish (or at least Muslim) students.[24] He preserved in writing about 350 instrumental compositions, including some of his own, using a notation system of his own devising.[25] His published compositions and transcriptions include nothing similar to our Melody; they are in the Ottoman "classical" tradition, with its complex melodies and its sophisticated use of oriental melodic modes (*makamlar*) and rhythms.[26]

By the eighteenth century a rich song tradition had developed in the social circles of the Phanariots, the Greek-speaking elite mentioned earlier.[27] Most of their compositions remain unpublished. However, Professor John Plemmenos, an expert on Phanariot song and other Ottoman musical genres, noted in an email that Phanariot melodies are mostly in the style of Ottoman art music, like those of Cantemir. He had never come across the Melody in his research.

Ottoman Istanbul was a vast cultural clearing-house, analogous to modern cities such as Chicago, Los Angeles and New York. Artists from

---

Greek Phanariots, Saarbrücken: Lambert Academic Publishing, 2010, pp. 37-41.

[24] See Panagiotis Poulos, "Greeks and Turks meet the *Rum*: Making Sense of the Sounds of 'Old Istanbul'", in *When Greeks and Turks Meet: Interdisciplinary Perspectives on the Relationship Since 1923,* ed. Vally Lytra, Abingdon: Routledge, 2016 (first published 2014), pp. 83-105, at p. 90.

[25] There is a selection on the 2009 CD *Istanbul. Dimitrie Cantemir (1673-1721)* by Jordi Savall and Hespèrion XXI (AliaVox AVSA 9870).

[26] Owen Wright, *Demetrius Cantemir, The Collection of Notations,* vol. 1, London: School of Oriental and African Studies, University of London (Musicology Series), 1992, and vol. 2, London: Routledge, 2000.

[27] Thirty-five Phanariot songs are transcribed in *Rediscovered Musical Treasures: Exegeses of Secular Oriental Music,* Part One, edited and transcribed by Thomas Apostolopoulos and Kyriakos Kalaitzidis, Bucharest: Editura Universității Naționale de Muzică, 2019 (open access). See also: Kyriakos Kalaitzidis,"Twenty-Seven Songs by Nikēphoros Kantouniarēs in Poetry by Athanasios Christopoulos", *Musicology Today. Journal of the National University of Music Bucharest,* 11 (2020), pp. 281-296.

many parts of the empire made their career there; the genres they developed (like the Armenian operetta) and their individual creations were re-exported to all corners of the empire and beyond.[28]

The Melody was presumably carried throughout southeastern Europe by travelers such as merchants, sailors, administrators and churchmen with their servants and secretaries, as well as by professional performers. Its travels did not necessarily end with the Ottoman empire's collapse. In 1918 the area of the present-day states of Slovenia, Croatia, Serbia, Kosovo, Bosnia and Herzegovina, Montenegro and North Macedonia was united to form the Kingdom of Serbs, Croats and Slovenes, renamed Yugoslavia in 1929. The absence of internal borders facilitated the movements of itinerant musicians and other travelers. Greek musicians and composers continued to be active in post-1922 Constantinople.[29] And, of course, from the early twentieth century, recorded music and the cinema allowed tunes to travel even more freely than before.

The musical cosmopolitanism of the Ottoman Empire is vividly illustrated by Kosmas Politis' novel *At Hadzifrangou's (Στου Χατζηφράγκου)*, first published as a book in 1963 but set in Smyrna at the turn of the twentieth century. One of its characters, the Greek priest Father Nikolas, creeps out of his house at night to visit a Jewish musician, Zacharias, and listen to him playing the outi (ud).[30] Zacharias himself grew up in Kerkyra, but developed his technique in Istanbul. While there, as well as studying songs in the şarkı tradition, he made a point of listening to cantors in Orthodox churches. A novel, of course, does not have the status of a documentary source; but Politis' book is based on personal memories and the reminiscences of refugees. Zacharias' story is not implausible.

So to whom does the Melody belong? Even if its original composer became known, no claim could be made for copyright after such a lapse

---

[28] On the diffusion and influence of Ottoman popular music, see also, for example, Thodoros Chatzipantazis (Χατζηπανταζής), *Της Ασιάτιδος Μούσης ερασταί... Η ακμή του αθηναϊκού καφέ αμάν στα χρόνια της βασιλείας του Γεωργίου Α΄. Συμβολή στη μελέτη της προϊστορίας του Ρεμπέτικου*, Athens: stigmi, 1986, and Risto Pekka Pennanen, "The Nationalization of Ottoman Popular Music in Greece", *Ethnomusicology* 48, no. 1 (2004): 1-25, with a Greek translation in the journal *Μουσικός Λόγος* 8 (2009): 119-153.

[29] See Tsiamoulis and Erevnidis, as above.

[30] Kosmas Politis (Πολίτης), *Στου Χατζηφράγκου*, επιμέλεια Peter Mackridge, Athens: Estia, 2007, pp. 40-43.

of time. For all intents and purposes it is a folk tune. It belongs to no one and to everyone, irrespective of ethnic affiliation.

Wandering words

It is the lyrics of a song that contribute most to the specific meaning it conveys to the people who sing or hear it, and to its cultural function in a given society. As we have said, different words can be set to the same tune, and each combination of words and melody will be perceived in effect as a different song.

The oldest set of lyrics known to have been set to the Melody is, of course, that of "D-ai şti, sufleţelul meu" in Anton Pann's collection, mentioned above. These lyrics are not the same or similar to those attached to the Melody in any other song that I am aware of, and their origin remains unclear.

The placing of the famous "Üsküdar'a gider iken" ("On the way to Üsküdar"), also known as "Kâtip" ("The Secretary" or "The Clerk"), as the starting-point of Peeva's film should not be taken to imply that this song, with its Turkish lyrics, is necessarily the source of all other songs with the same Melody. But it is logical to begin our discussion where the film begins. The song is also worth looking at more closely as it has become something of a cultural icon. Buchanan provides the text and a translation:[31]

Üsküdar'a gider iken aldı da bir yağmur.
Kâtibimin setiresi uzun, eteği çamur.
Kâtip uykudan uyunmiş, gözleri mahmur.
Kâtip benim, ben kâtibin, el ne karışır?
Kâtibime kolalı da gömlek ne güzel yaraşır.

Üsküdar'a gider iken bir mendil buldum,
mendilimin içine lokum doldurdum.
Ben kâtibin arar iken yanımda buldum.
Kâtip benim, ben kâtibin, el ne karışır?
Kâtibime kolalı da gömlek ne güzel yaraşır.

On the way to Üsküdar it began to rain hard.
My clerk wears a long frock coat; its skirt is muddied.
My clerk has just woken up, his eyes are sleepy.
The clerk is mine, I'm his, is that anyone else's business?
How well that starched shirt suits him!

---

[31] This is also the version heard in a well-known 1948 recording by Safiye Ayla, available on YouTube at https://youtu.be/SFwCw1mZd1g.

On the way to Üsküdar I found a handkerchief
and filled the handkerchief with Turkish delight.
I went in search of my clerk, and found him beside me,
The clerk is mine, I'm his, is that anyone else's business?
How well that starched shirt suits him!

Another version (using the word in its precise sense), has a revealing refrain: after "The clerk is mine, I'm his, is that anyone else's business?" it goes on: "Kâtibime elmas yüzük, ne güzel yaraşır!" ("How nice a diamond ring looks on my clerk!")[32]

As we mentioned, the first known recording of the song with these lyrics was made in 1902 by Felix von Luschan, in the province of Gaziantep, Anatolia. Presumably by 1913, when the Melody with the Turkish words was published in a Russian anthology of world folksongs (Buchanan, pp. 6-7), it was already widely known and popular. Since then, "Üsküdar'a gider iken" has been recorded in various arrangements, ranging from a work by the classical-style composer Ahmed Adhan Saygun, in 1943, to the Turkish shadow theatre.[33] The song gained a new lease of life from the film *Kâtip* (1968), excerpts from which are included in Peeva's documentary, featuring the richly talented singer and actor Zeki Müren.

The lyrics are the work of an unknown poet.[34] The speaker in the song is a woman who has fallen in love with a *kâtip*. With his long coat and his starched shirt, his appearance is that of an educated white-collar professional. His dress is a give-away, placing him firmly in the context of mid- to late nineteenth-century Istanbul. It reflects the requirement of Sultan Abdulmecid (reigned 1839-61) that public servants should wear European dress – together with the fez. In the extracts from the film *Kâtip* in Peeva's documentary, Zeki Müren gives a spirited interpretation of the handsome pen-pusher, and the nineteenth-century setting is clear. *Kâtip* has been described as a "historical" film, as it evokes a particular period, even though its story is not based on actual events.[35]

---

[32] Buchanan, p. 7, makes this a conditional clause, "would look so nice."
[33] The shadow-theatre version is on YouTube: https://youtu.be/onDUC7m4eZQ.
[34] The attribution to "Fuzuli" in the book accompanying the 3 CD set *Bal·Kan. Miel et sang / Honey and Blood*, by Jordi Savall and Hespèrion XXI (discussed below), is puzzling. Fuzuli is the pen-name of the Azerbaijani poet Muhammad bin Suleyman (c.1494–1556), who could not have written the words in their present form.
[35] Martin Stokes, *The Republic of Love. Cultural Intimacy and Turkish Popular Music*,

For the woman in the song, the clerk's western dress is part of his attraction: "How lovely the starched shirt looks on my clerk!" At least one commentator has interpreted these lines as satirical comment on the dress code imposed by the Sultan.³⁶ If so, the joke is at least partly on the woman, who seems highly impressed by the clerk's elegant exterior.

In the film, Peeva's next stop after Istanbul is the Greek island of Lesvos (Mytilini), where we hear first an unnamed man, then the famous singer Glykeria and finally the colourful Solon singing Greek songs set to our Melody. Here is a version of one of the songs, "Έχασα μαντίλι" ("I lost a handkerchief," Buchanan, pp. 14–15):

Poster for film *Kâtip* (1968) starring Zeki Müren

Έχασα μαντίλι μ' εκατό φλουριά,
κι έμαθα πως το 'βρε μια απ' τα Πλυθαριά.

Δώσ' μου το μαντίλι, κράτα τα φλουριά,
κι είμ' αραβωνιασμένος στα Νταμπακαριά.

Σα δε μου το δώσεις, θε να 'ρθω μια βραδιά.
θα σε φιλώ στο στόμα κι απάνω στην ελιά.

I lost a handkerchief with a hundred gold coins,
and I learned a woman from Plytharia had found it.

Give me the handkerchief, keep the coins,
for I am engaged to a girl from Dabakaria.

If you don't give it to me, I'll come one evening,
and kiss you on the mouth and on your beauty-spot.

Chicago: The University of Chicago Press, 2010, p. 47.
³⁶ Reşat Ekrem Koçu, quoted by Buchanan, p. 47.

The handkerchief is evidently to be understood as a gift from the speaker's fiancée. Plytharia, the home of the woman who finds it, was a district of the city of Ayvalık, on the Asia Minor coast, which had a large Greek population before 1922. In other versions the woman comes from Bornova, a suburb of Smyrna. In one well-known version, heard in Peeva's film, the narrator loses the handkerchief "between Athens and Piraeus", and the lady who finds it is "the priest's daughter". The term "version" is correct here, since, as well as the Melody, basic motifs (the male narrator, the lost handkerchief with the coins, the woman finding it, etc.) are common to all. The motif of the beauty-spot or mole (ελιά, literally an "olive") is shared with the second song (see below); a dark mole is seen as an enhancement as it highlights the fairness of the girl's complexion.[37]

Buchanan's suggestion that the motif of the handkerchief was triggered by the Turkish song is plausible; the word is similar in both languages, *mendil* and *μαντίλι* (*mandili*). Equally, though, the Greek lyrics could have been the catalyst for the Turkish. But the songwriters used the motif in different ways. In the Greek song the (male) speaker has *lost* a handkerchief full of coins; in "Üsküdar'a" the (female) speaker has *found* a handkerchief, and filled it with Turkish delight.

The lyrics of the other song are quite different. Here is a version performed by Glykeria on her 2008 CD set Όλα τα Σμυρνέικα (*All the Songs of Smyrna*), entitled "Από ξένο τόπο" ("Apo xeno topo", "From a Foreign Place"):

Από ξένο τόπο κι απ' αλαργινό (x2)
ήρθ' ένα κορίτσι, (φως μου), δεκαοχτώ χρονώ (x2).

Ούτε στην πόρτα βγαίνει ούτε στο στενό,
ούτε στο παραθύρι, δυο λόγια να της πω.

"Έβγα, κόρη του γιαλού, άστρο λαμπερό,
χάρισέ μου την ελιά σου πού 'χεις στο λαιμό."

"Δε σου τη χαρίζω, δε σου την πουλώ,
μόν' τη θέλω την ελίτσα να σε τυραννώ."

From a foreign place, from far away,
there came a girl, eighteen years old.

---

[37] As in Vamvakaris' famous song "Φραγκοσυριανή" ("Catholic Girl from Syros"): "Άσπρο πρόσωπο σαν κρίνο και στο μάγουλο ελιά" ("A face white as a lily and a mole on her cheek".)

She doesn't come to the door, or into the street,
or to the window, for me to talk to her.

"Come out, daughter of the sea, shining star,
give me the mole that you have on your neck."

"I won't give it to you, I won't sell it to you,
I want to keep it to go on tormenting you."

Some versions of the lyrics make the girl only twelve years old! One version, sung to a different tune, has the speaker seducing the girl with his "sly tricks" (μαριολιές); he makes her sit on his knee, undoes her blouse, and counts the moles on her chest. She refuses to lend or sell them to him, and tells him to go away, but to stop by again on his return – by which time, presumably, she will be much older (Buchanan, pp. 11–13).

The earliest documented version of the "Από ξένο τόπο" lyrics appears to be the one collected by Nikolaos Fardys in Smyrna, in 1887–88 (Buchanan, p. 11), with a different melody. About ten years later, as we have mentioned, Fardys noted a variant of the lyrics being sung to "our" Melody on the island of Samothrace. The Melody's appeal was apparently so strong that people transferred to it lyrics previously sung to quite different tunes. Curiously, and perhaps not fortuitously, the timing of Fardys' noting of the Melody would fit in well with the *Hor-Hor* theory.

In another old Greek song set to the Melody, a mother beats her daughter to make her reveal the identity of a man who has kissed her. The girl protests: "He is not a stranger from far away, not from a distant land; he is the clerk from our neighbourhood" ("Ούτ' απ' τα ξένα ξένος, ούτ' αλαργινός, / μόνε ο γραμματικός σιμά στη γειτονιά") (Buchanan, pp. 20–21). The clerk or secretary, γραμματικός, is the Greek equivalent of the *kâtip*, and the first line of the girl's reply recalls the beginning of "Από ξένο τόπο", except that here the concept is negated: since the man is a local whose background is known, there is less reason for the mother to object to the match. Apart from that, the lyrics have little in common with the other Greek songs mentioned above or with "Üsküdar'a". So did a Greek songmaker build upon hints from the Turkish and Greek songs? Maybe, but the common motif of the *kâtip* / γραμματικός could no doubt have occurred independently. In both cultures the educated man with an office job could be a desirable husband. He may not be rich but he has a respected profession and may be upwardly mobile.

Yet another example of the endless appeal of the Melody is "Don't Speak to me Again of Love" ("Μη μου ξαναπείς γι' αγάπη"), released on the 45 rpm disk Odeon DSOG 2791 in 1962 with the singer Marianna Chatzopoulou.[38] The song, meaning presumably both lyrics and music, is ascribed to Bambis Bakalis! The lyrics have no connection with "Üsküdar'a".

The only Greek song known to me that combines the Melody with lyrics more closely related to "Üsküdar'a" is "Eskoutari", recorded in the USA in 1948 or 1953 (according to different sources) by Virginia Mangidou (or Magidou, Mankidou, Μαγκίδου) from Constantinople, who made recordings in Greek and Turkish in the USA.[39] Both words and music are generally labelled "traditional" (παραδοσιακό).

Απ' την Πόλη είμ' εγώ, μέσα από το χωριό,
μέσα από το Σκούταρι κάποιον αγαπώ.

Ήτανε λεβέντης και γραμματικός,
σ' όλες τις Τουρκοπούλες πήγαινε για γαμπρός.

Κάποιαν αγαπούσε και της έπαιρνε
ένα κουτί λουκούμια τής επρόσφερνε.

I am from the City (Constantinople/Istanbul), from the village,
from Skoutari (i.e. Üsküdar) is the man I love.

He was a fine man, he was a clerk,
he seemed a good match to all the Turkish girls.

He was in love with a girl, and for her he would get
a box of Turkish delight and offer it to her.

Features shared with the Turkish song are the female speaker, her love for a "clerk", the link with Üsküdar (apparently described as a "village", χωριό!), and the gift of Turkish delight – although here it is the clerk who offers it to the object of his love, who is not the speaker. Although the rudimentary story-line differs from that of "Kâtip", it too expresses the appeal of a well turned-out, educated man.

---

[38] Available on YouTube https://youtu.be/a0CU2k1ezc0.
[39] On YouTube https://youtu.be/DSsvYlus0S4, from the collection "Songs and Dances of Vosporus. Recordings 1918-1948" (Greek Phonograph, 2002. Magidou's recording was also re-issued on Kalan Müzik's 2007 CD *Rembetika* (Istanbul 2007).

"Eskoutari" was revived in 2020 by the multinational Phemios Ensemble, co-founded by Spyros Halaris. The group incorporated the first two couplets, in Greek and with the original Melody, into the title song of their album *A Brama Ghjirandulona* (Corsican, roughly translatable as *Wanderlust*). The accompanying booklet refers to Peeva's film. The song's remaining lyrics are by the singer-songwriter Mighela Cesari, who expresses the spirit of her work in the line: "My song is of every colour and every land" ("U me cantu è d'ogni culori e d'ogni paesi").[40]

Linked to Greece, though in Judeo-Spanish, are the songs of the Sephardic Jews, who numbered over 50,000 in Salonica (Thessaloniki) before World War II, when most were deported and murdered in the Holocaust. A well-known song based on the Melody is "Selanik entero yo lo caminí", whose lyrics, however, are not related to the Greek songs discussed here: "I walked all over Salonika, / but could not find a girl as lovely as you. / How lovely is the air of Salonica; / there beautiful girls are two a penny. / Tell me you love me truly; / I will send a telegraph to all my people".[41] Another Spanish title, "En un lugar extranjero" ("In a Foreign Place") is attached to a version of the Melody played by the famous Greek folk violinist Yorgos Koros (1923-2014).[42] It could be the title of a Sephardic song inspired by the Greek "From a Foreign Place". However, this cannot be confirmed at the moment, as the version available on the internet is instrumental only.

From love to revolution in Slavic lands

In the central Balkan countries the Melody is attached to lyrics which in some cases really are "versions" or adaptations of the same text. Oral culture travels easily in this region, since its Slavonic languages and dialects are closely related and to a high degree mutually intelligible. Until recent decades, what are now the primary official languages of Serbia, Croatia, Bosnia and Herzegovina, and Montenegro were regarded as forms of one language, Serbocroatian; it is national ideology, rather than linguistic science, that demands they be treated as separate languages. Bulgarian and the language of North Macedonia

---

[40] The booklet, including the lyrics in the original and in translation, is available on the website spyroshalaris.com; choose "Phemios" in the Projects section.

[41] https://youtu.be/M-8BVVdIVvc. The word *metalik* (a small coin) relates to the Ottoman period, before 1912.

[42] Heard on https://youtu.be/ytajIG82Teg?si=kj6gk4UnJ3zzHqi5.

have a different morphology, but much vocabulary in common with the others. All these languages belong to the South Slavonic group.

In a love-song with the Melody popular in Serbia (Buchanan, pp. 30-31), "Ruse kose, curo, imaš", the lyrics form a dialogue: "Your hair, girl, is so fair, are you sorry for it?" "Had I been sorry for it, I wouldn't give it to you to mess up!" "You have such a honeyed mouth, my girl, are you sorry for it?" "Had I been sorry for it, I wouldn't give it to you to kiss." And so on.

In Peeva's documentary, "Ruse kose" is heard in a clip from the black-and-white film *Ciganka (The Gypsy Girl,* 1953*)*, whose heroine, Koštana, is said to have enchanted everyone with her singing. The film was based on the popular musical play *Koštana* by Bora (Borisav) Stanković, first performed in 1900 and set in the southern Serbian town of Vranje.[43] Stanković included different lyrics in the first printed edition of his play in 1902. The play had been made into an opera by Petar Konjović in 1931 and was adapted for television in 1976.

In Sarajevo, the capital of Bosnia, a characteristic type of old urban song is the *sevdalinka* or *sevdah,* from Turkish *sevda,* "passion, (erotic) longing". Traditionally, *sevdalinke* tended to have complex tunes in scales that recall oriental *makam* modes, though their eastern musical features are liable to be erased or disguised nowadays by the use of instruments such as the accordeon, designed for western scales and chordal accompaniments. The *sevdalinka* is often thought of as an exclusively Bosnian creation, as one of its great performers, the late Emina Zečaj, insists in Peeva's film. Nonetheless, the genre's appeal is not limited to this former Yugoslav region, and there is truth in the claim of a Bosnian speaker in the film that the *sevdalinka* genre unites East and West.

As well as its Muslim majority, to which Zečaj belonged – a legacy of the conversion of Christian Bosnians to the dominant religion under the Ottoman empire – Bosnia also has Orthodox and Catholic populations, who identify as Serbian and Croatian respectively, as well as a Sephardic Jewish community, almost totally annihilated by the Holocaust. The communities in multi-ethnic Sarajevo and other towns generally managed to co-exist, until they were swept into the conflicts

---

[43] For information in English see Wikipedia under "Borisav Stanković". On Balkan Roma (Gypsy) music, an important topic not discussed here, see for example Alan Ashton-Smith, *Gypsy Music. The Balkans and Beyond,* London: Reaktion Books, 2017, and Charles Keil et al., *Bright Balkan morning: Romani Lives and the Power of Music in Greek Macedonia,* Middletown, Connecticut: Wesleyan University Press, 2002. "Gypsification" is the theme of a Serbian priest's rant about 54 minutes into Peeva's film.

that led to war in the 1990s and the emergence of Bosnia and Herzegovina as a fragile federation.

"Ruse kose" is performed as a *sevdalinka* with our Melody (example in Buchanan, pp. 30–31), with little, if any, difference in the lyrics from the Serbian version. In one famous *sevdalinka*, the lines beginning "Your hair, girl, is so fair" are preceded by verses which integrate the song into the Muslim cultural environment. Its title "Anadolka" ("Anatolian girl"), already implies eastern connections. Different versions show varying degrees of adaptation. In one, the first line is simply: "Oh girl, Anatolian girl, be mine", after which the singer promises to serenade her with *sevdalinke* and ply her with almonds and rose-flavoured sherbet. In other versions, including the one heard in Peeva's film, the first line becomes even more distinctly Muslim: "Look at me, Anatolian girl, in Mohammed's name".[44] The Melody has also been attached to unrelated lyrics in another *sevdalinka*, "Poletjela dva goluba" ("Two doves took flight").[45]

In North Macedonia, or the Former Yugoslav Republic of Macedonia as it was then known, Peeva goes in search of Patsa of Drenovtsi, the heroine of romantic lyrics in the local language sung to the Melody. Ilija Pejovski, a western-trained musician, composer and writer on music, comments that the rhythm of the Melody is "not Macedonian".

In late nineteenth century Bulgaria, we are told, "every town and city in the country was 'drowning in this melody'".[46] Bulgarian lyrics quoted by Buchanan (pp. 34–35) form a dialogue about the girl's hair and/or eyes and/or figure. "'You have dark eyes, girl, are you giving them to me?' / 'Whether I have them or not, I'm not giving them to you to love.' / 'You have a slender figure, girl, are you giving it to me?'" And so on. There is clearly a relationship with "Ruse kose"; one was clearly inspired by the other.

So people with different languages and backgrounds have adapted existing lyrics or created new ones to make the Melody part of a new song fully assimilated into their own culture. "Anadolka" is as much part of Bosnian culture as "Ruse kose" is of Serbian, "Από ξένο τόπο" of Greek, and "Üsküdar'a" of Turkish. All these nations, and many more, can truly say that the song – lyrics plus music – is theirs.

---

[44] A translation of the song Bosnian 1 on everybodys-song.blogspot.com. I am grateful to Dr Zdenko Zlatar for a helpful discussion of this translation. A fine rendering by Nada Mamula can be found at https://youtu.be/FRH33GoM_zs.

[45] As sung, for example, by Rizo Hamidović, at https://youtu.be/QMGpe1h4BsU?si=ku3eEacD6D_RYZyQ.

[46] Buchanan, p. 33, quoting a 1973 article by Raina Katsarova.

But the film also shows how songs featuring the Melody can be made to serve very different purposes. Although the examples discussed so far been mainly lyrical love songs, the Melody has also been conscripted into several different and even mutually hostile national agendas. In Istanbul, before leaving, Peeva lets us hear it as a march at a celebration for the 550th anniversary of the Ottoman conquest of the City. It has become an anthem of modern Turkish nationalism.

In Sarajevo, the Melody is recycled in the Muslim religious song (*kasida* or *ilahije*) that a choir is rehearsing. The words are totally different from the gentle *sevdalinka* heard previously: "You ask, my brother, why there are tears in my eyes. / Listen to me, and then enquire into your own life. / Are we really, brother, the way we ought to be? / Allah is the highest judge, it's no use hiding. / Do we follow the holy Koran in our life, / or are we, you and I, just saying the words?"[47] Apart from the Melody, there is nothing in common, in words, tone or function, between this and the Bosnian *sevdalinka* or the Serbian "Ruse kose". Mehmed, the Sarajevo choirmaster, is aware that he is teaching a new song set to an old melody. The words, he says, were written by a lady 30–40 years earlier. Religion had become synonymous in Bosnia with ethnic identity, and religious lyrics could take on the function of a political anthem. Hence the dervish Baba Orel, in Skopje, regards it as a *jihadi* song; new text was added, he says, to a song which was originally "ours". We might remember the comment attributed to Martin Luther, when asked why he set religious songs to secular melodies: "Why should the Devil have all the best tunes?"

In Bulgaria, what Adela Peeva remembers as the tune of a gentle urban love song she now hears used in a nationalist anthem (Buchanan, p. 46): "A clear moon is already rising / above the green (or Balkan) forest. / Throughout all Strandža, slaves / strike up a new heroic song. / They hurry, hurry to arrive / before the roosters crow". It is connected to the Preobrazhenie ("Transfiguration") uprising of August 1903 in the Strandža region, which was still under Ottoman rule; the rebellion was linked to the Ilinden (Elijah's Day) uprising to the west. It was brutally crushed by the Ottoman authorities, though much of the area was allotted to Bulgaria after the Balkan Wars of 1912–13. The lyrics were written by a revolutionary leader, Yani Popov, after an event in

---

[47] See song Bosnian 2 on everybodys-song.blogspot.com. A longer version on http://najljepse-ilahije.blogspot.com.au/2013/03/zasto-suza-u-mom-oku.html (last consulted 3.11.2023) is, similarly, religious rather than overtly political.

April 1903 when conspirators planning the revolt were betrayed and two were killed.[48] Popov presumably attached his lyrics to a tune which he expected everyone to know – yet another indication of the Melody's early popularity. As the film shows, "A clear moon" had come to be sung at the annual commemoration of the uprising. The rally shown in the documentary appears to be dominated by nationalist groups in the Strandža district, which happens to be near the home of many of Bulgaria's so-called Turkish, i.e. Muslim, ethnic minority.

Another way of seeing things?

The final scenes in Peeva's film leave a bitter taste. Setting out to trace the "song's" travels and hoping to find elements of commonality among the people who sing it, Peeva finds her enquiries revive raw memories of murderous conflicts. When confronting Serbs in Vranje (the setting of Stanković's play) with the Bosnian Muslim lyrics, or suggesting to Bulgarian nationalists that their anthem was not Bulgarian, she must have been expecting a strong reaction, though possibly not as strong as that of her fellow-countryman who threatens to kill anyone who denies that the song is Bulgarian. Music is indeed an international language, but like any language it can express falsehood as well as truth, nonsense as well as wisdom, hatred as well as friendship.

Yet even in this age of rival nationalisms, there has been more artistic interchange than we might expect. Between Greeks and Turks in particular, cultural sharing did not end with the fall of the Ottoman Empire. To mention just two well-known examples: in the decades after the Greek-Turkish War of 1919–22, Deniz Kızı Eftalya, "Efthalia the Mermaid", a.k.a. Athanasia Georgiadou (1891–1939), was a favourite singer of Mustafa Kemal Atatürk. And in the early 1960s we find the great Greek singer Stelios Kazantzidis performing in Turkish.[49]

More recently, this musical interchange has been revived and intensified. From the 1980s Maria Farandouri and Zülfü Livaneli were performing together, with Turkish songs translated or adapted into Greek by Lefteris Papadopoulos. After the earthquakes in Greece and Türkiye in 2000 and 2001, there was a moving collaboration between the singers Charis Alexiou and Sezen Aksu. In recent years the singer Dilek Koç has worked with Glykeria and other Greek artists, focusing on the

---

[48] Dimana Trankova, "All quiet in Brashlyan", at https://www.vagabond.bg.
[49] Samples of both Deniz Kızı Eftalya and Kazantzidis singing in Turkish can be found on YouTube.

musical creations shared by the Greeks and Turks of Asia Minor.[50] Examples of such artistic collaboration could be multiplied indefinitely.[51]

Recent decades have also seen musical interchange through the genre known as *paradosiaká* ("traditional"). Greek musicians have learned to play eastern instruments such as the *saz* and the *kanun* (κανονάκι), have studied the Ottoman *makam* system, and have collaborated with Turkish artists.[52] Leaders in this movement were the groups Δυνάμεις του Αιγαίου ("Forces of the Aegean") and Βόσπορος ("Bosphorus"). The second of these, based in Istanbul and led by the musicologist Nikiforos Metaxas, featured Turkish musicians and presented, among other things, works by Greek (Ρωμιοί) composers of the City.[53]

Early proponents of *paradosiaká* had absorbed the ideas of the musicologist Simon Karas, who emphasized the continuity between Ancient Greek, Byzantine and modern Greek traditions, and tended to see ancient Greece as the main, if indirect, source of Ottoman music. This theory, Kallimopoulou points out, tends to minimize the Turkish element in Ottoman creativity; she notes, though, that this nationalist interpretation became less prominent later.[54]

Also since the late twentieth century, after studying musical traditions ranging from Greece and Türkiye to Afghanistan, the Irishman Ross Daly has brought together musicians from European, Asian and north African countries, as well as from Crete (where he is based) and the rest of Greece. Common to Daly and proponents of *paradosiaká* is an attachment to eastern monophony and heterophony as opposed to western chordal harmony.

As for the Melody, the fact of its dissemination to different cultures has been known for many decades. Thus from around 1990 the

---

[50] Dilek Kots (= Koç), *Karşı. Τραγούδια από την κοινή παράδοση των Ελλήνων και των Τούρκων της Μικράς Ασίας,* Undated [2005], MC 1972; Dilek Koç, *Sevdalım aman*, with the Glykeria as guest artist, 2010. EROS3091167073.

[51] See further Şebnem Susam-Saraeva, *Translation and Popular Music. Transcultural Intimacy in Turkish-Greek Relations*, Bern: Peter Lang, 2015.

[52] Eleni Kallimopoulou, *Paradosiaká: Music, Meaning and Identity in Modern Greece*, Farnham: Ashgate, 2009.

[53] Bosphorus / Βόσπορος, *Ρωμιοί συνθέτες της Πόλης*. Καλλιτεχνικός διευθυντής Νικηφόρος Μεταξάς, 1987, Minos EMI 064 – 1701423; see Panagiotis C. Poulos, "Greeks and Turks Meet the Rum: Making Sense of the Sounds of 'Old Istanbul'", in *When Greeks and Turks Meet. Interdisciplinary Perspectives on the Relationship Since 1923*, ed. Vally Lytra, London: Routledge, 2016, pp. 83–105

[54] Kallimopoulou, *Paradosiaká*, pp. 35-46, 214.

Canadian musician and musicologist Judith R. Cohen was performing a suite of songs with the same Melody in various languages, including Turkish, Greek and Judeo-Spanish.[55] Since Peeva's film of 2003 there has been an absolute explosion of interest. Reversing the impression given by the film, songs sharing the Melody have been used to express a desire for international peace, understanding and friendship. Between Greeks and Turks in particular, a search on YouTube will bring up multiple performances of "Από ξένο τόπο" and "Üsküdar'a" one after the other by various artists.

The famous Catalan musical director Jordi Savall has brought together singers and musicians from different cultures to present the Melody as a link between peoples.[56] One of his most ambitious projects, *Voices of Memory, Bal·Kan – Honey and Blood*, has participants from fourteen countries.[57] Sections of the work represent the cycles of life and the seasons, with the final section, "Reconciliation", featuring "Από ξένο τόπο", "Üsküdar'a" and "Ruse kose", as well as an instrumental version in Gypsy style.

At a time when, throughout the world, individuals, groups and states are promoting aggressive nationalism and/or religious exclusivism, spreading hatred and murderous conflict, distracting humanity from desperately pressing issues such as climate change, musicians have suggested through their work that these destructive ideologies can be overcome. Their message is an inspiration and a challenge. As Savall might put it, one day honey must prevail over blood.

---

[55] See her curriculum vitae and publication list on judithcohen.ca; she has kindly sent further information by email. Her *Üsküdara Suite* of 1991 features verses from songs in Turkish, Judeo-Spanish and Greek, the Bosnian "Poletjela dva goluba", the multilingual "Fel Shara", and the Ashkenazi klezmer "Der Terk in Amerika". The suite is included in her collection *Primavera en Salonica*, recorded 1992, on CD Saga KPD10.977 (released 1998, not to be confused with the CD with similar title by Savina Giannatou), and in her CD *Dans mon chemin j'ai rencontré*, Transit Productions, 1997 (TRCD9503). Her work *En medio del camino* (Montreal, c. 1990, with the Gerineldo ensemble), lacked the Bosnian item, but included a Moroccan Hebrew song.

[56] Savall's arrangements for Balkan folk and early music instruments are accessible in various versions; e.g. https://youtu.be/O_EPBFs-ylM and https://youtu.be/_OMh0u-ir9w (including the voice of his late wife, Montserrat Figueras). For a negative view, however, see the review by Francesco Martinelli (above, note 10).

[57] Jordi Savall (dir.), *Voix de la Mémoire / Voices of Memory. Bal-Kan: Miel et Sang / Honey and Blood*. Various soloists with Hespèrion XXI, 2013. Set of three CDs with book: Alia Vox AVSA 9902. Although *balkan* in Turkish denotes a wooded mountain chain, *bal* and *kan* separately mean "honey" and "blood".

GEORGE MICHELAKAKIS

Patriarchy And Nationalism In Adela Peeva's *Whose Is This Song?*

Adela Peeva's documentary *Whose Is This Song?* stands as evidence for the nationalisms which plague the Balkan region, to which Greece belongs. Certainly, the problem of nationalism which has plagued the tormented peoples of the Balkans is not unique to that region of the world; on the contrary, it is something wider, a global problem, which also affects immigration to Australia, ever since the land of the indigenous peoples was invaded by British imperialism, which exported the problems of hatred and racism beyond the borders of Europe.

We all know that no nation is absolutely autonomous or self-created culturally. The Balkan peoples, whose shared destiny was to be occupied for over four hundred years by the Ottomans, developed certain common cultural characteristics which define them to this day. Musical culture and song, as all other arts, are not created within sanitized and insulated national enclaves. They are created in immediate relation to the wider social context, which has patriarchy as its shared heritage. Patriarchy has been transmitted through religion since antiquity to the nation-states which were established gradually during the nineteenth century with the collapse of the Ottoman Empire.

This approach to Balkan studies is contemporary and is linked with the development of the humanities after World War I, as previously, especially in the nineteenth and early twentieth centuries, ethnography and anthropology were used to provide ideological justifications for the projects of "racial superiority" and "cultural purity and uniqueness", promoted by the newly established states after the collapse of the old empires.

We must not forget the ideological development of modern Greek ethnography, beginning, in particular, with Nikolaos Politis, who searched within modern Greek folk culture for "unique" elements connecting it to classical antiquity (and not to the surrounding peoples), while more recently Alki Kyriakidou-Nestoros produced a much more comprehensive analysis of the folk culture, paying more attention to similarities, especially between neighbouring peoples.

Adela Peeva is an ethnographer and film-maker from Bulgaria who represents the approach of modern scholars exploring the common cultural aspects that link all Balkan countries. However, the question posed by Peeva in the important documentary *Whose Is This Song?* does not simply bring to the fore the fact that Balkan peoples share many cultural roots; it also interrogates the strong nationalism which permeates their societies. As we will argue later, in a second viewing of the documentary the deep influence of patriarchal tradition and ideology on gender relations in the Balkans becomes obvious. We observe too how song and entertainment in general are impacted by the interpersonal relations defined by such an ideology.

Patriarchy and nationalism, nationalism and patriarchy are inextricably intertwined and permeate culture, hindering and delaying Balkan peoples from dissociating themselves from archaic superstitions and customs, which usually reflect rural-agrarian closed societies whose dominant worldview is founded always upon religion.

When, fifteen years ago, I visited the city of Ohrid with its 365 churches, in order to study the Byzantine frescoes at the central church of the city, built around the eleventh century, I remember how impressed I was by the pagan religiosity of the residents, who placed underpants, socks, hats and jackets under Christian icons, hoping that they would acquire the miraculous power to heal the ailments of their owners.

The word for the Balkans, as we know, originates from the Turkish word for the mountains. It designates the regions of Southeast Europe running from the Carpathian Mountains in Romania in a reversed S-shape through the former Yugoslavia and reaching down the mountain ridges of Pindos. The Turkish occupation of Serbia, Bosnia, Bulgaria, Albania and Greece over hundreds of years, ending only in the nineteenth or early twentieth century, didn't allow the development of a local bourgeois art. For this reason, popular culture especially thrived in the Balkans; and it belonged completely to the creativity of ordinary people.

Peeva's documentary depicts her journey through the Balkans. It starts off in Istanbul and travels through Greece, Albania, Bosnia, North Macedonia, Serbia and finally Bulgaria. It shows how a shared melody, which is found throughout the peninsula with different lyrics in each language, is employed either to express the desire of a man for a woman or the local nationalism of the specific ethnic group. In each case, whether erotic or militaristic, the voice expressing itself through singing is not the voice of an individual but the voice of patriarchy. It maks no difference if the singer is actually a woman. And in the Turkish song "Üsküdar'a gider iken", where, unusually, the "I" that speaks is female, the ideology is still that of patriarchy. The man she focusses on has a promising career, while all she can do is admire him from a distance.

The search for the authorship of the melody revealed that both patriarchy and nationalism are active factors in transforming it either into a male love song or into a militaristic anthem. The different lyrics associated with the tune in the film bring out, on the one hand, patriarchy's ideology on social gender, according to which a man has the right to express his desire for a woman but never a woman for a man (except, as we said, in "Üsküdar'a gider iken"), while on the other hand as a patriarchal, nationalistic and militaristic song it carries with it the full ideology of modern nation-states, according to which the defence of racial, religious and cultural purity and superiority justifies the hatred for the Other and the different, leading to the brutality of ethnic cleansing.

Despite the common elements of culture shared by the Balkan peoples, in music and other arts, we cannot really claim that these necessarily form a basis for the development of good relations between neighbouring societies. To the degree that they were created to serve the needs of patriarchy and its nationalisms, they simply exacerbate the enmity between genders and peoples.

The Balkans are the place where Christianity and Islam meet. Two sister monotheistic religions which in certain periods have exacerbated the subjugation of women, though not always in the same way. Patriarchy was predominantly embodied and made explicit in both religions. Furthermore, with the establishment of nation-states, these religions suspended their transnational character and were imbued with nationalism, as every state of the Balkans established its own national religious administration.

As we watch the documentary, we hear in astonishment an Albanian Muslim claiming that this song cannot be Serbian, because "Serbs have no culture"! What he meant was that Serbs are of another faith and believe in a different religion. The association between culture and religion becomes more apparent in Bosnia, where a music master teaches the same melody set to a militant religious anthem, claiming, in the interview given to Peeva, that the Bosnians won the war against the Serbs because their own Islamic religion is stronger than the Christian one!

The same scene is repeated in Christian Serbia and Bulgaria. Common people are deeply indoctrinated with the idea that their nation and religion are better and superior than the others. They even express anxiety and hostility when some dispute their own national and religious superiority. The Muslim representative of the Dervish community in Skopje believes that the mixing of religions in Sarajevo and especially amongst the members of the same family won't have a good outcome. He also expresses the fear that the same may take place in Skopje. The same negative approach is expressed by the Christian priest in Serbia who, while commenting on the feast of St George celebrated by the local Muslim Roma, speaks of the modern "gypsification" of Christian culture, although in reality the Gypsy influence enriching music in Serbia and other Balkan countries, shown in the work of great artists like Goran Bregović and Emir Kusturica, is deeply rooted and by no means new.

The Orthodox priest thinks that the mixing of Christian and Islamic cultural elements is inherently undesirable. He talks about an identity crisis experienced by the Serbian people. For a representative of tradition, as priests are, traditional purity is the holy chalice which must be protected by all means since cultural exchanges and mixings lead to catastrophe.

By examining this specific melody, as traced by Adela Peeva throughout the Balkans, we understand that its transformation from a love song to a military anthem expresses in both cases patriarchy in its twofold manifestations: its ideology on gender and its ideology on the superiority and purity of the race.

We saw that in Istanbul Adela Peeva encountered the same tune in two different performances that served two different needs: 1) as a song expressing erotic desire, in this case of a woman for a man, and 2) as a militaristic anthem played during the national celebrations for the conquest of the City by the Turks.

Usually, whether as a love song or military anthem, the voice speaking through the song is male. In one case to express the desire for a woman and in the other to incite war. The song is usually performed by a male voice, but when it is sung by a woman, as by Glykeria in Mytilene, Tereza in Albania and Emina in Bosnia, the voice speaking through the song is still usually male.

It is really impressive that so many related songs present man as having a voice to express his desire for the feminine whilst on the contrary there is an almost complete absence of songs showing the female voice expressing her desire for the masculine. When a female performer sings a male song, it functions as a love object for the male listener. The listener sings it along with them, creating in his mind the image of the woman about whom the lyrics are speaking.

> *Glykeria, Greek singer:* "Come out, girl, shining star of the sea / give me the little mole that you have on your neck..."
>
> *Tereza, Albanian singer:* "In the garden a bird twitters / and you made the royal basil blossom..."
>
> *Emina, Bosnian singer:* "I will wash you in dew, my flower..."
>
> *Koštana, Serbian Gypsy singer:* "Girl, you have a beautiful face. Will you let me kiss you?"

Adela Peeva's documentary depicts the extent of influence that patriarchal ideology has on the perception of gender in the Balkans and how the relations emerging from such ideology influence both song and entertainment in general. Moreover, it shows that men and women seem to exist within different spheres of expression, which nevertheless do not necessarily create two autonomous musical cultures.

The documentary also shows us something extremely crucial. In the patriarchal ideology on gender in the Balkans, the modern perception which distinguishes between biological and social gender does not exist at all. Nor can we find any perception of a polymorphous sexuality. There is still no expression of difference in the popular culture which seems omnipotent in the Balkans and which includes an internalized patriarchal law resisting all demands for change.

Draga Spasić as Koštana, 1914

The study of traditional culture in the Balkans is something of deep concern for us as it is transferred from the home country to the new countries of migration. The project of "maintaining our tradition", which all Balkan migrants promote with fanaticism, is in reality imbued with the anxiety of losing our cultural identity, which reflects patriarchy through religion and nationality.

Despite the fact that the constitutions of most migrant organizations in Australia state the "maintenance of tradition" as their reason for existence, no serious discussion has taken place to this day about the distinction between gender as a biological category and gender as a social construct. The failure to recognise this distinction defines the belief system which offers to each individual a latent conceptual framework about what is "normal" and what is not.

When in 2017 the Greek Orthodox Church in Australia fought hard to stop the growing realization by society that there is no correlation between traditional religious and patriarchal ideology on gender and the biological sexual reality, no Greek migrant organization, not even the progressive Left, dared to declare in public what modern science accepts. Today tradition functions as the barbed wire which keeps people captive to ossified institutions which the Church and the patriarchy struggle to protect by all means possible.

In the Greek communities of the Diaspora no discussion has ever taken place about the so-called "tradition". Discussion is always characterized by idealized generalizations without reference to any concrete analysis of reality. Multiculturalism is perceived as the promotion of tradition, even in entertainment, without any connection to the changed social realities in which the migrants now live. Consequently, tradition becomes an ideology which preserves nationalism and as such takes over everyday life by being lived without awareness and self-criticism.

The first generations of migrants maintain cultural characteristics of the agrarian patriarchal society within the framework of the private sphere at home, in the community and in their regional associations. Meanwhile, however, in the public sphere patriarchy has been replaced by the "nuclear" family structure. If the songs that Adela Peeva focussed on reflect patriarchal economies of low productivity, which needed an extensive kinship system through the exchange of women between men, in Australia today, a country with high productivity, women no longer function as objects for barter between men any more. The nuclear family with its loose bonds is promoted as something natural and takes over the reproduction of the labour force which capitalism needs.

In such new social realities, it is evident that tradition will exist in the mind of the first generation migrants as the lost "golden age". For artists, however, this same tradition will issue a challenge with which they can either come to a cowardly compromise or they can boldly reject it and move on to construct new forms of artistic freedom, reflecting their own particular reality.

PART TWO

The Balkans

Marian Țuțui

Four Views Of The Balkans From Down Under

There are more Australian movies referring to the Balkans and Balkan nations than anyone would think. This is mainly due to the significant immigration of Greeks and former Yugoslavs in recent decades, but also to the participation of a contingent of Australian soldiers in battles on the Gallipoli Peninsula during WWI. We have been able to distinguish four types of outlook on the Balkans.

The first view is obviously one of a typical country of emigration, namely that the Balkans is an area from which people had to flee, mainly because of war. This is the case with the film *The John Sullivan Story* (1979, Australia, dir. David Stevens). The main character in the title of this TV movie comes from a long and famous Australian TV series that ran from 1976 to 1983, *The Sullivans*, about a family during WWII, so the movie itself becomes a kind of prequel. After his boat is sunk by a submarine, John Sullivan is rescued "by Yugoslavian Chetniks who take him to their village to work as a doctor. The story evolves with some romance but also being captured by the Gestapo amongst other things".[1] As he is not allowed to leave, his story to some extent resembles that of *Doctor Zhivago*.

The Sound of One Hand Clapping (1998, Australia, dir. Richard Flanagan)[2] is about the reunion of a father and his daughter after 20 years of absence. Sonja Buloh (Kerry Fox) visits her father (Bojan Buloh) in Hobart, Tasmania. Her visit is also a pretext to remember their

---

[1] "The Sullivan Movie", https://www.themoviescene.co.uk/reviews/the-john-sullivan-story/the-john-sullivan-story.html. (Websites mentioned in this paper were last accessed in November 2020.)
[2] Nominated for the Golden Bear for this film at Berlinale in 1998.

hard life in Slovenia 30 years before. Both suffered during WWII because of Croatian Ustashe.[3]

Although at first sight *Ladies in Black* (2018, Australia, dir. Bruce Beresford) seems again a film about refugees, it is actually about mutual influence between peoples. The refugees finally find a haven in a sparsely inhabited country (thank God!), a sunny land where it seems there is no sadness. This is what a Hungarian, Rudi (Ryan Corr), says about his country of adoption, a man who fled both fascism and communism after the 1956 revolution. On the other hand, Europeans educate the backward locals. These are represented by Fay (Rachael Taylor), Rudi's fiancée, a beautiful but simple saleswoman, who left school when she was 15 years old, was once a kept woman and who learns from her boyfriend about the opera and Tolstoy. Although ironic, the most spectacular transformation is that of printer Miles (Shane Jacobson), the father of sales assistant Lisa (Angourie Rice), who learns from the continentals to drink wine, eat salami and duck liver and to accept that his daughter can go to university. The newcomers in the film are Hungarians, Slovenes, Croatians and Serbs, whom the locals call contemptuously "reffos" or, with a mixture of admiration and envy, "continentals". It is a film about Sydney in 1959 and more precisely about a group of women who work on the fashion floor of smart department store F. G. Goodes. But most of all it is about emancipation, especially of women. Slovenian Magda (played by star Julia Ormond) is a talented boss with a sassy sense of style who will leave the store to open her own fashion boutique. Until this step, she exercises her talent as a mentor for teenage Lisa and as a matchmaker, introducing Fay to Rudi. After being twice nominated for Oscars, director Bruce Beresford proved again his artistry in this bittersweet humorous screen adaptation (with co-writer Sue Milliken) of the novel *The Women in Black* (1993) by writer Madeleine St John. Her only novel set in Australia seems inspired by the experience of her French mother and her maternal grandparents, who were Romanian Jews.[4]

It is interesting that even for Australians the Balkans, and especially the Greek islands, are also places of refuge. In *Island* (1989, Australia, dir. Paul Cox) a formerly rich Czech-Australian emigrant comes to a small and sleepy Greek island to rethink her life. She develops a relationship

---

[3] A Croatian fascist, ultranationalist and terrorist organization, active between 1929 and 1945.

[4] Christopher Potter, "St John, Madeleine (1941–2006)", from *The Independent*, 6 July 2006, http://oa.anu.edu.au/obituary/st-john-madeleine-13361.

with two other women who each in their own way suffer from their pasts. One of them, Marquise, is portrayed by Irene Papas.

The third outlook on the Balkans can be found in the movies about the disastrous Gallipoli campaign, where Australians demonstrated the famous Anzac spirit. For many this was also the beginning of true Australian nationhood.

In 1915 the Entente Powers, and especially the British, at Winston Churchill's initiative, launched the Gallipoli Campaign against the Ottoman Empire, also known as the Dardanelles Campaign, the Battle of Gallipoli, or the Battle of Çanakkale. After suffering and inflicting many casualties and incapable of leaving the coast, the invasion force was withdrawn to Egypt in 1916.[5] It was the only major Ottoman victory during WWI and the first time Mustafa Kemal (Kemal Atatürk) proved his leadership qualities. On the other hand the disastrous campaign triggered the criticism of accredited journalists in Gallipoli. In September 1915, Australian Keith Murdoch wrote a letter to Australian Prime Minister Andrew Fisher about the disaster but also on the mood of Australian and New Zealand soldiers. The letter was initially stopped by censorship, but then reached *The Times* and its author became a famous journalist. After 66 years his son, billionaire Rupert Murdoch, was to be one of the producers of the film *Gallipoli* (1981, Australia, dir. Peter Weir). Today the campaign is often considered to be the beginning of Australian and New Zealand national consciousness, celebrated on 25 April, the anniversary of the landing. As early as 1928 two Australian amateurs, Keith Gategood and William Green, shot *The Spirit of Gallipoli*, a short silent film about "a high-spirited young man [who] discovers the benefits of army discipline".[6]

Peter Weir's *Gallipoli* is one of the best-known Australian movies. The film was nominated for the Golden Globe for the best foreign film and is about two Australian sprinters who face the brutal realities of war when they are sent to fight at Gallipoli. It is a gripping epic set in some truly beautiful landscapes with Mel Gibson, who was not yet an international star. It is impressive also for the authenticity of battle scenes and comradeship (recalling authentic photos from the campaign). As a result, this movie has itself become a symbol of Australian consciousness.

---

[5] The Australians had nearly 9,000 casualties. See https://en.wikipedia.org/wiki/Gallipoli_Campaign.

[6] Australia's audiovisual heritage online, https://aso.gov.au/titles/short-features/the-spirit-of-gallipoli/.

The fourth and final view can be seen again in Gallipoli-related films. Now Turkish enemies may deserve admiration and become friends, and Australians admit they had no reason to land in Türkiye. It seems, ultimately, a politically correct vision, but we have to keep in mind that some films are co-productions with Türkiye, which has recently been interested in recovering the values of the Ottoman Empire.

The credits in *The Water Diviner / Son Umut* (2014, Australia-USA-Türkiye, dir. Russell Crowe) are clearly intended to recall Arabic lettering. The allusions to the Orient and Türkiye can be perceived also in the first scenes of the film, where we have a parallel editing of scenes recalling a shadow play (Karagöz or Karagiozis). The scene has a Turkish soldier praying, seen through a semi-transparent curtain, and an Australian patrol filmed against the orange light of sunset.

The story moves forward and back in time. An Australian farmer, Connor (Russell Crowe) reads from the *Arabian Nights* to his three sons. It is a kind of anticipation of what will follow, and in the following scenes we can see premonitions, dreams and things seen in a trance; the scriptwriters have adopted a kind of mysticism favourable to the creation of an atmosphere of magical realism.[7] In fact, it is a premonition that his sons may still be alive that makes the farmer embark on a journey to the other end of the world.

Once Connor sets foot in Istanbul, the filmmakers try to capture our goodwill with charming stereotypes of Türkiye: he visits the Blue Mosque, his beautiful host Ayshe (Olga Kurylenko) provides a demonstration of Turkish coffee reading, he witnesses a Turkish circumcision party (sünnet) for Orhan (Dylan Georgiades), the boy from the guest house where he lives, and he pursues Major Hasan (Yılmaz Erdoğan) in the bazaar (as in Jules Dassin's *Topkapi* [1964]). On this occasion we have a glimpse of carpets, spices, donkeys, bird-cages and dyers on the streets.

Another of Connor's dreams shows a windmill back home in Australia and the whirling dervishes with his son Art (Ryan Corr) in the middle. The dream proves to be a prediction. When he sees a windmill in Anatolia he understands that his son must be somewhere near.

As stereotypes we have to add a cricket game on the train between Connor and Sergeant Jemal (Cem Yılmaz), as well as a scene of Turkish refugees chased by the Greek army, Greek soldiers looking like a gang of

---

[7] Jordan Adler, "The Water Diviner Review", 2015, http://wegotthiscovered.com/movies/the-water-diviner-review/.

armed bandits in contrast with the worthy Turkish soldiers, and even a cruel Greek executioner grinning at his victim.

Most of these stereotypes are connected with a new attempt to understand the Turkish enemy, but sometimes we have something more, a mirroring of the new Turkish policy to reconsider the Ottoman Empire. The same happened with a recent Türkiye-USA film co-production, *The Ottoman Lieutenant / Osmanlı Subayı* (2017, dir. Joseph Ruben), where an American heiress after WWI is bewitched by the exotic Turkish culture and a dashing Ottoman officer speaking English fluently. She is so fascinated that she will go to Türkiye and accept theoretically even the harem system of marriage. In *The Water Diviner* we have a similar situation. A ten-year-old boy and his mother, the owner of a guest house in Istanbul, have a good command of English, as do a Turkish major and even his sergeant. The Australian is so sure of the boy's English skills that he gives him his copy of the *Arabian Nights* in English (!) as a present.

At first the Australian farmer calls Istanbul the "wretched city" and Ayshe after seeing his copy of the *Arabian Nights* reproaches him: "Your guide is no longer valid. You should see the Blue Mosque". The scenes where the Australian farmer hears the muezzin's voice and thinks that somebody is selling something and the one where he says that "we do not have such a thing" after seeing the Blue Mosque symbolize a reversal of expectations: an English-speaker is overwhelmed by the civilization of the Orient!

After showing the little Turkish boy how he finds water in the desert the farmer says something relevant about his native country: "Hope's a necessity where I come from". But the most significant scenes in the film about what Türkiye means for the Australians and what Australia means for the Turks are in the train where Connor travels together with the Turkish soldiers. The sergeant asks: "What part of the empire did the Australians get after the war?"

> *Connor: No part.*
> *Sergeant: It is always about a struggle for land.*
> *Connor: We fought for a principle.*
> *Sergeant [looking towards his comrades]: I would like to do business with this country.*

Before he dies, the sergeant adds: "Anzac Bey, don't invade a country unless you know where it is".

However, at one point we have a situation revealing the Ottoman period in an unfavourable light, as quite a backward epoch. It is when Ayshe is told by her brother-in-law: "Act like an Ottoman woman; you have to cease to act like a European one".

We shall not linger on *Turkish Delight*, also known as *Anzac and the Johnny Turk* (2017, Türkiye-Australia), because it deals with similar stereotypes and the director is Turkish (Eris Akman).

At first glance, films like *The Water Diviner*, *The Ottoman Lieutenant* and *Turkish Delight* seem politically correct in their attitude to Türkiye, as they offer more complex images than earlier films, but they are in fact influenced by the idealization of the imperial period and the policy of President Recep Tayyip Erdoğan.

Marian Țuțui

The Visual Heritage Of The Manakia Brothers In The Balkan Countries

To which culture does the Manakia brothers' work belong?

The brothers Ienache (1878-1954) and Milton Manakia (1882-1964), even if not the first to make films in the Balkans, were certainly the first real filmmakers born in the Balkans, with a long career as cinematographers over 32 years, from 1907 to 1939, and as owners of a cinema theatre from 1921 to 1939.[1] Their first film, most probably shot in the spring of 1907 in their native village, Avdella, showed their grandmother Despina in the middle of a group of women weaving wool.[2] Meanwhile, their photographic activity received recognition during their lifetime (including being accepted as official photographers for the kings of Romania and Serbia) and was extremely long and productive. Milton was active for no less than 62 years.

Nowadays, Greece, the Republic of North Macedonia and even Albania all claim the Manakia brothers as part of their national cultural heritage.[3] Their affiliation to Macedonian cinematography and culture, even to that of Yugoslavia for a while, is more justified, since Bitola (a

---

[1] A version of this chapter was published in *Audio-Visual Heritage Space and its Protection. "It's Your Story, Don`t Lose it"*, ed. Deniz Bayraktar and Özlem Avcı Aksoy, Istanbul: Bağlam Publishing, 2017.

[2] In the fall of 1906 Ienache was still on his travels in Europe when, as a teacher of drawing and calligraphy at the Romanian high school in Bitola, he requested the Romanian Ministry of Education to extend his leave. See footnote 18 below.

[3] See also Igor Stardelov, *Manaki*, Skopje: Kinoteka na Makedonija, 2003, especially the chapter: "To Which Balkan National Culture do the Manakia Brothers Belong?" ("Na koja balkanska nacionalna kultura i pripaǵaat braḱata Manaki?"), p. 55.

The Manakia brothers, Ienache and Milton

town with which they are associated, formerly Monastir or Monastirion) is now part of North Macedonia, and even Avdella is part of historical Macedonia. Moreover, Milton had become a Macedonian citizen (within the Yugoslav federation) and had sold his collection of photos and films to the archives of what is now North Macedonia. The topics of the work of the Manakia brothers are also connected mainly to Macedonia. In the Republic of North Macedonia, the two photographers and filmmakers are considered with good reason to be among the greatest creators born in this land. North Macedonian researchers often mention their ethnic minority background (Vlach) and the fact that their work is a common heritage of the Balkan nations.

The two brothers considered themselves Romanians.[4] They studied in Romanian schools, as did Ienache's son, while Ienache worked as a teacher in several Romanian schools, in Ioannina, Bitola and Thessaloniki, among other towns. In fact, after the bankruptcy that followed the fire which destroyed their cinema, Ienache went to Thessaloniki to teach again in the Romanian high school there and in order for his son to study there in Romanian, as in Yugoslavia the Romanian schools had been abolished. Ienache left his photo studio to his younger brother, who had married recently and who did not have any other professional skills.[5]

Greece claims the Manakia brothers because Avdella, their native village, is nowadays in Greece. As we mentioned, Ienache lived his last

---

[4] Since the Vlach language is related to Romanian, the Romanian government funded schools in various Vlach communities, encouraging the students to develop a Romanian identity.

[5] Igor Stardelov (as in note 3 above) agrees with me on this topic. See pp. 55-59.

years in Thessaloniki. The Greeks consider the Vlachs to be not Romanians or some other nation, but Romanized Greeks. Last but not least we have to mention that two of their films, *Manifestations* (1908-1909) and *The Burial of Bishop Emilianos of Grevena* (1911) have Greek inserts.

The Manakia brothers can also be claimed by Türkiye as they were Ottoman subjects until 1913, while Avdella, Grevena, Ioannina and Bitola, where they worked, were part of the empire.

In the inter-war period, in 1936, Anastase Hâciu wrote a book in Romania about the Vlachs, in which he mentioned the cinematographic activity of the Manakia brothers.[6] Meanwhile, several Romanian magazines published their photos. After WWII, the two brothers were almost forgotten in Romania, mainly because the Communist authorities hardly tackled the problem of Romanians abroad. In 1985, in a short history of Romanian photography, Constantin Săvulescu mentioned some photos by Ienache as the first printed photos in Romania.[7] In 1989 Cristina Corciovescu and Bujor T. Rîpeanu mentioned the brothers' pioneer cinematographic activity[8], using as their source *L'Encyclopédie du Cinéma* by Roger Boussinot.[9]

At the end of the 50s, Yugoslavia began to claim the Manakia brothers, and through Boussinot's encyclopaedia the information was spread all over the world. In 1958, Croatian director Branko Ranitović made the film *Kamera 300*, in which he interviewed Milton in the Serbo-Croatian language, analysed his activity and finally proclaimed him the first cinematographer in the Balkans.

Although contemporary Greek newspapers knew at least about the photographic activity of Ienache, they did not cherish but rejected it as the reprehensible activity of a Romanian nationalist. Thus, the newspaper *Η Φωνή της Ηπείρου* (*The Voice of Epirus*) considered him an "instigator" or "ape", *Πύρρος* described him as "the photographer of Avdella", while *Ο Αγώνας* (*The Struggle*) called him a "photographer and propagandist".[10]

---

[6] Anastase Hâciu, *Aromânii. Comerț, industrie, arte, expansiune, civilizație*, Focșani: Tipografia Cartea Putnei, 1936.

[7] Constantin Săvulescu, *Cronologia ilustrată a fotografiei în România. Perioada 1834-1916*, Bucharest: 1985, p.11.

[8] Cristina Corciovescu and Bujor T. Rîpeanu, *Secolul cinematografului*, Bucharest: Editura Științifică și Enciclopedică, 1989, pp. 10-11.

[9] Roget Boussinot, *L'Encyclopédie du Cinéma*, Paris: Bordas, 1967.

[10] Christos K. Christodoulou, *The Manakis Brothers. The Greek Pioneers of the Balkanic Cinema*, Thessaloniki: Organization for the Cultural Capital of Europe, 1997,

The Greeks started to understand the merits of the Manakia brothers only in 1971 when Kostas Stamatiou dedicated a piece to them, published in the newspaper *Ta Nea*.[11] However, the information was again from Roger Boussinot's encyclopaedia! In 1978, Nikos Zervos and Christos Christodoulou made a TV documentary, *The Filmmakers of Northern Greece* (Οι κινηματογραφιστές της Βόρειας Ελλάδας). Two years later, T. Papayannidis dedicated to them another TV documentary *You, Mountains of Greven*a (Εσείς, βουνά των Γρεβενών), while Fotos Lambrinos and L. Loisios used footage from their films in the documentary *Panorama of the Century* (Το πανόραμα του αιώνα) in 1984.

Film archives, libraries, collectors and countries owning works by the Manakia brothers

At the beginning of the 90s, the director of the Albanian Film Archive, Abaz Xoxha, began to claim that the Manakia brothers were Albanian.[12] He quoted an old teacher, Irfan Tershana, who had a photo taken by Ienache, and claimed that he had talked with "Manakia" in Albanian! On the occasion of an exhibition of photos by the Manakia brothers that I organized in Tirana in 1999, I met Irfan Tershana and spoke with him. I realized that the old man did not know that there were two brothers Manakia. On the other hand, he could speak Macedonian,[13] Italian and even Romanian and was not very sure in what language he talked with "Manakia"! However, later on the next director of the Albanian Film Archive claimed the same thing, while www.imdb.com published as a fact that the two brothers were Albanians and even the titles of some of their films were translated into Albanian. After 2000, I tried myself to correct the information about the Manakia brothers on www.imdb.com. When IMDb replied that they had acquired the information from an institution, I drew this to the attention of my colleagues at the Cinematheque of North Macedonia. They managed to introduce the titles of the films in Macedonian, along with a brief biography from which one could learn that the two brothers "were ethnic Macedonians".[14]

---

pp. 22, 23 etc.

[11] Takis Galaitsis (Γκαλαΐτσης), Αφοι Μανάκια. — Οι Κλεισουριώτες που ξεκίνησαν την κινηματογράφηση στα Βαλκάνια! (2017). Available from: http://oladeka.com/2017/08/αφοι-μανάκια-οι-κλεισουριώτες-που-ξεκ/.

[12] Abaz Xoxha, *Art i shtatë në Shqipëri*, Tirana: Albin, 1994, p. 21.

[13] The term "Macedonian", in this paper, refers to the Slavonic language of the Republic of North Macedonia, and its dialects.

[14] Milton Manaki, Biography: http://www.imdb.com/name/nm1046054/bio?ref_=nm_ov_bio_sm.

So in Albania one can find a photo by the Manakia brothers in the collection of the family of Irfan Tershana. Probably one can also find about 20 copies of the photos of Albanian topics from the exhibition I put on in Tirana in December 1999. Some of them include images from the Dibra (Debar) Congress (1909, July 20-23) that decided on the adoption of the Latin alphabet for the Albanian language and took the first steps towards establishing an Albanian state. All the photos in the exhibition are copies of photos from the collection of the Library of the Romanian Academy.

In 1952 Milton Manakia sold his collection of photos to the Bitola branch of the National Archives of Macedonia and in 1963 he made over his films to the Cinematheque of Macedonia.[15] In 2013 the cinematheque finalized the restoration of 1,460.5 metres of film, 42 titles of films and 70 minutes of material at the Hungarian Film Laboratory in Budapest.[16] Although the Cinematheque of North Macedonia has made impressive efforts to capitalize on the cinematographic work of the brothers Manakia, we may observe that they were not able to determine the place and date of some of the films, and they still use some erroneous information. The most important error is the statement that it was for reasons of national pride that the Manakia brothers made their first film in 1905. In fact, this was impossible. Ienache went to Paris, where he purchased Bioscope camera no. 300 in the fall of 1906. On the other hand, the village of Avdella, the place where the first film was made, was always deserted after St. Demetrios' Day (26 October). Avdella is a mountain village situated at 1,400 metres altitude, which is abandoned by shepherds after St. Demetrios, when they move down to the little town of Grevena. Also, the Manakia family owned a house in Avdella and another one in Grevena. Documents published by the National Archives in Bitola prove that in the fall of 1906 Ienache wrote a letter to the Minister of Education in Romania in order to extend his leave at the Romanian High School in Bitola,[17] and to continue the journey through Europe that King Carol I of Romania had offered him. On the other hand, Milton recalled in an interview that he had first seen moving images in

---

[15] State institutions such as these have been renamed since the republic's recognition under the name North Macedonia.

[16] See Igor Stardelov, "Preservation of the Manaki Brothers Film Heritage", *Journal of Film Preservation* 54 (1997), pp. 27-30.

[17] *The Creation of the Manaki Brothers,* Skopje: Matica makedonska, 1996, p. 68.

Bucharest in 1906, and the next day his brother began to dream of buying a camera.[18]

The Cinematheque of Macedonia is inconsistent in their publications regarding the number of films left by the Manakia brothers. For instance, in a catalogue we find the film *The Visit of Minister Istrati in Macedonia* (*Poseta na ministerot Istrati vo Makedonija*) with a length of 216 metres.[19] In the DVD they made in 2013, this film turns into three films: *Romanian Delegation Visiting Bitola* (*Romanska delegacija vo poseta na Bitola*), *Romanian Delegation Visiting Gopeš* (*Romanska delegacija vo poseta na Gopeš*) and *Romanian Delegation Visiting Resen* (*Romanska delegacija vo poseta na Resen*). It is the same film made in 1911 that the Manakia brothers themselves entitled *A Trip to Turkish Macedonia* (*Excursie în Macedonia turcească*), which is preserved in the Romanian Film Archive. The edited copy, with titles and inserts in the Romanian language, is 168 metres long.[20] The National Archives in Bitola own more than 5,000 photos and the Bioscope Camera no. 300 bought by Ienache from Paris.

In the Romanian Film Archive, one can find two edited films made by the Manakia brothers. The titles and explanatory inserts are in the literary Romanian language with the syntax characteristic of the early 20th century. They are *Scenes from the Life of the Vlachs in the Pindus* (*Scene din viața aromânilor din Pind*)[21] and *A Trip to Turkish Macedonia* (*Excursie în Macedonia turcească*) of 160 metres and 168 metres, respectively The first is in fact edited material that reproduces the contents of six original reels that become episodes in this film, while the Cinematheque of North Macedonia considers each reel a distinct film with its own title. The episodes are: "A Scene of Feasting at a Vlach Fair" ("O scenă de petrecere la un bâlciu aromânesc"),

---

[18] "In the capital of Romania, we found out that in England and France they sell cameras that make 'living' photos. Such news for us was that time incredible, even shocking, however we could not doubt it as we had seen a short projection of films. People looked like puppets, their moves were jerky, as if they were tied with strings by their noses and hands. It did not stop us from being intoxicated, enslaved, charmed by a magic force. Ienache already could not escape from the thought of coming back to Bitola with a shooting camera. Even in his sleep, he pined for it. While I came back home he left for London where he got a Bioscope camera." See Dimitar Dimitrovski-Takec, *Manaki i Bitola*, Bitola: Rabotničkijot Univerzitet Krste P. Misirkov, 1977, p. 18.

[19] *Katalog na nacionalniot filmski fond 1905-2000*, Skopje: Kinoteka na Makedonija, 2001, p. 4.

[20] Silvia Borcan and Bujor T. Rîpeanu, *Catalogul filmelor documentare românești 1897-1948*, Bucharest: Arhiva Națională de Filme, 1981, p. 10.

[21] Borcan and Rîpeanu, p. 132.

"The National Circle Dance with the Vlachs in the Pindus" ("Hora națională la aromânii din Pind"), "The Celebration of Epiphany with the Vlachs in Veria"[22] ("Serbarea Bobotezei la aromânii din Veria"), "A Scene of Vlach Primary Education. Abella Village. Epirus" ("O scenă din învățământul primar aromânesc. Comuna Abella. Epir") and "Domestic Life with the Vlach Women in the Pindus" ("Viața casnică la aromâncele din Pind").[23] On the lower part of each frame, we read in Romanian: "F-ții Manakia. Pindo-Balkan Film", which in translation is "Manakia Bros. Pindo-Balkan Film".

A Trip to Turkish Macedonia (*Excursie în Macedonia turcească*) also has six episodes with explanatory inserts in Romanian but without any mention of the authors or of the studio as in *Scenes from the Life of the Vlachs in the Pindus*:

1. *On the Plain of Pelagonia before the Town of Bitola; the Cavalry Vanguard, Carriages with Visitors and Carts with Luggage*

2. *The Reception of the Visitors in the Union and Progress Park by the Turkish Authorities and by the Christian Communities in Bitola*

3. *The Way to Resen*

4. *The Reception of the Visitors by Niazi Bey in his Home Town of Resen*

5. *A Road through the Forest over Bukova Saddle*

6. *The Departure of the Visitors for Thessaloniki. The Bitola Railway.*

It is interesting that Bujor T. Rîpeanu, one of the specialists in old Romanian cinema and named as co-author of the catalogue, expressed some doubt over the identification of the cinematographer as Ion Voinescu.[24] In 1994, after watching the Macedonian version in Skopje, I was able to prove that the Manakia brothers were the authors of this film. Ion Voinescu was the official photographer of the Romanian delegation, whom the Manakias probably met in Bucharest in 1906 when Voinescu and the two brothers received awards for photography.

---

[22] Veria is also called Ber (in Macedonian) or Karaferye (in Turkish). See the article Karaferye in Turkish Wikipedia.

[23] The Cinematheque of North Macedonia considers these episodes as films, under the titles: *Fair in Veria* (*Panagur vo Ber*), *Vlach Circle Dance* (*Vlaško oro*), *Ephiphany* (*Vodici*), *The Open-air School* (*Učilište na otvoren prostor*) and *The Weavers* (*Predilki*). In fact, we can also add *Grandmother Despina* (*Baba Despina*). See http://www.imdb.com/name/nm1046054/?ref_=nv_sr_1.

[24] Borcan and Rîpeanu, p. 10.

From the information we have, Ion Voinescu shot his first film during the Second Balkan War in 1913: *The Operation of the Romanian Army in Bulgaria* (*Operațiunea armatei române în Bulgaria*).

Several institutions and private collectors in Romania have photos and postcards made by the Manakia brothers, as well as books and magazines featuring their photos or their advertising, in which they mention "selling moving pictures with ethnographic content". The Library of the Romanian Academy has albums of photos donated by Ienache in 1906: *Faces and Landscapes from Macedonia* (*Chipuri și vederi din Macedonia*), *Macedonia. Landscapes, Faces and Scenes from the Romanian Settlements (1906)* (*Macedonia. Vederi, figuri, scene din așezările românești (1906)*), *The Vlach Teaching Staff in Turkey* (*Corpul didactic aromânesc din Turcia*), *Macedonia. Types, Costumes and Views from the Regions Inhabited by Romanians about 1900* (*Macedonia. tipuri, costume și vederi din regiunile locuite de români pe la 1900*) and *Landscapes and Memories from Macedonia. 10 July 1908* (*Vederi și amintiri din Macedonia. 10 iulie 1908*). The albums were donated by Ienache to the Romanian Academy on 29 June 1907.

Over 200 photos on glass plates are preserved in the collection of the Museum of the Romanian Peasant in Bucharest. In 1906, Alexandru Tsigara-Samurcaș, the first director of the museum, purchased them from Ienache Manakia.

The Romanian newspaper *Universul* (*The Universe*) published in 1903 a series of illustrations reproducing photos dedicated to the events in the Balkans, especially the Saint Elijah's Day (Ilinden) Uprising, taken on the spot, according to some explanatory notes. One of them, "Hora națională a aromânilor din Avdella, din Macedonia" ("The National Round Dance of the Aromanians in Avdella, in Macedonia") in issue no. 77 (Thursday 20 March. 1903) has the following explanation: "Today's illustration, reproduced from a photo taken on the spot by Mr I. Manakia, Aromanian photographer from the village of Avdella, represents a group of Aromanians in Avdella doing their national round dance."[25] The historian of Romanian photography Constantin Săvulescu considers this to be one of the first photos printed by engraving in Romania.[26] He also mentions that the first photo ever reproduced by zincography in Romania was the portrait of D.

---

[25] The Vlachs are also called Macedo-Romanians or Aromanians. They call themselves Aromâni (Aromanians).

[26] Săvulescu, as above, p. 11.

Theodorescu, secretary of Sidoli Circus, taken in 1909, again printed in *Universul*. According to Mircea Tomescu, a researcher on typography, in 1902 in Romania there were five lithography studios, two zincography workshops and 17 engravers, who worked mainly in wood.

Having a closer look at *Universul*, we may notice that there are at least two other reproductions of photos taken by the Manakia brothers. No. 61 (4 March) includes "The Town of Monastir (Bitola) in Macedonia", while no. 76 (19 March) has "The Romanian Village of Avdella, in Macedonia". The two illustrations strikingly resemble photos by the Manakia brothers in the albums of the Romanian Academy. It is more plausible that Ienache had sent the photos than that he would have brought them himself to Bucharest. The captions for the photos are important, as well as the reports from the conflict area, even if there is no mention of their authors for explicable reasons. We can assume that the "correspondent" of *Universul* is obviously a Vlach, mainly from the fact that in the beginning he presents the Ilinden Uprising as a regrettable event; later on, his sympathy for the cause of the insurgents can be sensed, but also his concern for impartial and accurate information. The reports on the 1903 events in other Romanian periodicals usually contain fewer details. Other photos in *Universul* (according to their captions) show: "The Costume of Albanized Serbians in Ipek (Old Serbia)" (Ipek is in present-day Kosovo, Peja in Albanian and Peć in Serbian) in no.101, "Bulgarian Peasants in the Vilayet of Thessaloniki (Macedonia)" in no. 59, "An Albanian Girl" in no. 80, "A Christian Albanian Woman" in no. 60, "Serbian Peasants in the Vilayet of Monastir (Macedonia)" in no. 95, "Macedonian Insurgents Throwing Weapons in Houses" in no. 95, "Macedonian Insurgents Arrested by Bulgarian Troops" in no. 78, and finally "How the Turks Act in Macedonia" in no. 26. Besides these, there are another 11 images of seven places in Macedonia but also from Epirus, Greece, Serbia and Kosovo, photos of Ottoman high officials, as well as of religious monuments in Macedonia, Epirus and Kosovo. During the period January-February, the news and illustrations on the Ilinden Uprising in Macedonia compete only with other events in the Balkans such as the Italian-Turkish war, the assassination of the king and queen of Serbia and in fact with only one other event from outside the Balkans — the Boer War in South Africa. One may notice the impartiality of the captions, with the exception of the moment when the author refers to the victims of the Turkish reprisals. More surprising, as they imply a great capacity of historical anticipation, are the distinctions between Albanians and Albanized Serbians in Kosovo or the Muslim Bulgarians (Pomaks) in Macedonia, while in the articles there is a distinction between the Macedonian representatives of VMRO and Bulgarians. For many people such distinctions are not clear even in the third millennium, but a Vlach could make them even as early as 1903! Unfortunately, we do not know the name of this matchless "correspondent in Macedonia", but since we know that at least partly the photos belonged to the Manakia brothers, it is not very risky to assume that they were the correspondents, or at least war photojournalists.[27]

In my collection, I have the album printed in 1907 in Paris by Ienache Manakia, *The Macedo-Romanian Ethnographic Album. Types, Costumes and Villages of Aromanians* (*Albumul etnografic macedo-român. Tipuri, porturi și localități ale aromânilor*).

The Cinematheque of Serbia, as the primary inheritor of the Cinematheque of Yugoslavia, has preserved in its collections copies of many films made by the Manakia brothers, as the Cinematheque of Macedonia was only founded in 1974. It also has the negative of the only film where one can see Milton talking, the documentary *Kamera 300* (1958, directed by Croatian director Branko Ranitović). Many photos by the Manakia brothers which were published in Yugoslav magazines can be found in various libraries.

In the little town of Vršac in Vojvodina, the Bocșan family has a letter written by Milton Manakia to teacher Nicolae Bocșan in 1951. The letter is important because it is in Romanian and Milton says that he is Romanian and is interested in Romanian culture. In 1951, when he sent the letter, Romanian-Yugoslav relations were tense after the conflict between Stalin and Tito, as the Romanian Communist leader Gheorghe Gheorghiu-Dej denounced Tito as a Western agent. On 6 February 1951, after reading in the newspaper *Libertatea*[28] about the staging by Nicolae Bocșan of the play *The Cabinet Minister's Wife* by Branislav Nušić (1864-1938)[29] in Romanian at the Romanian high

---

[27] Marian Țuțui, *Frații Manakia și imaginea Balcanilor*, Bucharest: Noi Media Print, 2010, pp. 26-27.

[28] *Libertatea* was a newspaper of the Romanian minority in Voivodina, Yugoslavia. After 1945 all the Vlach magazines and newspapers in Yugoslavia, Greece and other Balkan countries ceased to exist. So it was the only Romanian periodical that Milton could read in 1951 in Yugoslavia.

[29] Branislav Nušić's real name was Alkibijad Nuša and he was a Vlach at least on his

school, Milton wrote to teacher Bocşan in Vârşeţ (Vršac): "I am a Romanian and when I see and read that Romanians make progress in culture, I am glad and my heart fills with joy." In the same letter he sent a photo of Branislav Nušić and wrote that he had met Nušić in 1912, while the dramatist was a Serbian consular clerk in Bitola. He added that Nušić was the son "of Romanian parents from Klisoura, a pure Romanian village".[30] At the end of the letter, he mentions with pride: "my film about the sultan is screened all over Yugoslavia". He signs it "Milton Manakia".[31]

Photos and postcards made by the Manakia Bros. can probably also be found in other Balkan countries and outside the Balkans. For instance, the 1918 German publication *Dreizehnter Jahresbericht des Instituts für Rumänische Sprache (Rumänische Seminar) zu Leipzig* (Thirteenth Annual Report of the Institute for the Romanian Language [Romanian Seminar] in Leipzig) hosted articles on Romanian dialects written by the German linguist Gustav Weigand and illustrated with several photos. In 1907, his study "Rumanen und Aromunen in Bulgarien" ("Romanians and Aromanians in Bulgaria") included at least one photo by the Manakia brothers, which I was able to recognize.[32] In Greece one cannot find original footage by the Manakia brothers but only photos and postcards in private collections.

Conclusions

Although to a certain extent the Manakia brothers belong to a national culture, the Macedonian one, if not to the Romanian and Greek ones, it can be said with greater certainty that they belong to the Balkans. Not only because the borders in the Balkans have changed very often and people like the Manakia brothers had no less than three citizenships in their lifetime, but also because, in its beginnings, cinema was not a national phenomenon, it was not related to any language as it was mute and many of the pioneers travelled from one country to another. We could say that the Manakia Brothers were European artists *avant la lettre*.

---

father's side. See https://en.wikipedia.org/wiki/Branislav_Nu%C5%A1i%C4%87.
[30] Like most historians and linguists at the time Milton considered the Vlachs as Romanians.
[31] I received a copy of the letter from the late film director Pompiliu Gâlmeanu, who met the recipient.
[32] Ţuţui, as above, p. 27.

The last century is closer to us than earlier ones not only chronologically, but also because of the images preserved on photosensitive film, among which are the ones left by the Manakia brothers. Our ancestors waged wars in the Balkans, traced out borders and wrote histories to the transient rulers' liking, but some photos and images on silver nitrate have preserved with accuracy the images of our past. Time is a whimsical antiquary: many of the photos ordered by individuals in the past are now heritage assets; moving images without pretensions from 80-100 years ago are more valuable than films with artistic pretensions, made by lots of people and with a lot of money. Maybe on a scale of millennia people will consider that the Manakia brothers have left to posterity an image of the 20th century as important as Herodotus or Strabo in ancient times. However, what moves us when watching their photos and films is that they had such an early intuition of what was moving in the Balkans, in both senses of the word.

Helen Vatsikopoulos

The Balkans In Europe:
And The Curse Of Too Much History

By way of a definition:

The Balkans, which in Turkish means "mountains", run roughly from the Danube to the Dardanelles, from Istria to Istanbul and is a term for the little lands of Hungary, Romania, Jugoslavia, Albania, Bulgaria, Greece and part of Turkey, although neither Hungarian nor Greek welcomes inclusion in the label. It is, or was, a gay peninsula filled with sprightly people who ate peppered foods, drank strong liquors, wore flamboyant clothes, loved and murdered easily and had a splendid talent for starting wars... Karl Marx called them "ethnic trash".[1]

The geography is right. The rest needs some urgent rectification: Cyrus Leo Sulzberger, the author of this entertaining but somewhat stereotypical description of my ancestors, was a scion of the *New York Times* newspaper dynasty and knew the Balkans well. A Pulitzer Prize-winning journalist, he was a chief foreign correspondent for decades. Writing in his memoir *A Long Row of Candles,* on the Balkan people he adds: "I, as a footloose youngster in my twenties, adored them". What fun C.L.S. must have had. But I, as a Greek-born Australian who hails from the Balkans, with some Macedonian ancestry, just have to step in here. I have some issues with this reductionist stereotype because it seems to be repeated time and time again. Other Greeks might object to being lumped in the Balkan region – the Mediterranean Greeks who live in white sugar cube houses and swim in clear azure seas – but my Greece is different.

---

[1] Cyrus Leo Sulzberger, *A Long Row of Candles: Memoirs and Diaries 1934-54,* London: Macdonald, 1969, p. 35.

For the first five years of my life I lived in a house built of stone, each piece roughly hewn from the surrounding mountains of granite or limestone, and we swam in a lake created by a geological fault some five million years ago alongside fish who exist nowhere else in the world. Instead of tentacled octopuses hanging like decorations on the porch, we had bright red spicy peppers drying for the harsh winter.

The noun Balkan I have no issue with, it's the verb that taints. To Balkanize is to "divide into smaller mutually hostile states". The Oxford Dictionary also adds another noun:

"Balkanization: (from the Balkans where it was done in the late 19th and early 20th centuries)". And then an italicized example if anyone is left in doubt: "*ambitious neighbours would snatch pieces of territory*".[2]

That Marx thought us "ethnic trash" is amusing. But if French Prime Minister Emmanuel Macron does – well, that is a game changer. In October of 2019, two Balkan nations waited to be officially escorted into the European club – Albania and the newly named Republic of North Macedonia. Accession talks had been a long time coming, and eagerly anticipated. For North Macedonia it had been a long and divisive journey to appease neighbouring Greece so it could remove its decades-long veto on membership. The country referred to by the UN and other countries, at Greece's insistence, as the Former Yugoslav Republic of Macedonia since its independence in 1991 had appeased its neighbour and finally changed its name to North Macedonia. It had agreed to change its flag, it had agreed to rename its monuments and rewrite its history books. It was a big sacrifice and at times a national humiliation. A referendum on the name change was largely boycotted. But North Macedonia had fulfilled all its promises leading to membership. Greece and Macedonia had done it. The past was behind them. They looked towards the future. A historic window of opportunity had opened up and the two countries had seized it. In 2018 they came together in a tiny village called Psarades, near the border on the shores of Lake Prespa, to sign an agreement. They had worked hard, ignoring their nationalist brethren, wearing abuse and condemnation. But they had done it in line with what Prime Minister Macron had declared was a time ripe for a "European Renaissance". A European renewal built on the pillars of freedom, protection and progress. What he did not want for Europe, he

---

[2] *The Australian Concise Oxford Dictionary*, sixth ed., Melbourne: Oxford University Press, 2017.

Lake Prespa, shared by Greece, Albania and North Macedonia

said, were anger-mongers backed by fake news who promised anything and everything but were in fact nationalists who threatened all of Europe. North Macedonia and Greece were confident that they had slayed the Balkan stereotypes and buried the Balkanized past. They had done the hard work, now it was time for their reward.

In October 2019 France, the Netherlands and Denmark refused Albania entry. And then, to everyone's shock, Prime Minister Macron used his veto and said "Non" to North Macedonia and Albania.

"Pourquoi?" Albania and North Macedonia were still a bit too Balkan for comfort, not quite European enough, not ready to join the real Europe; the ghosts of Sulzberger's stereotypes were yet to be slain. A historic opportunity had been squandered, those who worked for compromise had been betrayed. The North Macedonian Prime Minister resigned, having staked all on this compromise. His people would judge this failure at the polls. France had unwittingly rewarded Sulzberger's stereotypes. Irredentism, the desire to see some past territory or past period of glory restored, had won. As Europe closed the door, Russia's remained wide open. Prime Minister Macron had warned Europe: "Retreating into nationalism offers nothing, it is rejection without an alternative". When he rejected North Macedonia's entry into Europe it was Macron who forced this retreat into the past.

If only this nationalism stayed in the Balkans where it originated and where it belongs. But it never does. It wouldn't take long to travel around the world.

The Balkans in Australia

It began in Sydney with a text message from an ABC producer and former student of mine. "Saw this at my gym in Marrickville. First I've seen of its kind in my 22 years here." And there it was, an image, just a sticker on a stair handrail in a suburban gym, but he had also seen a few posters in the traditionally Greek neighbourhood. A blue and white sticker, the colours of the Greek flag and the message in Greek script: "Macedonia is Greek". Here we go again. Just a sticker? Just a few posters? A closer look and the logo was disturbingly familiar. An ancient Greek key symbol framed by an olive wreath. It was unmistakably Golden Dawn, the neo-fascist, Greek extremist right-wing group that aspired to a Greater Greece all the way up to Istanbul and, yes, all of North Macedonia.

This was the organization that came to prominence at the height of the Greek Financial Crisis in the late 2000s when the European Union powers demanded austerity. Muscle-bound Golden Dawn members were seen escorting the elderly to their ATMs and helping with soup kitchens. At one stage Golden Dawn was the third largest party in Greece. But since then its popularity has waned. The 2019 Greek elections saw them lose their one remaining seat in parliament, though they retained one in the European assembly. In October 2020 a court in Athens found Golden Dawn to be a criminal organization and ordered its leaders jailed.

But the party still has a foothold in Australia with branches in New South Wales, Tasmania, Victoria and South Australia. Golden Dawn Australia even has its own flag, the Union Jack replaced by the Greek key and the Southern Cross made up of small starburst symbols. These are the ones associated with the dynasty of Alexander the Great and ancient Macedonia. And this is what it is all about. Who has the right to claim the legacy of that superhero Alexander the Great. From Athens to Skopje to Marrickville: this is what the Macedonian Question is all about.

Some background to the Macedonian Question

On 8 September 1991 the Former Yugoslav Republic of Macedonia declared its independence. Some other republics of the Socialist

Federated Republic of Yugoslavia, which they had been a part of since 1945, did the same. Croatia, Montenegro, Bosnia-Herzegovina and Slovenia all pulled away from the USSR-modelled Yugoslavia, which had been soldered together by Socialist leader Marshal Josip Broz Tito's iron fist. Only Serbia stood firm but soon pursued its own "Greater Serbia". Bulgaria immediately recognized the new state of Macedonia but would not recognize its nationality or language, as it believed that Macedonians were really regional Bulgarians who spoke a Bulgarian dialect.

Its other neighbour, Greece, could not accept an independent state at all under this name. It would only call this politically inconvenient entity "the Former Yugoslav Republic of Macedonia" or by its acronym, FYROM, or by its capital, The Republic of Skopje, or just Skopje. And Greece made it clear that it would use its veto as a member of the European Union to block entry until the name was dealt with. To the Greeks, this was just the latest iteration of the hundred-year-old "Macedonian Question".

A few months after the independence split, on 17 February 1992, the Greek Foreign Minister Antonis Samaras explained to his European Political Cooperation (EPC) counterparts why Greece would not accept recognition on the grounds of FYROM's alleged irredentist expansionist plans and the theft of Greece's cultural inheritance: "Skopje found necessary to usurp Greek historical and cultural heritage in Macedonia from antiquity to the present. Thus, Alexander the Great and Aristotle have been added to the Skopjan pantheon!"

Prior to the World War II communist victory, from 1929 to 1941, during the time of the Kingdom of Yugoslavia, it was a province known as Vardar Banovina. Samaras explained that Tito always had plans for expansion and projected his Macedonia as the only legitimate state: "It was a political move fitting the Yugoslav leader's hegemonistic plans at the time. The Skopje Federative Republic was seen as the nucleus – or Piedmont – for the annexation of the adjoining Macedonian provinces of Greece and Bulgaria".

In 1992, the first democratically elected President of this state, Kiro Gligorov, clarified Macedonia's ancestry in a front-page story in the *Toronto Star*:

> *We are Macedonians but we are Slav Macedonians. That's who we are! We have no connection to Alexander the Great and his Macedonia.*

The ancient Macedonians no longer exist, they had disappeared from history a long time ago. Our ancestors came here in the 5th and 6th century (AD).[3]

The Macedonian Question was a highly emotive one and it could even make grown men cry. It was in the Ashmolean, Oxford University's 17th-century Museum of Art and Archaeology on 6 April 2011 that Emeritus Professor Robin Lane Fox was reduced to tears. The classics historian and author of *Alexander the Great* (1974) and the *Search for Alexander* (1981) was attending the opening of a rare exhibition of Macedonian antiquities: *Heracles to Alexander the Great – Treasures from the Royal Capital of Macedon, a Hellenic Kingdom in the Age of Democracy*. The sight of gold crowns that had graced the heads and elaborate silver cups that had touched the lips of Alexander the Great and Philip of Macedon elicited an emotional moment for the professor.

But the likes of Gligorov were soon replaced by a new, younger generation of politician and ancient Macedonia was claimed as theirs. Under the leadership of nationalist Prime Minister Nikola Gruevski, they embarked on a major reinvention of the capital under the project "Skopje 2014" – complete with giant statues of Alexander the Great and Philip of Macedon – and commissioned new public buildings in the ancient style so that visitors would see a city that looked as if it was created in antiquity. Just like Athens. This was a complete reversal of what the country's first prime minister, Kiro Gligorov, publicly stated in 1992 – that Macedonians today are descended from the Slavs who migrated to the area in the fifth and sixth centuries, and therefore have no connection to Philip and Alexander of ancient Macedon. At the exhibition of Macedonian antiquities, Lane Fox was asked about this turnaround by the latest leadership; he was unequivocal:

I think there is a message that is historical but still politically has to be said. Macedon is a Greek speaking kingdom in northern Greece populated by people using Greek names, Greek months of the year, worshipping Greek gods. Those who live in Skopje and say that that is Macedon and Alexander's homeland, are as ignorant and outrageous as if someone were to say that Oxford University was really in Belarus and Oxford was Minsk.

In an interview with a Greek journalist, posted on YouTube, Lane Fox reiterated the historic record:

---

[3] Dusko Doder, "History Never Dies in the Balkans", *The Toronto Star*, 15 March 1992.

Let's be generous for one moment, they may want to be part of Alexander's world and we should respect that and encourage it but they are nothing to do with his homeland. They must remember they were on the margins; some of the cavalry perhaps came from Paeonia on the edges of Skopje. But Alexander himself? It is nationalist nonsense. To annoy Greece.

And annoy Greece they did.

Everyone wants to claim Alexander the Great

The Nationalists of North Macedonia, and particularly the Internal Macedonian Revolutionary Organization (VMRO-DPMNE) political party, dispute that the ancient Macedonians were a Hellenic civilization. Ancient texts from Greeks of the time refer to them as barbarians, the name Greeks gave to "others". Aristotle was Alexander's tutor but Macedonian extremists deny that this means that the ancient Macedonians only spoke Greek and did not have their own language. So, if they were barbarians, they could not be Greek and therefore Greece cannot claim them. Thus, Macedonians can lay claim to the name Macedonia, the Macedonian language and their own Macedonian culture. Their national flag was created with the star of Vergina, the royal insignia found in the tomb of Philip of Macedon, discovered by Greek archaeologist Manolis Andronikos in 1977.

But there is another reason why everyone wants to claim Alexander the Great as their own and it has to do with a very modern phenomenon, that of *Soft Power,* in line with Joseph Nye's theory. Nye claimed that apart from military and economic power, soft power or the power of culture was able to make countries popular and attractive in the international sphere. Today's nations market and promote themselves with cultural diplomacy. This is what Pierre Bourdieu refers to as *cultural capital* or its cultural acquisitions, like ruins and museum exhibits and literature and films; and *symbolic capital* or its accumulated prestige like historical legacies. As such, antiquities are symbolic capital, used for national profit. Yannis Hamilakis writes in *The Nation and its Ruins* that a nation's ancient past and its archaeological finds are the primary symbolic capital of the country. He regards antiquities "as a symbolic resource of the nation"; therefore, the state is keen to safeguard them and guarantee their "profitable investment".[4] This is

---

[4] Yannis Hamilakis, *The Nation and its Ruins: Antiquity, Archaeology, and National Imagination in Greece*, Oxford: Oxford University Press, 2007.

one of the main reasons that Greece and North Macedonia were battling to secure their ancient and cultural legacies. The past is of benefit not only to the present but also the future. Nationalism and archaeology are almost in a symbiotic relationship. While Skopje boasted the biggest Alexander, the Greek city of Thessaloniki has had one for decades. Athens erected theirs only last year. Everyone wants to claim the ancient superhero.

Skopje, the ancient new city

I decided to see Skopje for myself. In a taxi travelling from the northern Greek border town of Niki, I crossed over into North Macedonia. The countryside looked the same, the same mountains of granite and limestone, the same wooded hills and farms stretching across the plains, even the people looked the same too. The only giveaways were the Titoist sprayed concrete, Brutalist apartment blocks that didn't have any balconies. As we passed through towns I noticed the starburst of Vergina, the symbol of the house of Macedon, emblazoned everywhere, from small fountains to the logos of private companies and public buildings. The socialist-era monuments stood out like sputniks, space-age globes and satellites fashioned with determined-looking proletarians brandishing scythes and sheaves of wheat; all promising a socialist paradise. And then came the modern ancient statues. I counted several Alexander the Greats before I got to the capital Skopje and then the anachronism of Skopje 2014 hit me – it felt as if I was either in a classical Disneyland or in a transplanted Caesar's Palace casino-land in a reinvented Las Vegas in the Balkans.

In the main square of Skopje stood the world's largest bronze statue. Alexander the Great on his steed Bucephalus. Towering as big as a multi-storey building, Alexander was raised high on a giant plinth, guarded by a circle of armed, muscled soldiers, who were in turn raised above a circular fountain that gushed synchronized sprays of water that changed colour with rotating rainbow lights. The tiles at the base of the fountain were copies of the originals found in the tomb of Philip of Macedon in Vergina. Albanian Muslim women in hijab brought their babies in strollers and their toddlers to play with in the water sprays. Chinese tourists photographed the new antiquities and families wandered the square on a night out. Across the square from Alexander the Great and over a historic bridge was his father, Philip of Macedon. He too stood tall and strong and the two men faced each other from opposite sides of the River Vardar. I remember a smaller Philip in Thessaloniki, smaller in scale and more historically accurate with a battle scar on his face. There were other statues too; historical figures like Byzantine Emperor Justinian and the medieval Tsar Samuel. There were also statues of nineteenth-century revolutionaries who fought against the Ottomans. Many of these are also claimed by Bulgaria – but that is another story. When the statues got repetitive, there were the two restaurant hotels in the river that resembled sixteenth-century Spanish galleons. From there I could see the new government buildings – the Ministry of Foreign Affairs, the new Archaeological Museum, the Museum of the Macedonian Struggle amongst many – all built in the classical style with large ancient Greco-Roman columns. Elsewhere, the communist-era buildings were getting facelifts, rococo facades giving the city the appearance of a European city that had been designed well before 2014 and more likely a few centuries ago. My eye caught a semicircle of marble maidens in the style of Greek *kores*. They were the nine muses of ancient Greek mythology, the daughters of Zeus. And there she was, Clio. The proclaimer, the herald and the muse of history. I wonder what she would have made of this historical pastiche of a city. Was there a look of puzzlement on her marbly visage? Perhaps it was my imagination or bias. Perhaps it was all a case of bread and circuses, but at an estimated cost of $700 million it was also a soft power project that was meant to define the nation. Every morning, in the days I stayed in Skopje I would wake to multicoloured paint splashed over the ancient-modern statues. Clearly not everyone thought it was money well spent. In 2016, the architect of Skopje 2014, Prime Minister Nikola Gruevski, was ousted from power and fled to Hungary, where he was granted political asylum. Within two years, the new government would begin to attempt to correct his kitsch and historical reinventions.

The Prespa Agreement

On Sunday June 17, 2018, under a temporary awning on a stage erected by the shores of Greater Prespa Lake, the prime ministers of Greece and its northern neighbour, still referred to as FYROM, and their foreign ministers and entourages, met in the village of Psarades. The village, my paternal grandmother's birthplace, is located only minutes from the border.

Also present was Matthew Nimetz, the American diplomat and UN envoy who, for the past 24 years, had worked behind the scenes to bring the two sides to agreement. Representing their countries were two youthful prime ministers unencumbered by the past. The then Greek Prime Minister Alexis Tsipras is a socialist, leader of the Coalition of the Radical Left, or Syriza. A communist in his youth, he oversaw the most austere negotiations over Greece's debt bailout. In a country dominated by the socially conservative Greek Orthodox faith, Tsipras has not married and lives out of wedlock, with his partner and their two children. He doesn't wear a tie. North Macedonia's Prime Minister at the time Zoran Zaev is an economist by profession and was leader of the Social Democratic Union of Macedonia. He sports a small scar on his forehead from the time he was beaten in parliament after his party elected an ethnic Albanian to the speaker's chair. The ethnic Albanian Muslims comprise a third of his country's population. The two men were born within four months of each other in 1974. The whole event was a photo opportunity for the times. They shook hands as their foreign ministers signed the agreement that would rename FYROM to North Macedonia, with an agreed geographic qualifier. The twittersphere was abuzz. Johannes Hahn, the EU commissioner for European Neighbourhood and Enlargement Negotiations, could hardly contain his excitement. "Signed – sealed – delivered!" he tweeted to the world.

Alexis Tsipras, who had just survived a parliamentary no-confidence motion over this move, told the gathering: "We are here to heal the wounds of time, to open a path for peace, brotherhood and growth for our countries, the Balkans and Europe."

The father of North Macedonia's then foreign minister Nikola Dimitrov was born in Greece and became a Macedonian refugee during the Civil War. Zaev, who had only become Prime Minister a year earlier, wasted no time in seeking a solution to this diplomatic impasse: "Our two countries should step out of the past and look to the future. Our peoples want peace ... we will be partners and allies."

After the signing, the official party boarded a boat and crossed the watery border to a village on the other side for a celebratory lunch. It was a perfect photo opportunity for the digital age. The two men would soon be nominated for the 2019 Nobel Peace Prize.

So, what did they agree on? The Former Yugoslav Republic of Macedonia would henceforth be known as North Macedonia, its language recognized as Macedonian and its identity as Macedonian. The flag would change, removing the ancient symbol of the house of Macedon, and the airport would no longer be named after Alexander the Great. The parliaments of both countries eventually ratified the agreement, though the numbers for a referendum in North Macedonia were poor. One year later Alexis Tsipras would lose power for what his enemies said was a sell-out of their heritage.

Two weeks after the signing, I went to Psarades. I sat at the same spot where the two leaders created history, ending the protracted fight with Greece over which country has the right to use the name Macedonia. At a restaurant closest to the jetty where the men signed and then left for lunch over the border I sat and took in the landscape and the significance of the Prespa Agreement. I ordered the local fish, the fiery red peppers and some of the local fire water, the *tsipouro* made by the farmers from the distilled skins of grapes. There was no mood for celebration there. None of the residents were invited to attend the ceremony. None of the residents of neighbouring villages were welcomed either. *Al Jazeera* had reported: "Security was tight at Sunday's venue, with police cordons in place many miles from the village. Anybody seeking to approach had to pass through successive identity checks."

In fact, there had been dozens of buses full of protesters, who travelled from all over the country to protest the agreement and were prevented from entering the one road to Psarades by a cordon of riot police. People I spoke to in the village were upset and several cried. They said the village church bells rang during the signing – the only way they could object to what they said was a sell-out of a 3,000-year-old Hellenic history. To them, the youthful prime ministers were, of course, too young to remember the Greek struggle for Macedonia in the 19th century; nor did they experience the Greek Civil War of 1946-49. They had no emotional investment in the issue, nor had they experienced the trauma of fratricide. Zaev and Tsipras were not people of the border area. This might have been an historical event but it was not the first one and it wouldn't be the last. Edith Durham, one of the generation of 19th century British travellers who frequented the Balkans, wrote in *The Burden of the Balkans* that "History in the Balkan Peninsula repeats itself with surprising regularity".[5] And academic John Agnew claims the Macedonian issue is "one of the best examples of ancient hatred to be found anywhere".

---

[5] Edith Durham, *The Burden of the Balkans*, London: Edward Arnold, 1905 (Reprint: Dodo Press, 2018).

Too much history

It's my favourite quote about the Balkans (apart from Sulzberger's) and it is attributed to Winston Churchill:

> *The peoples of the Balkans produce more history than they can consume, and the weight of their past lies oppressively on their present.*

Scholars are in dispute on whether the wordsmith leader actually said it or not. But it is spot on. Nothing happens in the Balkans without a trauma, a hurt, a betrayal that happened in the past and memories in this part of the world are very long. I sit in the restaurant, the meal over. I slowly sip the thick Turkish coffee, though I must call it Greek here in Greece. I look out over the lake and the mountains. The migratory birds have made their journey from Africa, they are breeding in the still waters. To the locals, the Prespa Agreement is just one more of many that they have seen come and go. The others were usually planned, discussed and drafted in gilt-decorated rooms with damask-covered furniture in the salons of cities they could only ever dream of visiting. Too much history here. Near the cliffs by the lake archaeologists had found evidence of settlements dating back six thousand years, Hellenistic settlements, Roman ones, evidence of Slavic invasions and the empires of Tsar Samuel the Bulgarian, the Byzantines, the Serbs and then the Ottomans. Two Balkan wars, the First World War, the Second and then the Greek Civil War whose scars have not yet healed. Too much history and now another chapter.

Just over one hundred years ago this village was part of the Ottoman Empire, my grandparents were born subjects of the Sultan. I look over at the smaller lake, wholly within Greece, and the larger Prespa Lake. Like the geographical region of Macedonia, this bigger lake is also divided. The Albanian, Greek and North Macedonian borders cut through it, subdividing its waters with national boundaries.

Is this latest historical chapter going to bring everlasting peace? I call my father in Adelaide. What does he think of the Prespa Agreement? He is happy. He says it's about time. About time that the past was buried so that healing could begin. And he would know. This area was the frontline of the Greek Civil War (1946-49). As a child during this little-known conflict, he was kidnapped by the losing communists, the ones whose fighters were once supported by Tito's partisans across the border. He then spent eight years in Skopje, one of 28,000 children transported out of the border war zone either to safety or to be brainwashed to the communist cause. This is still living history.

Later I would catch up with his brother, who was on holiday in Greece. He was one of those who came by bus wanting to protest the agreement but was not allowed through. I ask him what he thinks of the Prespa Agreement and the tears roll down his face, he is inconsolable. He was only eight years old when the retreating communists took him, his other brother and their mother to be resettled in Poland. It would be nearly a decade before the Poles would grant their release and long-awaited return home. This is not the solution, my uncle tells me, it is just another treaty, yet another wound. Tsipras he says has sold the Macedonian name to the "Skopians". He cannot bring himself to call their identity Macedonian, which the agreement does. A meme appears on Facebook: an image of the Greek Civil War Communist leader Nikos Zahariadis in Psarades surrounded by Slavic-Macedonian fighters who fought with him, hoping this alliance would lead to the annexation of this area to Tito's Macedonia. At the bottom of the page is a mournful looking Alexander the Great. Uncle Tony shakes his head. "Zahariadis failed but Tsipras has succeeded". More and more history and so little time to process it.

I get up and walk around the village. The traditional stone houses have two storeys and balconies. They are timeless, they could be used as locations for films set anytime from the early 20th century to the present. About one hundred people live in this village, but there are more people from Psarades living in Perth, Western Australia, than there are here in the ancestral homeland. The whole area defined as the municipality of Prespa is according to the Greek 2011 census the least densely populated region in Greece. Before the Greek Civil War around 12,000 people lived in 16 villages, today it's home for around 1,500. Many who were communist sympathizers or spoke the local Slavic language, which is now the official language across the border, fled in the dying days of the civil war and many either didn't want to or were not allowed to return. Scattered around the villages are ruins, the homes left behind, while several villages remain completely abandoned. And Greece still insists that there are no minorities in the country. Just Greeks who speak a different language. The sounds of that language can still be heard in hushed tones.

How do you write about the Balkans? How do you get away from the stereotypes that speak of Marx's "ethnic trash"? Lily Lynch is the editor of the Balkanist website, a former Californian who now lives in Belgrade, Serbia. Her "handy guide for journalists on how to write about this mysterious and brooding region" is of course satirical.[6] Set the scene, she writes, by describing the landscape using terms like "a vampiric maw of limestone" or an "accursed" geography that looks like "God gouged its surface with his fingernails". Write about the "barbarity or bloodshed" and of the recent history that "has been written in blood". And then, she says, trot out the quote from Churchill about the Balkans having "more history than they can consume". Guilty as charged.

But seriously there is truth to this. Like the patronizing depictions of the Middle East and 19th-century Ottoman world as some sort of Oriental exotic fantasy called out by Edward Said; the Balkans has been condemned in a similar way. In her seminal book *Imagining the Balkans* (Oxford, 1997) Maria Todorova calls out the culturally constructed Balkans that depict its people as "the other". Nowhere has this been more demonstrated than in the reporting of the Bosnian War (1992-95). I too am guilty. As Yugoslavia was breaking up, I was there reporting for the Special Broadcasting Service's international current affairs program Dateline and marvelling at the characters that seemed to be out of central casting. Serbia's Vuk Drašković and his long grizzly Chetnik beard. And who can forget Radovan Karadžić, the psychiatrist with that crazy hair. I interviewed these men and saw a Balkan distinctiveness that was hard to ignore. At the same time, nowhere has the curse of too much history been better exemplified than in the call to arms made by then Serbian Prime Minister Slobodan Milošević. The disintegration of Yugoslavia was inevitable so Slobodan Milošević, the consummate politician, decided to call up the ghosts of the past to shore up his future. On the 28th of June 1989 at the Field of Blackbirds he commemorated Serbia's defeat at the hands of the Ottomans back in 1389. The 600th anniversary of the Battle of Kosovo was used as an emotive political tool telling Serbs that he would never allow them to be victims again. Medieval Serbia was brought back from the dead to inflame the modern Serbs against their Yugoslavian neighbours.

---

[6] https://balkanist.net/how-to-write-about-the-balkans/.

Better to forget? Or to remember?

David Reiff is a journalist who has covered many wars. He reported on the breakup of Yugoslavia, as did I, then the conflict in Kosovo and the Bosnian war. Rieff questions the value of remembering the great wars, the great defeats and tragedies and injustices of the past, because they are subject to selective memory and are often misused through politicization.

Reiff questions George Santayana's iconic phrase: "Those who cannot remember the past are condemned to repeat it". In his work on the dangers of remembering, *In Praise of Forgetting: Historical Memory and its Ironies*, he introduces a prime example: "the Bosnian War, which was in large measure a slaughter fuelled by collective memory, or, more precisely, by the inability to forget".[7]

Forgetting is not that simple in the Balkans, as Prime Minister Macron well understands. But the weight of Balkan history should not be a burden carried on the shoulders of migrants in Australia. And it should not be a matter concerning the second generation. In the twenty-seven years since the Former Yugoslav Republic of Macedonia was declared, our cities have seen streets aflame in red flags with Vergina symbols of Macedonia and streams of blue and white flags proclaiming Macedonia can only ever be Greek. Those demonstrations faded after a while. They should never return.

The citizens of Sydney's Marrickville might be confronted with stickers and posters of "Macedonia is Greek", but in Whittlesea, a suburb of Melbourne, things seem to have taken a turn for the worse. The Mayor of Whittlesea is twenty-two-year-old Emilia Sterjova, making her the youngest mayor in Australia. She is also of Macedonian ancestry – not Greek-Macedonian but what we now call North Macedonian. Australia recognizes the Prespa Agreement, which among many things insists the Vergina symbol no longer occupies the flag, replaced now with a stylized sun. But Melbourne is a long way from Brussels. It was perhaps a normal Facebook post, Mayor Sterjova is looking happy. She has a white handkerchief in one lifted hand as if she is leading a line dance and in the other she is holding a flag. But it is the wrong flag. It is not the flag sanctioned by the Prespa Agreement. It is

---

[7] David Reiff, *In Praise of Forgetting: Historical Memory and its Ironies*, Yale University Press, 2016.

the old flag. It is the controversial flag of the nationalists.[8] Whittlesea in suburban Melbourne is to the Macedonians what Sydney's Marrickville is to the Greeks. Both sides claim ethnic majorities in these two migrant strongholds. But Greeks also live in Whittlesea and sit on the local council. This did more than upset the two Greek councillors, it caused a storm of protest. There were reports of a bashing and Mayor Sterjova claims to have received death threats. Irredentism has arrived in Whittlesea.

Back in Marrickville I followed the provenance of that sticker. Golden Dawn, the Greek fascist and racist political party, now banned in Greece, that once held the third largest presence in the Greek Parliament, has its own website. The photo gallery is somewhat alarming. Black shirts and Nazi salutes. A photograph shows members cutting the traditional News Year *vasilopita* cake. On the wall are Byzantine-style icons of dour-looking saints. On the table in front of the cake are the "Macedonia is Greek" stickers and flyers that promise a new victory: "We will return and the earth will tremble."

The site states its aim is to "Struggle for Our Hellenic Homeland" and, despite being migrants or the children of migrants in Australia, they are fighting to stop Greece's 1.8 million illegal immigrants. Their call is not limited to the Greek migrants but to second and third generation Australian-born "Hellenes". And anyone else who shares their vision:

> *We invite all Australians, including those of non-Greek background, to support the Nationalists of Greece in their struggle against the international powers that seek to destroy Hellenism and the birthplace of Western Civilization.*

And the Australian representatives of Golden Dawn have been busy making new friends, including Serbian Chetniks and Russian Cossacks. The Russian Cossacks of Australia, dressed in khaki uniforms, presented Golden Dawn with the flag of Novorossiya, the pro-Russian separatists of Ukraine. It looks almost medieval. What connects them is religion and in particular the Christian Orthodox faith. In another photograph I see an Orthodox priest blessing the gathering. And then I see a familiar face, it's of their special guest; he is none other than home-grown far-right extremist, Dr Jim Saleam, representing the Australian

---

[8] https://neoskosmos.com/en/154233/greek-communitys-outcry-as-whittlesea-mayor-holds-up-vergina-sun-as-a-symbol-of-macedonia/.

Nationalists. Greeks, Russians and Australians – yes, it's a multicultural country after all and there is freedom of speech and association. But there is a troubling development here.

In February of 2020, the director-general of Australia's Security Intelligence Organization (ASIO) Mike Burgess warned: "In Australia, the right-wing threat is real and it's growing." It is going to be, he said, among the country's most challenging security threats. We have enough challenges of our own in Australia, we should not import the perceived injustices of Europe's past. There is no room for irredentism in Marrickville, Whittlesea, or anywhere else in this country.

Macron and the European Project

Back in the Balkans and The Joint Inter-Disciplinary Committee of Experts on historical, archaeological and educational matters has begun meeting regularly in the country now called North Macedonia. The Committee of Experts is going through history books, public bodies, monuments, statues, maps, school textbooks and street signs making sure there are no "irredentist or revisional" references and when it finds them it calls them out and demands they be erased. It sounds like a scene in a dystopian novel by Ismail Kadare. Except it is real.

The Alexander the Great statue that once stood inside the Alexander the Great airport is gone. It was a gift of the Turkish government. The giant Alexander the Great statue in the main square of Skopje now has a plaque that explains he symbolizes "the Ancient Hellenic period" and remains in the square as a token of friendship between Macedonia and Greece. It is often graffitied as are other explanations of these "symbols of friendship". In the spirit of rapprochement, Greek fighter jets are policing North Macedonia's airspace and the latter is about to join NATO.[9] But not all is running smoothly. The opposition is threatening to revoke the Prespa Agreement if it wins power and opposition members of parliament continue to stand in front of the old flag and use the old name. Greece is getting rattled. Irredentist claims will continue. The 16th of June, 2018, may be a date worthy of celebration, when two young Prime Ministers risked their political careers in the spirit of compromise. But in a region with so much history it is also one of those dates that is selectively plucked out as a day of betrayal. That is the way of the Balkans.

---

[9] http://www.ekathimerini.com/240711/article/ekathimerini/news/greece-flies-first-fighter-jet-over-north-macedonia.

The Prespa Agreement is signed. The French who first said "No", then said "Maybe", and then along with the other twenty-six member states finally said "Yes". Was it the Russian alternative that changed their minds, or the Turkish or the Chinese or the Gulf Arab states all vying for influence in the Balkans? And is it now a done deal? Well, no. Nothing is ever that simple in the Balkans.

North Macedonians after nearly three decades fighting the Greeks on the name issue are now facing another adversary: the Bulgarians. It is no longer about the name but the language. The Prespa Agreement recognized the Macedonian language, but the Bulgarians do not. It is, they insist, a "variant" of the Bulgarian language and the door to Europe will remain locked until North Macedonia admits to it. And so it goes. On and on. Only in the Balkans.

Further References:

Tertrais, Bruno, "The Revenge of History", *The Washington Quarterly*, vol. 38, no. 4, **2016**, p. 8.

https://www.aljazeera.com/news/2018/06/greece-macedonia-sign-agreement-change-180617074429644.html

https://balkaninsight.com/2018/06/15/divisive-skopje-2014-landmarks-find-new-purpose-06-14-2018/

https://edition.cnn.com/travel/article/macedonia-changes-name-intl/index.html

http://www.macedonian-heritage.gr/OfficialDocuments/Samaras2.html

https://www.theguardian.com/commentisfree/2019/mar/04/europe-brexit-uk

https://web.archive.org/web/20091021145008/http://geocities.com/dagtho/yugconst19310903.html

http://xa-australia.blogspot.com

https://www.youtube.com/watch?v=6OYx-29Z3xE

(All internet references in this chapter were correct at 22 September 2023.)

Vrasidas Karalis

Greek Music And Its Formal Complexities

I

"This musical art comes not only from folk music, but from our past, our desires, our imagination and stories, and our tradition, which is the tradition of the Greek nation."

Manolis Kalomiris

Throughout the centuries, Greek music has been as polycentric and diverse as Greek culture itself. Despite the tremendous historical changes, music production in areas that today belong to the nation-state of Greece remained alive and constantly reinvented itself through its regional differences together with their intra-regional variations. Because of its geographic fragmentation, the music of islands (Aegean, Crete, Ionian islands, Cyprus) and Pontus was in many ways quite different in structure and tone to the music produced on the Greek mainland or in the urban centres like Constantinople and Smyrna.

In all these separate and, to a degree, parallel traditions, however, there was a deep distinction between the dominant demotic music (performed at religious festivals and folk fairs) and the high urban culture used by the bourgeois elite in their social festivities and ceremonies. The dichotomy between demotic and high art is probably the most salient characteristic of musical production throughout the development of Greek music, especially after the fall of Byzantium.

As Greek populations were dispersed both in the mainly Ottoman east and the Italian west as well as in the north, in Russia, and in the south, in Egypt, or settled in the urban centres of the Balkans, they encountered different traditions and practices. Moreover, music is always a fusion of sounds composed mostly around instrumental exchanges and the possibilities that new instruments and orchestrations create. Despite the fact that we know of a number of instruments, such as the lyre and the *aulos*, already mentioned in the Homeric epics, it seems that in ancient times, through their encounters with Egyptians, Persians and Phoenicians, Greek musicians adopted or adapted many non-Greek instruments, which then became part of the Greek music repertory. All major changes in music begin with the introduction or the invention of a new instrument which provides new tonal possibilities and rearranges the previous experiences at both the collective and the individual level.

By the time of Alexander and the expansion towards the east, the orientalization of Greek music became more prominent. Syriac, Hebrew, Egyptian, Persian and even Indian elements and their respective instruments became permanent characteristics of the Greek melodic tradition, enriched later through encounters with the Arab, Slavic and Turkish traditions. (To this day, some of the most popular songs and tunes originate from India and Persia, whereas the difference between Greek and Turkish music is slight, involving the employment of intervals which differ from western tones and semitones.)

For many centuries Greek music was the field of multiple cultural productions in which diverse aural experiences stood next to each other, a situation that became problematic only after the establishment of the Greek nation-state and the quest for ideological expressions of uniform national identity. Yet it didn't stop the aural experience changing in new compositions, as the introduction of the clarinet shows in the early decades of the nineteenth century – an innovation which led to the abandonment of the bagpipe or the traditional flute and transformed completely the soundscapes of music production, especially of demotic music. The addition of a fourth string to the bouzouki in order to "westernize" its sound was analogous.

Despite such continuity in instrumental or vocal innovations, it is rather difficult to establish a grand narrative on the history of Greek music in an "essentialist" or even "constructivist" manner. There is definitely both continuity and discontinuity, as well as the paradoxical situation that, until the invention of the recording studios, Greek music was extremely fluid and diverse, and even if it was produced by Greeks (for it was sometimes produced by non-Greeks) it was in a constant dialogue with other traditions and cultures. The fixed categorization of a core musical style and its regional variations as "Greek" started in the nineteenth century, when national traditions were organized discursively along historiographic lines of continuity, similarity and correspondence with certain salient traits of what became dominant in the institutionalized self-perception of the nation-state.

However, the in-between, polymorphous and somehow anarchic character of Greek culture can be detected in all forms of its music as an inexhaustible aesthetic capital and diachronic musical heritage. As with the ancient Greek dialects used in different artistic genres and styles of music and poetry performance, something analogous happens in modern Greek culture. The folk-demotic songs, the ecclesiastical chant, the subcultural *rebetika*, the improvised songs, the urban popular music or even modern classical music have always been in a constant dialogue with other traditions and frequently with each other. More than with linguistic forms, poems, stories and fairytales, the appeal of music as a universal language of emotions and experiences could never be restricted by official proclamations or even professed principles of nationalism, especially in periods when a society reimagines itself and looks outwards for points of reference.

The father of modern Greek music, Nikolaos Mantzaros (1795–1872), for example, best known for composing what is today the Greek national anthem, created his music through the Italian tradition. Living in the liminal area of the Ionian Islands with a strong and self-conscious aristocracy, Mantzaros was able to envision a transition from the basically monophonic Greek tradition to the harmonic polyphony of the Western traditions, something already tested in certain polyphonic liturgies by Frangiskos Leontaritis (1518–72). Mantzaros also tried new orchestral arrangements, differentiating himself, especially towards the end of his life, from the Italian tradition of Zingarelli and Rossini, discovering the "noble art of counterpoint", as he stated. (It is also rumoured that he composed a now lost (?) symphony in the German style *Sinfonia alla Tedesca*.) His appropriation of new harmonies from western Europe paved the way for the Greek National School, which would later flourish in Athens as the new political and cultural centre of the nation-state.

Greece's geographic position between Italy and Türkiye always had a deep impact on the aural culture of the new state. A good Turkish song or a catchy Italian tune were easily appropriated by Greek composers and audiences even in the bleakest historical moments of war and conflict. Very few paid any attention to the origin of these melodies because the song itself, its performance, dissemination and reception relied more on the actual confluence of events around it than on its preceding history. Music was always a realm of appropriation. Songs belong to their performers and not to their origins. Greek and Turkish musicians continued to work together despite the war and the alienation following 1922.

Composing music also belongs to the historical circumstances of its reception more than to the specific biography of its composers. After the establishment of the Greek Conservatorium in 1871 (and its curriculum reforms in 1891), the necessity of a Greek national music evolved into a veritable "civil war" between musicians. This can be seen in the story of two of its most popular classical composers. First, the case of Manolis Kalomiris (1883–1962) and then that of Nikos Skalkottas (1904–49). From the early twentieth century, there was a fierce debate in Athens about "the poison of Germanicism" that was said to be destroying "the polyphonic song of the Greek psyche". This accusation against the main advocates of the modernizing school was made by George Lambelet (1875–1945), whose short essay "National Music" (1901) tried to find a formal platform for the convergence of demotic and high art, of the westernizing tradition and its folk local counterpart.

Kalomiris consolidated the so-called "national school" of music, influenced by the emerging tradition of the Five Russian composers around Rimsky-Korsakoff and at the same time of Richard Wagner in Germany. Kalomiris insisted that Greek music was not close only to the Italian but to many other traditions and its diversity has nothing to do with geographic proximity: "To me at least," he wrote, "our national music reminds me more of a Norwegian or Russian song than of ten Italian operas!" The debate was fierce and, in a way, precedes the question of "Greekness" as discussed by the literary generation of the 1930s some decades later.

Kalomiris' operas, symphonies, piano works and chamber music created a space of symbiotic existence between Wagner's continuous melody and the Russians' harmonic orientalism, which in his opera

The Mother's Ring (1917, revised in 1938), for example, or his *Symphony of Manliness* (1918–20) or in his underrated finest work, the opera *Constantine Paleologos* (1961), takes on a completely surprising character. Kalomiris' rhythmic dynamism, as he called it, relocated local melodic lines from the folk and ecclesiastical traditions into a Wagnerian sonic atmosphere and mythological landscapes (as can be seen in the Fourth Movement of his *Symphony of Manliness*). He considered the trisemitone as the most permanent feature of "Greek" music, exploited throughout the centuries in a series of elaborations and employed in folk songs, shared of course by many Middle Eastern music traditions but also found in the West.

His final opera constitutes an exciting space of thematic motifs and variations in which the diverse sounds of the Greek tradition are all "unified" under his ingenious orchestration and successful use of Greek language in the work's melodic tonality and in his attempt to heal the lingering trauma of the fall of Constantinople and by extension of the Asia Minor Catastrophe of 1922 in an era when everybody wanted to forget it. His minor works *Triptych for Orchestra* (1937), *Piano Concerto* (1935) and especially his *Concertino for Violin and Orchestra* (1955) show how successfully he moved beyond a dichotomy of East versus West to polysemic sounds with strong Mediterranean resonances, with constant reference to the past of the Hellenic tradition but also with a pronounced hybridity in his orchestral experimentations.

However, if Kalomiris shows an inspiring yet conservative introspection, testing the value of modernity through the measures and the needs of the tradition, Nikos Skalkottas moved to a point outside the Greek tradition, while struggling to re-establish a point of returning to it. Probably the most permanent pattern in all his work is that of exodus and return, an Odyssean *nostos*, as the return is not simply a homecoming but also a movement inwards. Skalkottas departed from the culture of national music as established by the Athens Conservatorium, and opened himself up to the experimental radicalism of Arnold Schoenberg in the Weimar Republic and the culture of "new objectivity" before the rise of the Nazis in Germany. His *36 Greek Dances* (1931 and re-orchestrated in 1948–49) indicate the compromises that his artistic vision had to go through in order to fuse the popular tunes of folk tradition with the new "absolute music" of modernity.

Skalkottas re-wrote the dances twice in the thirties and then finally just before his death, in an attempt to have them performed. Despite the fact that today they are his most successful composition internationally, performed frequently by many outstanding orchestras, at the time of their composition they sounded alien and alienating. Skalkottas' radical modernism was an attempt to create new sonic spaces by testing the limits of his personal oscillation between tonal and atonal music, using dissonance and infusing the music with incongruous sub-tonalities, in the way Shostakovich did in his symphonies. This leads to the feeling of something incomplete in his work, or something which is promised but never delivered. Skalkottas understood the need for the gradual convergence of demotic and bourgeois art through experimentation in form and orchestration, and was the first composer to attempt a new synthesis with the urban song-tradition of the *rebetiko* underground music in his *Concerto for Two Violins* (1945), a project that remained unfinished and was rejected, due to his early death.

Skalkottas was in fact continuing a movement inaugurated by Emilios Riadis (1880–1935), whose "foreign" impressionistic music, deeply influenced by Maurice Ravel, was hardly performed during his lifetime. His work however shows an inspiring dialogue with European modernism and his piano work *Homage à Maurice Ravel* (1925) is still one of the most intricate and suggestive experiments with sound.

On the other side of the spectrum, in the urban popular music known as *rebetika*, the songs of Markos Vamvakaris (1905–72) became extremely popular with the urban proletariat, as he made them more acceptable by introducing a new form of orchestra with *bouzouki* and *baglama*, replacing the oriental *sandouri*. This also changed their performance venues, especially after the War, whereas until then they were heard only in underground hashish dens. Vamvakaris reinvented and to a certain degree mainstreamed the *rebetika* performance after giving his songs to popular singers to be sung in urban bourgeois entertainment centres. His early recordings from the 1930s probably represent to this day some of the most "authentic" sounds of *rebetika* music, as they were composed in their own un-commercialized style with their inextricably connected vernacular lyrics. All recordings after the 1950s are to a large degree sanitized, domesticated or politicized to suit the entertainment needs of the emerging middle class who were trying to gentrify their remembered origins.

Marginalization was the predicament of most innovators during the so-called "stone years" of poverty, even after 1945 when the *bouzouki* was marginalized by the juke-box. Dimitris Mitropoulos, who understood Skalkottas' significance and tested the performability of the *Dances*, had to leave the country and become a world-renowned conductor in New York. Despite Mitropoulos' few compositions, like his magisterial *Concerto Grosso* (1928) and his experiment with dodecaphony *Ostinata in Tre Parti* (1926–27), the new generation of composers appeared outside the usual framework of the Greek Conservatorium despite its institutional domination.

From Kalomiris to Skalkottas, Greek music had to move from premodernity to radical modernity, from classicism to romanticism and from impressionism to expressionism while responding effectively to the new medium of recorded sound and dissemination through the radio, moving simultaneously out of the local towards the global. This transition happened extremely fast and led to the exclusion of Skalkottas from the official canon of national music and the rise of the recording composer. (Skalkottas' work was to be rediscovered in the eighties as a European composer in the manner of Béla Bartók, who also struggled to achieve a synthesis of East and West.)

The new soundscapes, however, were not broadcast by the Greek radio of the post-war period, from which they were excluded as decadent and anti-social, but through the rising new medium of technological modernity, the cinema. With Manos Hadjidakis (1925–94) and Mikis Theodorakis (1925–2021) the perception and the reception of Greek music as national culture changed radically and organically, not only with their popular songs but also with their more ambitious compositions, starting with their film soundtracks. Hadjidakis' music for Nikos Koundouros' *Magic City* (1954) and Theodorakis' epic composition for Gregg Tallas' *The Barefoot Battalion* (1953), and later his *Electra* (1962), paved the way for orchestral innovations and compositional changes that have redefined Greek music to this day. Hadjidakis' music fuses American sounds with the local instruments (the *bouzouki* becomes the central instrument at the new performance space of public taverns, being until then accepted only for underground *rebetika* performances), whereas with Theodorakis' work the grand Western European tradition of symphonic music becomes part of the popular culture, something that was to reach maturity in the 1960s and 70s and find its ultimate expression in his *7th Symphony* (1984).

In a way, the tension between Kalomiris and Skalkottas was to be resolved by the medium of cinema and not by another composer. Both Hadjidakis and Theodorakis were simultaneously and alternatingly modern and premodern, struggling to deal with creative originality in the era of the mechanical replication of music by the entertainment industry. Furthermore, as composers of the period of fusion they consciously tried to bring together high and popular music, while grafting their compositions with references to other traditions, mainly from the Balkans and especially from Türkiye, but also from Italy and the Arab world, as well as from wider global music. But music does not create only national, or even tribal, identity but also class consciousness; the convergence of musical styles meant also the gradual domination of the middle class, which appropriated subcultural and high cultural identities within a new framework of democratic equality of idioms. This was consolidated with the establishment of a bourgeois subjectivity and its uneasy quarrels with the established order of power, which never led to a complete disengagement or critical confrontation with the past.

Yannis Dalianidis' *Commoners and Aristocrats* (1959) and Orestis Laskos' *Beethoven and Bouzouki* (1965) can be seen as emblematic films which paved the way for a gradual convergence of various musical styles in a form of substitute class reconciliation. Usually both movies have been used to imply the artistic endorsement of the *bouzouki* by the upper bourgeoisie, but in reality they also implied the acceptance of classical high art by the working class in specific venues of performance and sites of coexistence. Especially after 1974, the restoration of the Republic allowed for the first time the free exchange of practices and ideas in all forms of the creative imaginary.

The truth is that for decades it was obvious that an interesting fermentation was taking place in the country. Dimitris Mitropoulos, who became famous as conductor, not as composer, and of course the great performer Maria Callas demonstrated that, despite the domination of demotic tradition, high bourgeois culture was also thriving in one way or another, in a country without strong institutional structures or indeed aristocratic protocols.

Jani Christou (1926–70), however, with his "metaserial music" totally shatters this un-nuanced view of music production and occupies a special place that needs more careful study. If Kalomiris and Skalkottas had to deal with the Greek musical past and make it relevant to contemporary audiences and modes of production, Christou with his iconoclastic meta-modernism attempted to completely dissociate music from sound and harmony, assembling a primeval performance-happening of body, movement, theatricality and instrumental experimentation in a way that many cannot accept to this day (the unperformability for example of his *Strychnine Lady* (1967) is probably the case at hand).

Christou's music indicated that premodernism, modernism and postmodernism existed symbiotically in the Greek creative imaginary with the audiences moving freely and somehow unselfconsciously between genres, instrumental potentialities, sonic landscapes and performance spaces. In an interesting metaphor for this multiple identity, the classical composer Giannis Konstantinidis (1903–84) released some of the most popular Greek songs under the pseudonym Kostas Giannidis while composing the most demanding chamber music of the post-war era.

Such versatility produced composers as diverse as Ianis Xenakis (1922–2001) and Vangelis (1943–), who started composing in Greece before moving to the international stage, in a way that brought them to prominence in both popular and experimental music – although Vangelis' soundtrack for the movie *Blade Runner* is a strange amalgam of both, paving the way for the new genre of electronic music. Xenakis' "stochastic music" also established the new architectonics of sound first heard in his *Metastaseis* (1953–54), dis-assembling the great form of music, the orchestra and the symphonic structure.

The cultural situation that stifled and killed Skalkottas was gradually opening up and new voices and performers were claiming visibility, despite the restrictive institutional framework, state censorship and the domination of popular music. Soon the song cycles or the grand oratorios composed in the 70s and 80s, like the *Magnus Eroticus* (1972) by Hadjidakis or the *Canto General* (1974) by Theodorakis, were abandoned by the local recording studios. From the mid-eighties the rise of the star performer through the commodification of the industry and the rise of private television channels started changing again both the mode of production and the space of performance.

Meanwhile even Theodorakis, the patriarch of the convergence of musical styles, spent most years of his long life composing operas and symphonies or revisiting the orchestral works of his early youth, as the music landscape of the country was increasingly dominated by the populist byproducts of the entertainment industry. Despite all, however, it seems that the convergence between high/urban and demotic cultures that took place in Hadjidakis' and Theodorakis' scores in the late 1950s still inspires new sonic landscapes both inside and outside the official system of production or channels of dissemination. It is also obvious that contemporary Greek music is still searching for its new identifications, which roam through diverse and frequently contradictory mainstream cultural, subcultural or cross-cultural identities.

II

Silence is the most beautiful sound because it contains everything.

Eleni Karaindrou

Greek music was and still remains the most visible example of Greek culture's liminal condition, occupying an in-between position defined by the diverse potentialities of its structural heterogeneity. Despite its prevalent demotic character there always existed a counter-tradition of high culture, not always in competition with the popular musical production but in a way expressing a critical view of its own physiognomy. If popular music with its long history and collective appeal expressed the central core of Greek cultural imaginary, high culture as developed first in the Ionian Islands represented a critical self-reflection on the limits of its provenance. It also functioned as the central secular expression of cultural creativity that counteracted the profound appeal and domination of ecclesiastical music which determined the creative imaginary after the destruction of the Byzantine aristocracy.

Demotic culture is by its nature *syllectic* – it gathers tunes, performances and instruments from everywhere. High culture is *eclectic* – it chooses and appropriates under a pattern of existing genres, styles of performance and forms of expectation. Demotic culture is based on subtle repetitions and archetypal rituals that bind a community around its festivals and ceremonies of social bonding. High culture, especially of the urban bourgeoisie, is based on the constant change of styles of composition and performance, that allows new audiences from diverse backgrounds to make claims to social visibility and political power.

Furthermore, historically, high-bourgeois culture meant participation in modernity and the new symbolic order encapsulated by its institutions. It was a process that indicated not only modernization but also secularization and individual emancipation: it led to the understanding of pieces of liturgical music not as part of timeless ecclesiastical ceremonies but as works of aesthetic imagination. It also reinterpreted anonymous folk music as the expression of spontaneous creative imaginary transcending the customs and the rituals that defined it, with a continuing relevance beyond their social and cultural horizon. Skalkottas' *Greek Dances* are not about regional folksy tunes but about a supra-geographic symbolic territory for an imaginable community of listeners everywhere.

Greek music was always an amalgam of both, having liminality of compositional patterns as the most permanent element of its morphoplastic potentialities. Despite the small market and the smaller audience, Greek music continues the challenging task of being renewed from elsewhere by absorbing new elements (jazz, soul, rock, disco, electronic, etc.) and by establishing novel melodic attractions through instrumental experimentation. Its multimodality remains the foundational grammar of its tonal repertory. It bridges cultural configurations and aural experiences and at the same time repositions itself within its geographical context by incorporating new patterns through the composers of the diaspora and the new voices emerging after the demographic change of the nineties.

One of the most tortuous questions of the past, especially for seekers after cultural purity, was about the "belonging" of Greek culture, as they always underestimated or downplayed the trans-cultural and indeed cross-cultural nature of all music production in Greek regions since antiquity and the rapid repositioning of its cultural physiognomy according to the demography and the ideological projects of the dominant political order. Music is never owned; it is always reimagined by various people under different conditions of performance and reception.

Music production by Greeks drew from and gave back to all those music traditions that it came in contact with: it was and still is a synthetic but also a synthesizing configuration of sonic potentialities. Its main structural conflict was not its affinity with other overlapping traditions in the region but the internal dichotomy between high and demotic styles of production, between the urban and the rural, the *syllectic* and the *eclectic*. With the assistance and the osmotic function of technology, as introduced after World War II, the cultural imaginary became able to establish forms of convergence and consilience that ended such dichotomy. Because of its liminal and marginal position, the Greek music industry was able to avoid the pitfalls of extreme commercialism and the dangers of bureaucratic standardization: and it can still provide an open space for new sound synergies and imaginative reinventions of its past.

Following a significant tradition of women composers, like Suzanna Nerantzi (1830–1900), Sophia Dellaporta (born c.1850), Mario Foskarina–Damaskinou (1850–1921), Eleni Lambiri (1889–1960), Eleni Econopoulou (1912–99), Rena Kyriakou (1917–94), Calliope Tsoupaki (b. 1963) amongst others, Konstantia Gourzi (b. 1962), who today lives in Germany, is continuing the synthesizing work of previous generations; she states that: "I make my contribution in that I bring sounds and ideas from different religions and cultures, and longingly let one of the previously seeming opposites take shape in a transcendent, sonic coexistence." The same can be said about Eleni Karaindrou (1939–), whose film music fuses modes and tunes through the haunting sonorities of wind and string instruments, creating an atmosphere of meditative nostalgia through its minimalistic self-replicating psychological de-realization, which has already gained wide international recognition. With Karaindrou, Greek music becomes part of the global music traditions not as an ethnic or exotic form of aural experience but as a significant contributor to the changes that are taking place world-wide today with the extreme commercialization of music production in the globalized society of "total spectacle".

Despite the ongoing financial and cultural crisis, new performance venues are constructed, like the new Megaro Mousikis (Recital Hall), and new composers from diverse backgrounds delineate the future orientation of Greek music, or rather the global music produced in Greece. The internet and the use of electronics has both democratized and trivialized music production – and this is one of the great dilemmas and ambiguities of all contemporary music. But the future holds many surprises and the Greek diaspora might bring one of them. The new field of research could be the music composed in different parts of the world by musicians of Greek origin – like John Psathas in New Zealand for example, Constantine Koukias in Australia and the Netherlands, Georges Aperghis in France or Georges Tsontakis in the States. And through them we will probably be able to better understand and interpret the dilemmas about self-expression and collective identity, between authenticity and innovation, of contemporary Greek music in its appropriate global context.

Certainly, there are some epistemological questions raised by the narrative presented so far. However, even if we accept the most radical constructionist approach, what we call today Greek music could not have been created out of nothing. Other communities understood that there were specific tunes called Greek, or motifs and phrases, and they called them so. In a Medici wedding in 1589 a composition for solo voice (monody) *alla Greca* was sung as a polemic against the prevailing polyphonic madrigal. In the Balkans and the Arab world there are dances called Greek indicating their origin and sound – just as in Greek the *Chamiko* and the Serbian dances suggest by their names a non-Greek origin.

With the beginning of the Enlightenment, the need to delineate clear patterns of classification led to the gradual separation of such inter-communal cultural customs and ceremonies in multiethnic empires. Like most traditions with long recorded linguistic history, Greek music followed the upheavals and the transformations that took place over the centuries in all of them, due to the Greeks' geographic dispersion and topographic fragmentation. In a way, there was always a recognition of homologous sonic experiences that were characterized as Greek (despite the fact that on many occasions until today the Byzantine-Orthodox melos is semantically conflated to mean Greek music.)

Yet when talking about Modern Greek music many intellectuals condemned the aristocratic "foreign" music of the Constantinopolitan upper classes or denounced the Oriental influence of its folk songs. The quest for authentic music and indigenous sounds began as a result of romantic nationalism. The project for "authentically" Greek music was gradually formed in a rather random and vague way (since there was no political centre). Its organizing principles changed when from the polycentric communities of the eighteenth century it moved to the homogenizing nation-states of the nineteenth. Within the new state, music defined national identity and established a specific political order. As part of a nation-building strategy, it was made and composed for an imagined community of listeners but definitely not for an imaginary social utopia. Its actual performance, production and ultimately its funding established its very materiality; its imagined character produced in actual terms its very specific and concrete historicity.

However, the real rupture began with the establishment of the nation-state, during which a somehow self-contradictory process was inaugurated: the transition from the diverse cultural communities of dispersed Hellenisms to a unifying political nationhood of singular Hellenism (or even Helladism). This transition, both in social organization and symbolic self-perception, meant the privileging of specific discursive practices which led to an enforced hierarchization amongst existing regional idioms. Yet none of them won absolute legitimacy or complete acceptance.

Despite all, music production in the nation-state always maintained its central being as expressing a reality of boundaries and thresholds. It was always comprised of multiple converging and diverging conversations about national character, class consciousness and political conviction plus, for the educated few, about form, structure and orchestration. It developed around fragile institutional infrastructures and in the absence of research centres. Following the political vicissitudes of the state that sponsored its development, it became both an agent of political and cultural conformism as well as a radical project of modernist renewal. The industry itself sometimes gives the best answer: usually Kalomiris' works on CD are coupled with works by Skalkottas, and the national school style of music is quite frequently complemented by cosmopolitan experiments with sound.

The social polity in the nation-state remained indeterminate, an interstitial space and therefore a zone of diverse, contradictory and somehow anarchic interactions. The famous oscillation between East and West was also an expression of such interactions following the gradual convergence of the political centres of Greek populations to the single and singular political centre of Athens – established and ruled by members of urban bourgeoisies from various cities, like

Constantinople, Alexandria, Smyrna, Odessa, Venice, Petersburg, even Vienna, Paris and London.

The convergence happened only after a monumental catastrophe that changed the worldview of the previous four centuries. The fact that after 1922 Athens became the centre of Hellenic culture was predominantly a traumatic event: it presupposed loss and absence, indeed it predicated all existential realities as modalities of a foundational trauma. Music gave specific expression to the quest for healing and closure. Only in the middle sixties did it become possible to address the trauma that has established contemporary urban culture in the country and defined its artistic expressions.

Yet no homogenization can ever be complete – and definitely it is never absolute. The grammar of melodic production in Greece always remained multimodal and based on diverse scales and performance styles. The central question therefore should be not "Whose song is this?" but "Whose performance is this?" Music exists as performance: *its form defines the content of its identity*. In this respect, the music poetics in contemporary Greek creative imaginary is still in the making. No musician, not even Nikos Skalkottas, ever produced, beyond his personal reflections, any theoretical conceptualizations of the act of music composition in Greece. We only have descriptive sociological contextualizations but not interpretations of music as morphoplastic activity in the country. This is something which remains to be constructed after extensive research in the archives of oblivion by bringing back to life the neglected work of forgotten composers, performers and instrumentalists.

From the Greek (Rum) composers of Ottoman Constantinople to the works of Giannis Konstantinidis, Marios Varvoglis, Nicolas Astrinidis, Yorgos Sisilianos, Harilaos Perpessas (1907–95) to Theodore Antoniou, Haris Vrondos, Pericles Koukos and Michail Travlos, a thriving tradition of classical composers stands next to the more popular but equally interesting composers like Mimis Plessas, Nikos Mamangakis, Argyris Kounadis, Kostas Kapnisis, Dimitris Papadimitriou, Savina Yannatou, and Lena Platonos, amongst others.

It seems that during the last decade of crisis the convergence that took place in the fifties is disintegrating and a new disconnect between sound and performance is taking place. Music is composed for the performers' sake and around their personality. But thanks to the persistent work of committed researchers, it has also been revealed that the Greek musical past is much richer and more complex than previously thought. With them, the project of understanding Greek music is still evolving: disregarded works are found frequently in many libraries and new ambitious and adventurous experiments are composed, inspired and motivated by forgotten moments in history. Greek culture has lived with many identities in the past; it seems that more identities are already in the making and are having an impact on its creative imaginary. Fortunately, the poetics of music in Greece still remain an inconclusive plausible narrative of ever multiplying complexities.

николас Doumanis

The Mediterranean World, Identity And Migration: Some Ancient And Modern Examples

When it comes to the relationships between cultural, ethnic, racial, religious and national groups, the focus of academic literature has been on difference. Each group is usually imagined as a solid entity with hard edges, and most attention is drawn to moments of confrontation and friction. Much less interest is shown in how each might peacefully engage, overlap and even meld together. Middle grounds are rarely noticed. After all, conflict is more interesting to readers. It promotes a more graspable, albeit simplistic, way of understanding how groups relate. Western history has traditionally been dominated by the study of large political units (imperial states) and their mutual struggles for mastery, and these inter-state struggles are often described as if they were between solid things called "peoples": between *the* British, *the* French, *the* Russians etc. It was the anthropologist Eric Wolf who noted the tendency of historians to assume nations to be as solid as billiard balls that clash violently in play:

> *By endowing nations, societies and cultures with the qualities of internally homogeneous and externally distinctive and bounded objects, we create a model of the world as a global pool hall in which entities spin off each other like so many round and hard balls.*[1]

---

[1] Eric R. Wolf, in Eric R. Wolf et al., *Europe and the People without History*, Berkeley: University of California Press, 1982, p. 6.

The problem, as Wolf goes on to explain, is to fatally distort the nature of relationships. Consider ethnicity and the ethnic group in the Iron Age Mediterranean. From about 900 BC, indeed throughout the Archaic period (c. 800 to 500 BC), *the* Greeks and *the* Phoenicians were said to have fanned out westwards across the sea, transmitting Greek and Phoenician culture to places as far as Spain. The sea was thought to be the setting of a contest between the two dominant colonizing cultures of the era, with the former succeeding in claiming much of the northern coastal areas, and the latter dominating the south. Until relatively recently, this idea of a colonial contest between two well-formed and distinct cultures was the orthodox line.[2] Nowadays, this line is no longer accepted. Archaeological research and critical revision of the concept of ethnicity has seriously undermined any notion that the Archaic Greeks and the Phoenicians knew themselves to be "Greeks" or "Phoenicians". For by ascribing them *with the qualities of internally homogeneous and externally distinctive and bounded objects* we have overlooked the myriad ways in which Mediterranean cultures interacted and often created new cultures. Recent studies in world or global history have also made it clear that peoples have, more often than not, interrelated, cooperated, traded, socialized and coexisted peacefully. Groups have interacted for millennia, sometimes quite violently, but the typical mode of engagement was one that was more profitable in economic terms, and it is one that promoted a much greater deal of social and cultural confluence.[3]

One of the claims that arise from recent historiography and archaeological research, and a claim that is reinforced below, is that the Greeks and Greek culture were formed as a result of mobility and cultural sharing. The Greeks became a people as a result of mixing with other groups.

The problem of ethnicity in the ancient world

Since 2000 there has been renewed interest in the history of the Mediterranean, and particularly in Fernand Braudel's idea of the Mediterranean as a subject in its own right. In *The Mediterranean and*

---

[2] See Moses Finley, *Early Greece: The Bronze and Archaic Ages*, London: Chatto and Windus, 1970; Oswyn Murray, *Early Greece,* 2nd ed., London: Fontana, 1993; John Boardman, *The Greeks Overseas*, 4th ed., London: Thames and Hudson, 1999; John Boardman and N. G. L. Hammond (eds), *The Cambridge Ancient History*, vol. III, part 3, *The Expansion of the Greek World, Eighth to Sixth Centuries BC,* 2nd ed., Cambridge: Cambridge University Press, 1982.

[3] See Nicholas Doumanis, *Before the Nation: Muslim-Christian Coexistence and its Destruction in Ottoman Anatolia*, Oxford: Oxford University Press, 2013.

the Mediterranean World in the Age of Philip II (1972), Braudel argued that the sea and the coastal natural environment had indelibly shaped, if not determined, the historical destinies of the peoples that lined its shores and inhabited its islands. The natural environment and its complex ecologies conspired into forcing peoples to eke out an existence on the sea and to interact with peoples via the sea. *The Mediterranean* was a monumental work that drew attention to the fundamental relationship between humans and the natural environment, but such was the scale of the book's achievement that historians were content to talk about it rather than follow its example. That changed belatedly in 2000 with the publication of the equally monumental *Corrupting Sea* by the medievalist Peregrine Horden and the ancient historian Nicholas Purcell. Since then, Mediterranean history has enjoyed a renaissance. Historians have been working on the sea's geography and ecology in order to elucidate how each managed to shape the social destinies of the peoples who live around "the Inner Sea", and how peoples moved and were reconstituted culturally by their movements. In *The Corrupting Sea*, Horden and Purcell deal explicitly with the idea of connectivity: that rather than representing a barrier to relationships, the sea facilitated intense interactions between peoples to a degree that it destabilized such categories as ethnicity, or facilitated the making of ethnicities through intense interactions. Horden and Purcell do not, however, have a great deal to say about ethnogenesis, but the connections they draw between Mediterranean ecology and mobility make it clear that peoples or cultures were in frequent contact with other peoples or cultures, and that this was the normal mode in antiquity and in the Middle Ages.[4]

A close examination of ethnogenesis is offered by the most significant intervention in the field of Mediterranean history in recent years, the Wolfson Prize-winning book *The Making of the Middle Sea* (2013) by the Disney Professor of Archaeology at the University of Cambridge, Cyprian Broodbank.[5] As the title suggests, Broodbank brilliantly considers the emergent properties that came together to transform the Mediterranean into a connected space. *The Making of the Middle Sea* covers thousands of years of history, including the Copper Age, the Bronze Age and the Iron Age, and it details the history of early

---

[4] *The Corrupting Sea: A Study of Mediterranean History*, Oxford: Blackwell, 2000.
[5] *The Making of the Middle Sea: a History of the Mediterranean from the Beginning to the Emergence of the Classical World*, London: Thames and Hudson, 2013.

agriculture, urbanization and early states, not just in the relatively densely populated east but also in the more sparsely populated regions of the western Mediterranean. Given that most of his evidence is archaeological, he typically offers plenty of discussion of metals, tools, various technologies, and about the incremental advances in technologies that relate to socio-economic changes. Broodbank nevertheless succeeds in making the material evidence speak, and he succeeds in showing how new identities were being formed all the time.

For the Bronze Age, and particularly for the Near East (Egypt, the Levant, Mesopotamia and Anatolia), we have abundant archaeological evidence and some written evidence. The latter often provides the names of cultures or ethnic groups. There are some cultures that endure throughout the period, like the Egyptians, Assyrians and Babylonians, but there are numerous cultures that arise suddenly in the historical record, and then seemingly disappear just as quickly. What about the Hittites, for example, the people of Mitanni, the Hyksos, the Kassites? One could rattle out a huge number of peoples about whom we know very little. In the Iron Age, we have the Lydians, the Phrygians, the people of Moab and Edom. The Arameans, for example, whose language became the language of the Assyrian, the Persian empire and Jesus, first became a force in Syria and northern Mesopotamia around 1000 BC. But they seem to come from the Syrian fringe of the Arabian Desert nearby. They are locals who nevertheless come *out of the blue*.

Why did so many ethnic groups seem to emerge in the Bronze and Iron ages? How important were these identities to the peoples in question? Were these primary or secondary identities? Were they prepared to die for these identities? Unfortunately, archaeological evidence cannot provide enough detail to answer such questions. There is certainly not enough information to explain in detail specific cases of ethnogenesis: how ethnic groups like, say, the Samaritans, first emerged and developed. What archaeology does provide, however, is enough clues to suggest broad patterns of ethnic group formation.

The Iron Age Mediterranean and the Near Eastern empires

One reason why groups kept forming was because of movement or migration. Empires were powerful enough to force migration, while the opening up of the Mediterranean Sea allowed for unforced migration. Because of these movements, peoples had greater opportunities to mix and share ideas, which in turn saw the formation of new identities.

In the Bronze Age (c.3000–1200 BC), the Mediterranean was an under-developed space. The central and western regions were sparsely populated, featuring small, village-sized settlements, whereas in the east towns and cities concentrated in the Levant (i.e. the Syria-Palestine region) and to a much lesser extent in the Aegean. Travel across the sea was rare. Ships preferred to hug the coast. But by 1200 the situation had changed. Because of improvements in shipping technology, merchants from the more developed east were frequenting establishing settlements in the centre and west. Towns were beginning to emerge independently in this other Mediterranean, and these were linking up with other towns to form regional networks. By 500 BC the Mediterranean had become a heavily trafficked and connected space, in which various Italian, Spanish, Gallic and North African peoples were mixing with Greek and Levantine peoples. Archaeological research suggests that the mixing process had structure. Networks that emerged in the western half of the basin were being linked up with trading networks in the east by intrepid Cypriot, Aegean and Levantine ships. Broodbank's idea is that the Phoenicians and Greeks could only do serious business in the west once western peoples had grown in number, accumulated enough surplus wealth, and had elites that were willing to buy luxury goods from the east. In other words, the two halves of the Mediterranean linked up once the under-developed western half achieved enough social complexity of its own accord.

In the meantime, empires were integrating the Near East. In the Bronze Age (c.3000–1200 BC) empires had formed in the region but these were relatively short-lived and left a minimal impression on the many cultures subjected to their authority. A much greater influence was generated by trade, as happened with the Mesopotamian region that came under the influence of Uruk, and when Egypt extended its influence over the Levant.[6] The same could not be said of the series of massive empires that dominated the Near East in the Iron Age: first the Neo-Assyrian Empire (911–612 BC), then the Neo-Babylonian Empire (626–359 BC), and finally the great behemoth (Achaemenid) Persia (550–330 BC). These were the world's first purpose-built empires – purpose-built to consolidate imperial authority over huge territories – and therefore wielded enormous power over large portions of humanity. These super-states

---

[6] G. Algaze, *Ancient Mesopotamia at the Dawn of Civilization*, Chicago: University of Chicago Press, 2008; David Wengrow, *What makes Civilization? The Ancient Near East and the Future of the West,* Oxford: Oxford University Press, 2010.

had the capacity to mobilize massive resources – manpower, finance, knowledge – and build massive cities, infrastructures, reclaim agricultural land, and move millions of people about in Stalinist fashion. They were capable of ethnically cleansing populations in the Middle East and greatly disrupting cultural life.

It is with these two vast systems in mind, the Mediterranean on the one hand and the world empires on the other, that I wish to consider the impact of forced and unforced movement on identities. Take the Phoenicians. The Mediterranean created "the Phoenicians". The term "Phoenician" was ascribed to the peoples who built trading cities along the shores of the Levant from the Late Bronze Age, who grew rich on being the middlemen in material exchanges between the wider Mediterranean and the urbanized Near East. The Phoenicians were based in port cities like Sidon, Byblos and Tyre. They brought metals and other raw materials from Spain and Sicily and Tunisia and supplied the aristocracies in the Near East with high-value goods. The Phoenicians are mentioned in Homer's epics as a Levantine people who are sea traders par excellence. In *The Iliad* and *The Odyssey* they are shifty, clever, and know the sea intimately.

But this is what the Greeks said of them. Did the Phoenicians believe they were a group? Did they have Phoenician consciousness, or was the name "Phoenician" an ascription applied by outsiders, and which only made sense to outsiders? It is certainly true that we know far too little about them. The Phoenicians invented a phonetic writing system, but they left very little for us to read that tells us much about them. We do not know what they called themselves: it is possible they called themselves "Canaanites" and identified as a group, but we cannot be certain. A recent book by Josephine Quinn argues that the Phoenicians are, in a sense, a Greek invention, and that they "did not in fact exist as a self-conscious collective or people".[7] They did, of course, *become* Phoenicians in due course, and what made then a group was the Mediterranean. The Phoenicians, claims Broodbank, developed into a recognzable group through their common experiences in the Mediterranean, where they explored the basin and set up relationships with peoples in Spain, Provence, Italy, Greece and North Africa. They borrowed, adapted and reconfigured cultural elements. They learned about the sea and its idiosyncrasies from these peoples and used their

---

[7] Josephine Quinn, *In Search of the Phoenicians,* Princeton: Princeton University Press, 2018.

accumulated knowledge to master the sea and build the best sea-craft. It was these experiences, and the traditions and practices that were developed through these experiences, that made the Phoenicians *the Phoenicians*.

Nowadays historians and archaeologists of this early Iron Age period, between 1000 and 500 BC, are reluctant to use the ethnic ascriptions "Phoenicians" and "Greeks" because we are not at all sure that these people had a group identity until the very end of that period. Better, perhaps, to use geographical ascriptions like "Levantine" and "Aegean". We do know that identities were forged to a marked degree through inter-Mediterranean interactions. The sea provided mobility and opportunities that made peoples mix, borrow, shed blood and intermarry.[8]

Take the Greeks, of whom we know a great deal more.[9] The Greeks were already an identifiable group in the time of Homer (if not before), in so far as they shared the same gods, spoke Greek and shared some cultural traits. In *The Iliad* he refers to them as "Achaeans", yet he also uses other names, while "Hellas" refers to a region in western Thessaly, whose people, the "Hellenes" were supposed to be named after an early king Hellen. This apparent confusion over names if anything indicated that the group later known as Hellenes were in the making. Historians of Archaic Greece agree that they would acquire a concrete identity by the fifth century, and differ only on the manner in which that identity took shape.[10]

Experts on Greek expansion in the Iron Age Mediterranean recognized that the Greeks developed a common identity over time by travelling amongst other peoples who were unlike themselves, and from whom they borrowed freely. They adopted influences to invent a common culture they could all agree on. There are numerous indications that non-Greek engagement in the Black Sea region, in Italy, Spain, France, and Sicily, as well as in the well-developed cultures of Egypt and

---

[8] Robin Osborne, *Greek History: The Basics,* 2nd ed., New York: Routledge, 2014, pp. 25-40.
[9] Much of what follows is drawn from Robin Osborne, *Greece in the Making, 1200-469 BC,* 2nd ed., London: Routledge, 2009; Jonathan Hall, *A History of the Archaic Greek World, ca. 1200-479 BCE,* 2nd ed., Oxford: Wiley Blackwell, 2013; Harvey A. Schapiro (ed), *The Cambridge Companion to Archaic Greece,* Cambridge: Cambridge University Press, 2007; Kurt Raaflaub (ed.), *A Companion to Archaic Greece,* Oxford: Wiley Blackwell, 2009.
[10] An excellent summary of the debate on early Greek identity is found in Margalit Finkelberg, *Greeks and Pre-Greeks: Aegean Prehistory and Greek Heroic Tradition,* Cambridge: Cambridge University Press, 2005, pp. 16-23.

the Near East, contributed to the making of Greek culture, from something formless or loose into a broadly recognizable identity. This identity was forged through interactions with other Greek-speaking peoples and non-Greek-speakers. The non-Greek "barbarians", who made incomprehensible "ba-ba" sounds, presented a point of difference that helped the Greeks recognize their commonalities.

Indeed, in recent years historians of the Archaic Period (800–500 BC) have ceased to refer to Greek settlement movements as "colonization", for the term implies that the Greeks were already Greeks before they had transplanted themselves and their cultures into southern Italy, Provence, northeastern Spain, Sicily, eastern Libya and around the Black Sea; Greek culture had not taken its classical form yet. The urban plan of a *polis*, for example, with its orthogonal pattern, its public spaces and its public buildings, was not something that was exported to the "New World" of southern Italy and Sicily. Rather, it was a concept that was developed through interactions between the old and new Worlds. If anything, the *polis* as a physical environment was probably created in the new world where settlers had the chance to develop cityscapes afresh. Thus, places like Megara Hyblaia in Sicily looked like a Greek *polis* before old cities like Athens, which was forced to clear some of its built environment in order to create its *agora*.

Just as important was the role of non-Greeks. "Barbarians" inspired Greek identity formation in a positive sense. For example, Etruscan elites, who bought massive quantities of Greek pottery – some 30,000 Greek pots have been found in Etruscan tombs – had potters in Greece catering to Etruscan tastes. As a consequence, Etruscan tastes had an impact on Greek pottery in terms of style and its uses. From the Phrygians of central Anatolia, whose wealth and splendor beguiled the Greeks, the Greeks borrowed ideas about aristocratic consumption and the *megaron*, a central hall that served as a public space, and which would become one of the many public buildings that the Greeks would use. The alphabet they took from the Phoenicians and used it to write prose literature. "Sculpture" they borrowed from the Egyptians and made it Greek. All of this was put together to create a recognizable "Greek" culture. The Israeli historian of Greece, Irad Malkin, concludes that the Greeks learned to see themselves as Greeks as they sailed further and further apart. "The 'centre' of their world", Malkin claims, "was the entire Archaic Mediterranean... [their world was] multiethnic, multicultural, and, most important, multidirectional", but in all this they defined themselves.[11]

Greek and Phoenician identities were therefore in flux during the early Iron Age. Between 800 and 500 BC, the Greeks were "in the making". But politics or events were also important. It took a political event, an experience that inspired them as much as the myth of the Trojan War, to make being Greek meaningful. That was the Persian War in 480–479 BC, when the world's greatest military power was successfully resisted by a small number of Greek city-states: only 31 of about 1000. It was only then that the Greeks appeared to settle on a meaningful name for themselves as "Hellenes".[12]

Short-term political factors also affected identity formation in the Near East. Centuries earlier, the Assyrians and Babylonians made a habit of deporting peoples and relocating them to places that suited imperial interests. They did it to break up cultural solidarities and to redeploy labour where it suited them. The process nevertheless served to create new cultures. And if deportations generally had the effect of breaking ethnic solidarities, for the Hebrews/Jews exile to Babylon in 597 and 586 BC was evidently a source of renewed strength. In this case, at least, those exiled, including the prophets Jeremiah and Ezekiel, were elites from Judah who struggled against assimilation and reformed the Jewish faith in the process. The exiles returned in 539 with a well-defined version of Judaism. That harder sense of Jewishness conflicted with Jewishness in the homeland, which had melded with other cultures of the region. The Babylonian exile appeared to crystallize Jewish identity, whereas for other groups the experience of deportation led to integration into larger cultural units.[13]

What I have sought to explain is how identities were affected within a particular period of early Mediterranean history: when the Mediterranean was *in the making* and when the first world empires took shape. What about recent Mediterranean history? Historians have tended to see the ancient and modern worlds as completely separate entities,

---

[11] Irad Malkin, *A Small Greek World: Networks in the Ancient Mediterranean*, New York: Oxford University Press, 2011, p. 164.
[12] Paul Cartledge, *Thermopylae: The Battle that Changed the World*, New Work: Vintage, 2006)
[13] Charles E. Carter, "(Re)defining 'Israel': The Legacy of the Neo-Babylonian and Persian Periods", in Susan Niditch (ed.), *The Wiley Companion to Ancient Israel*, Oxford: Wiley Blackwell, 2016.

but the factors that transformed identities in ancient times would continue to apply long after.

Mobility and ethnicity, 1850–1970

How did the identities of Mediterranean peoples like the Greeks fare in modern times? How did the great modern changes of the nineteenth and twentieth centuries, so brilliantly described by Christopher Bayly in his *Birth of the Modern World, 1780–1914* (2006) and his posthumously published *Remaking the Modern World, 1900–2015* (2018), or in Eric Hobsbawm's brilliant Age of tetralogy: *Age of Revolution* (1963), *Age of Capital* (1975), *Age of Empire* (1987), *Age of Extremes* (1994)? This modern age has been the age of nation-building, colonialism, and of industrialization, when capital and the middle classes came to define the world. It was also an age when more people moved around the globe than at any time in the past. Millions of people not only crossed the Atlantic, but also moved from East and South Asia into South-East Asia, and people from Russia and East Asia moved into Central and North-East Asia.[14] There were also millions that would be forcibly removed from their homelands – nowadays it is called "ethnic cleansing". The "unmixing" of the multi-ethnic Russian, Habsburg and Ottoman Empires involved the movement of millions of eastern Europeans westwards, millions of Muslims out of the Russian Empire and the Balkans, and millions of Christians out of Anatolia.[15]

That these great population movements coincided with the invention of modern nationalities was not a coincidence. Most historians agree with Benedict Anderson, Ernest Gellner and Eric Hobsbawm that nationalism as it is understood today is modern: that modern nationalism is different to the kind of patriotic cultures that existed before the modern era.[16] Nation building required intensive social engineering and often a great deal of violence and trauma. Even the French had to be smelted out of the multitudes of patois-speaking peoples that existed within the hexagon; most eastern Europeans had to be convinced not to be indifferent to the callings of nationhood; and if they were not convinced, then the

---

[14] Adam McKeown, "Global Migration 1846-1940", *Journal of World History* 15.2 (2004), pp. 155-89.

[15] Donald Bloxham, "The Great Unweaving: Forced Population Movement in Europe, 1875-1949", in Richard Bessel and Claudia Haake (eds.), *Removing Peoples: Forced Removal in the Modern World,* Oxford: Oxford University Press, 2009, pp. 167-208.

[16] Ernest Gellner, *Nations and Nationalism,* Ithaca: Cornell University Press, 1983; Benedict Anderson, *Imagined Communities,* revised edition, London: Verso, 1991; Eric Hobsbawm, *Nations and Nationalism since 1780,* Cambridge: Cambridge University Press, 1990.

First World War traumatized them into being exclusively German, Czech, Slovenian and so on.[17]

Mass migration played a major role here. The great influx of peoples into receiving states had the locals focusing more intently than ever before on what made them distinct from the newcomers. This also happened to be the age when borders were being policed and passports issued. The newcomers, in turn, were forced to think about their identities. Who were they? Italians, for example, often *became* Italian rather than Sicilian or Calabrian only when they arrived in the United States, where ethnic categories were used quite routinely in everyday discourse in order to differentiate the immense variety of peoples that had streamed into the country. People returning to their homelands, as Greeks in the United States did in large numbers, would also be transformed by their experience of having lived in the United States.

How were Greeks made by migration? The Greeks of the Ottoman Empire were transformed indelibly by forced relocation. Historians and foreign observers have always referred to the Greek Orthodox Christians of Constantinople, Smyrna and other parts of the Ottoman Empire simply as "the Greeks", and it was certainly the case that many of them spoke Greek and all of them observed the church liturgy in (Koine) Greek. The ascription made sense, but it also belied complexities. There were Turkish- and Armenian-speaking Greek Orthodox Christians that were also described as "Greeks", and speakers of Greek dialects, such as the Pontic speakers of the Black Sea region.[18] (Not included were the Greek-speaking Muslims of Crete, Macedonia and the Black Sea region.) Another reason for labelling these people "Greeks" is that it was assumed that these Ottoman subjects would always *become* "Greeks", which was also said of Greek-speaking Cypriots.

But what if the Greek Orthodox Christians of the Ottoman Empire had been allowed to stay in their homelands? What if the Young Turk Revolution of 1908 had succeeded in creating a functional inclusive order that made it possible for Greek Orthodox Christians to remain in Smyrna, Cappadocia and the Trabzon region? These "Greeks" did not

---

[17] Roger Markwick and Nicholas Doumanis, "Nationalization of the Masses", in Nicholas Doumanis (ed), *Oxford Handbook of European History 1914-1945*, Oxford: Oxford University Press, 2016.

[18] Sia Anagnostopoulou, *Μικρά Ασία, 19ος αι. – 1919: Οι ελληνορθόδοξες κοινότητες από το Μιλλέτ των Ρωμιών στο ελληνικό έθνος*, Athens: Ellinika Grammata, 1997; much of what follows is drawn from Doumanis, *Before the Nation*.

describe themselves as "Hellenes", nor indeed were they known as such by the Muslim majority. In Turkish they were known as "Romans" – *Rum, Rumlar*. These people called themselves Romans too: as Ρωμιοί (*Romii*) or Ρωμαίοι (*Roméi*). For them, after 1821, "the Hellenes" were the Greek nationals. The Turkish-speaking Karamanlidhes of central Anatolia already had a publishing industry that produced books in Turkish using the Greek script. As was made clear much later when Ottoman Greeks became refugees (πρόσφυγες) and acquired new names (Μικρασιάτες, "from Asia Minor" and Πόντιοι "Pontians"), they had their own cultural traits, many of which they had shared with their old Muslim neighbours in Anatolia and eastern Thrace.

It was the forced expulsion of the Greek Orthodox Christians or Greek Ottomans across the Aegean that would transform them eventually into "Hellenes", making them within a generation indistinguishable from the autochthonous Greeks. Similarly, the many Muslim peoples that were expelled from their ancestral lands in Greece, the Balkans and southern Russia and forced to reconstitute their lives in Türkiye, were expected to discard their mother cultures and become "Turkish". Refugee peoples in post-1922 Greece and Türkiye were subjected to xenophobia from the indigenous population, the effect of which was to encourage the refugees to remember their homelands on the one hand, but to also strive to became "better patriots" than the indigenous people. Cretan Muslims, for example, earned a reputation in Türkiye for the intensity of their Turkish patriotism. The population exchange between Greece and Türkiye in the long run did create Turks and many more Greeks.[19]

Migration also worked to create Greeks in another way. Since the 1890s, Greeks had emigrated across the Atlantic and throughout much of the world thereafter. As Greek nationals and Greeks from the Ottoman Empire arrived in their thousands in New York and then spread across the country, they also clustered to form communities. In major cities like New York and Chicago, in manufacturing towns like Lowell, Massachusetts, and Lancaster, Pennsylvania, or in the West where male émigrés worked in railway construction, the Greeks formed "Greektowns" and became one of the better-known ethnic groups in the United States. These Greektowns or Greek

---

[19] Nicholas Doumanis, "Peasants into Nationals: Violence, War, and the Making of Turks and Greeks, 1912-1922", in Daniela Baratieri et al. (eds), *Totalitarian Dictatorship: New Histories,* London and New York: Routledge, 2013, pp. 172-189.

neighbourhoods consisted of various kinds of Greeks, people with different accents and dialects, who nevertheless found that they had enough in common to form communities. As a group they developed a composite sense of Greekness to which they could all identify, albeit one that was also mediated by their "American" environment. Thus these communities would in due course have their own church, their Greek spaces (cafes, sweetshops), organizations (AHEPA), Greek schools and newspapers.[20]

Tellingly, when Greece along with Serbia, Bulgaria and Montenegro declared war on the Ottoman Empire in October 1912, thousands of young Greek Americans enthusiastically tried to enlist in the Greek Army.[21] That level of patriotism was inculcated by the experience of living in a country in which xenophobia and popular culture reinforced ethnic identities. "America" made Greeks feel much more "Greek" than they did in Greece.

Conclusion: Greek Australians

Ironically, therefore, cultural sharing did not dilute Greek identity. When Greeks migrated in large numbers to Australia after the Second World War, they generally arrived with a primary school education, which meant that they had been exposed to basic elements of Greek nationalist culture. They therefore valued the Greek flag, were schooled in nationalist Greek history, and supported Greek national causes. In the meantime, however, living in Australia with Greeks from different parts of the Greek world, such as Cyprus, the Peloponnese, Macedonia, the Aegean and Ionian islands, also impressed upon them the need for a common Greek culture that suited all of them. Over time, Greeks in Australia developed their own wedding traditions, their own kinds of social engagements, cultural spaces and their own organizations. Living together in Australia also gave them a sense of common struggle in a xenophobic yet economically accommodating environment, in which a disproportionate number of Greek migrants became shopkeepers and small businessmen. Such common experiences made for the development of a *Greek-Australian* identity.

They also became Greek-Australians by acquiring Australian approaches to time, work practices and engagement with the law and

---

[20] Charles Moskos, *Greek Americans*, 2nd ed., New Brunswick (New Jersey): Transaction, 1989.
[21] Theodore Saloutos, *The Greeks in the United States,* Cambridge (Mass.): Harvard University Press, 1964.

authorities. Migrants had to adapt to local ways and make it part of what the French sociologist Pierre Bourdieu called their *habitus* – their everyday dispositions and tendencies. The test was when they returned to Greece as returnees or visitors, and discovered that the ways of the locals, even their own siblings, seemed alien to them. Migration changed them.

Michael Karadjis

The Balkans: Europe's Periphery

Dominating the Balkans for centuries, the Ottoman Empire held back the development of its nations, which therefore belatedly emerged as Europe's periphery. As the first Balkan nation to emerge, Greece's proximity to the sea and regional trade gave its incipient capitalist economy the status of regional leader, while markedly less developed than western Europe.

If events such as the 1967 CIA-backed colonels' coup make Greece resemble a Latin-American US-client state, its accession into the EU implies full membership of the western club. Yet, as its economic crisis demonstrates, there is little room for new entrants, Greece remaining, in "world-systems" theory, Europe's "semi-periphery", the leading part of its Balkan periphery.[1]

Countries like Greece, midway between developed western "imperialism" and the semi-colonial world,[2] have also been conceptualized as "sub-imperial" powers, relatively developed parts of the "Global South" with their own regional ambitions, e.g. Iran, Saudi Arabia, India, Brazil etc.[3] Arguably, Greece was joined in this status when modern Türkiye was born in 1923, emerging as Greece's regional "sub-imperial" rival.

---

[1] On World-Systems theory, see Immanuel Wallerstein, *The Capitalist World-Economy*, Cambridge: Cambridge University Press, 1979.
[2] Here the term "imperialism" is not used to mean direct colonialism, but indirect economic domination of global scope, conceptualized as "neo-colonialism" by Kwame Nkrumah, *Neo-Colonialism, The Last Stage of Imperialism*, first published London: Thomas Nelson & Sons, 1965.
[3] On "sub-imperialism", see Patrick Bond, "Towards a Broader Theory of Imperialism", *Review of African Political Economy*, 2018, http://roape.net/2018/04/18/towards-a-broader-theory-of-imperialism/.

Despite the popular association of the Balkans with "ethnic conflict", other European nations were at war for a thousand years to 1945. Only the relatively recent emergence of Balkan nations makes ethnic conflict appear a "Balkan" phenomenon. This article will begin with a theoretical discussion of the national question, before examining how this has led to a number of "frozen conflicts" in the region today.

The National Question

Modern nations differ from state formations such as empires and principalities of pre-modern Europe. The concept of a "nation" *based on language* only emerged in the nineteenth century. Today's nations differ even from earlier sovereign states which roughly corresponded to later nation-states, such as France and Spain. Without transport or communications, medieval peasants knew little beyond their local world of manor and church.[4]

Vladimir Lenin explained how the development of capitalism led to the development of the modern nation, as it brought about "increasing exchange among regions ... growing circulation of commodities, and the concentration of the small local markets into a single, all-Russian market".[5] Emerging during the transition from feudalism to capitalism, nations arose in western Europe between the seventeenth and nineteenth centuries, while eastern Europe and the Balkans remained captive to multi-national empires until the early twentieth century.

Lenin followed German Marxist Karl Kautsky's definition of a nation as an entity formed through this economic development in combination with a common language, culture, literature and territory,[6] the corollary of which was the right of nations to self-determination, therefore advocating the break-up of Russia's "prison-house of nations".[7]

---

[4] The following passage on Russian feudalism explains this: "...the landlords and the monasteries acquired peasants from various localities ... one could hardly speak of national ties ... the state split into separate 'lands', sometimes even principalities, which preserved strong traces of the former autonomy, peculiarities of administration, at times their own troops ... their own tariff frontiers, and so forth", Vladimir. I. Lenin, "What the 'Friends of the People' are and How they Fight the Social-Democrats", *Collected Works*, vol. 1, Moscow: Progress Publishers, 1972 (original publication 1894), pp. 154–155.

[5] Lenin, op. cit., pp. 154–155.

[6] Karl Kautsky (Ben Lewis translation), "Nationality and Internationality", *Critique*, 37: 3 (1908; 2009), 371 –389.

[7] Vladimir I. Lenin, "The Right of Nations to Self-Determination", *Collected Works*, Volume 20, Moscow: Progress Publishers, 1972 (original publication 1914), pp. 393-454.

Benedict Anderson elaborated that nations were constructed as "imagined communities", based around common language and culture, by middle-class groups (writers, intellectuals, teachers) as the rising bourgeoisie strove to create a national market.[8] In particular, while European books were long written in Latin, which only a privileged minority could read, the invention of the printing press led publishing businesses to publish in the "national" vernaculars, creating a hugely expanded middle-class market for books and newspapers, facilitating linguistic uniformity and national consciousness.[9]

However, this new *literate* "national" community "below Latin" was also "above the spoken vernaculars" of the masses. E. G. Hobsbawm explains that "the popular masses – workers, servants, peasants – are the last to be affected by" national consciousness.[10] However, some vague identity, based on language, religion, "consciousness of belonging to a lasting political entity" or some historical view of themselves, often did exist, termed by Hobsbawm "popular proto-nationalism".[11] This facilitated national construction "as existing symbols and sentiments of proto-national community could be mobilized behind a modern cause or a modern state".[12]

The birth of the modern Greek nation

In the 2000 years between the ancient Greek city-states and modern Greece, neither the Byzantine Empire nor the Greek Orthodox Church (the "Patriarchate") represented anything "national" in character or scope, though perhaps representing "proto-national" aspects. During medieval times, today's Greece was occupied by Slavic, Aromanian (Vlach) and Albanian-speaking immigrants, in addition to the Greek-speaking population. The Orthodox Church brought these peoples to Christianity, but there was little in the way of "Greece".

However, the early rise of a merchant bourgeoisie in Greece – due to its exposure to the sea and regional trade and a strong diaspora – led to early signs of national consciousness by the 1790s. At its revolutionary beginnings, however, its ideological expression was more internationalist than nationalist;

---

[8] Benedict Anderson, *Imagined Communities: Reflections on the Origin and Spread of Nationalism,* London: Verso, 1983 (revised edition 2006), p. 5.
[9] Ibid., pp. 44–45.
[10] Eric G. Hobsbawm, *Nations and Nationalism since 1780*, Cambridge: Cambridge University Press, 1990, p. 12.
[11] Ibid., p. 46.
[12] Ibid., p. 77.

revolutionary leader Rigas Feraios (Velestinlis) called on Greeks, Bulgarians, Albanians, Vlachs, Armenians and Turks to unite against Ottoman despotism and construct a Balkans where all were equal.[13]

The revolution in the 1820s forged the nucleus of the Greek nation-state. Church, state and bourgeoisie now joined hands to set up schools to teach the Greek language and Hellenize the non-Greek speaking or bilingual Arvanites (Albanians), Vlachs and Slavs.

Even the Greek-speaking peasantry needed to be won; speaking a vernacular Greek different to the state's official "katharevousa", their national identity lagged. Most called themselves "Romaioi", identifying as former inhabitants of the East Roman (Byzantine) Empire. While hardly an expression of Greek nationalism, this neatly accords with Hobsbawm's "proto-nationalism". In time, not only the "Romaioi", but also most Arvanites and Vlachs and many Slavic-speakers were won to Greek national identity.

The emergence of other nations

Beyond the borders, this Hellenic nation also strove to draw in the Greek and non-Greek populations still under Ottoman rule, particularly in the Macedonian region. In the late nineteenth century, it faced competition from Bulgaria and Serbia, which had both independent states and Orthodox churches whose languages were related to that of Macedonia's Slavic peasants.

Statistical takes on the region's ethnic demography differed sharply, often due to different ways of classifying language and religion in different censuses.[14] A 1904 Ottoman census shows 307,000 Greeks, concentrated near the Aegean, whose national identity was clear. The 1.5 million Muslims included Turks, Muslim Slavs and Albanians. Estimates of Slavic-speakers ranged around 1.5 million. Apart from

---

[13] Dimitrios Karaberopoulos, *Rhigas Velestinlis (1757-1798) and his Revolutionary plan for a democratic state at the Balkan area*, Academia, https://www.academia.edu/37563503/RHIGAS_VELESTINLIS_1757_1798_and_his_Revolutionary_plan_for_a_democratic_state_at_the_Balkan_area.

[14] The discussion below covers a 1904 Turkish census, cited in Dimitris Lithoxoou, *Minority Issues and National Consciousness in Greece* (in Greek), Athens: Leviathan, 1992, p. 43, and Greek (1899), Serbian (1889), Bulgarian (1900) and German (1905) censuses, from Jovan Cvijić, *Questions Balkaniques,* Vol. 1, Paris: 1916, sourced in Henry Clifford Darby, "Macedonia", in Stephen Clissold (ed.) *A Short History of Yugoslavia from Early Times to 1966*, Cambridge: Cambridge University Press, 1966, p. 136, The total population was around 2.8 million.

a small number of Serbs, the Turkish census classified most Christian Slavs (895,000) as "Bulgarian", distinguishing between Greek Orthodox (320,000) and Bulgarian Orthodox (575,000). However, the national consciousness of neither group was solely determined by religion, ranging from Greek through independent "Macedonian" to Bulgarian.[15] An 1889 Serbian survey found all Slavs in the region to be Serbs, a 1900 Bulgarian survey found them all to be Bulgarians, and a 1905 German survey thought they were all "Macedo-Slavs", while a Greek census in 1899 showed ć also propounded a separate category of "Macedo-Slavs".[16]

In 1912–13 Greece, Bulgaria and Serbia seized the region. Serbia incorporated the Slavic Muslim Sanjak, largely Albanian Kosovo and 40 per cent of Macedonia. Greece took half of Macedonia, incorporating both ethnic Greek and Slavic-speaking regions; Bulgaria got the remainder. The Balkan Wars were followed by the collapse of the multi-national Ottoman and Austro-Hungarian Empires in 1918.

In 1910, the Balkan socialist parties called for "a free federation of the Balkan republics";[17] "free" meant that federating was a voluntary decision by independent nations, "federation" recognizing the difficulty of building nation-states where ethnicities were interspersed.

When Austria-Hungary broke up after World War I, its South-Slav subjects joined with the Serbian monarchy to form the "Kingdom of the Serbs, Croats and Slovenes", a prison-house of nations, especially for Macedonian Slavs, Slavic Muslims of Bosnia and Sanjak, and Kosovar Albanians.[18]

---

[15] According to Greek-Canadian writer Leften Stavrianos, "Those inhabitants of Macedonia that lived close to the Greek, Bulgarian and Serbian frontiers could be classified as Greek, Bulgarian and Serbian, respectively. The remainder of the population, with the exception of such minorities as Turks, Vlachs, Jews and Albanians, may be considered as being distinctively Macedonian. These Macedonians had a dialect and certain cultural characteristics which justify their being classed as a distinct south Slav group." See Leften S. Stavrianos, *The Balkans Since 1453*, New York: Holt, Rinehart and Winston, 1961, p. 518 (first published 1958).

[16] As did Greek professor G. Soteriades, see Henry R. Wilkinson, *Maps and Politics: A Review of the Ethnic Cartography of Macedonia*, Liverpool: Liverpool University Press, 1951, pp. 177–179, 189–193. Though this Greek and Serbian adoption of "Macedo-Slav" in the period before and after the Balkan Wars of 1912–13 may have been motivated by wanting to fight Bulgarian claims, this nevertheless emphasizes the very fluidity of all these ethnic designations at the time.

[17] Leften S. Stavrianos, "The Balkan Federation Movement: A Neglected Aspect", *The American Historical Review* 48.1 (1942), pp. 30-31.

[18] The Albanians furiously resisted Serbian occupation in 1913, and the Serbian monarchy was pitiless in its suppression: "Houses and whole villages reduced to ashes, unarmed and innocent populations massacred en masse, incredible acts of

World War II saw this clash between socialist and bourgeois-chauvinist ideals writ large. The multi-national resistance against Nazi occupation, led by Broz Tito's "Partisans", fought to turn Yugoslavia into an equal federation of nations, confronting Serbia's Nazi-collaborationist Nedić regime, the Serb nationalist Chetniks,[19] and Croatia's genocidal Ustashe regime.

Meanwhile, when Kemal Atatürk began forging the Turkish nation-state upon overthrowing the Ottoman Empire in 1919 (following the Armenian and Pontian genocides perpetrated by the dying empire), his first problem were the Greeks on the Aegean coast.

Greek leader Venizelos' invasion in 1919 invoked the principles of self-determination, given Smyrna's large Greek population. However, questions of where to draw new borders in ethnically mixed regions, initial massacres of Turks[20] and the context of the wider British-French-Italian imperialist attack on Türkiye, complicated the issue.[21] By taking its war deep into Anatolia, the royalist regime which succeeded Venizelos enabled Atatürk's counteroffensive to "solve" the Greek "problem" by driving Smyrna's Greek population into the sea.

The Asia Minor Catastrophe led to Greece and Türkiye consolidating their bourgeois national projects via the 1923 exchange of 1.5 million Christians from Türkiye with hundreds of thousands of Muslims from Greece. In contrast, Greek Communists, who had opposed the invasion, argued that each ethnically disputed or mixed area should have the right to a referendum on which state to join.[22]

---

violence, pillage and brutality of every kind – such were the means which were employed by the Serbo-Montenegrin soldiery, with a view to the entire transformation of the ethnic character of regions inhabited exclusively by Albanians" (Carnegie Endowment for International Peace, *Report of the International Commission to Inquire into the Causes and Conduct of the Balkan Wars*, Washington, D.C.: 1914).

[19] The Chetniks' aims were outlined in 1941: "To cleanse the state territory of all national minorities and anti-national elements. To create a direct continuous border between Serbia and Montenegro and between Serbia and Slovenia, by cleansing Sanjak of its Muslim inhabitants and Bosnia of its Muslim and Croatian inhabitants." See Jozo Tomasevich, *War and Revolution in Yugoslavia 1941-45: The Chetniks,* Stanford: Stanford University Press, 1975.

[20] Michael Llewellyn-Smith, *Ionian Vision: Greece in Asia Minor, 1919–1922,* New York: St. Martin's Press, 1973, pp. 89–90.

[21] A look at the map of the imperialist-imposed Treaty of Sèvres (1920) starkly reveals this reality; see for example Wikipedia under "Treaty of Sèvres".

[22] "The Anti-War Conference of Thessaloniki in 1918", from G. B. Leontaritis, *First World War*, Athens: Exantas, pp. 178–181 (sourced from Anti-War Anti-Nationalist League, *Without Borders: Anti-War Pages,* Athens: 1993 (in Greek).

Socialist Yugoslavia

The constitution of the Socialist Federal Republic of Yugoslavia, promulgated in 1945, proclaimed "the right of every nation to self-determination, including secession". Each constituent "nation" had its own "republic", while Kosovo and Vojvodina were autonomous "provinces" within Serbia. This attempt to create an equal federation of (socialist) nations was a foremost experiment reflecting Marxist views on the national question.

That there were imperfections – such as effective Serbian domination of the central political and military apparatus,[23] and economic decentralization favouring the northern republics (Slovenia's GDP was seven times that of Kosovo)[24] – is hardly remarkable.

But just as the experiment with "workers' self-managed" socialism promoted national equality, so Yugoslavia's later descent into capitalism buried it. From "market socialism" in the 1960s, in which socialized factories competed with one another, leading to massive unemployment, through decentralization of economic decision-making to the republics in the 1970s, leading to irresponsible borrowing and a $20 billion debt, to the imposition of federation-wide austerity by the International Monetary Fund (IMF) and World Bank to squeeze the debt from Yugoslav workers,[25] this evolution grew into capitalist restoration in the 1980s.

Nationalism became the ideology of the republic-based capitalist classes, utilized as they competed to seize control of Yugoslavia's resources,[26] either by trying to capture the federation and re-centralize it (Serbia under Slobodan Milošević) or to split away and grab some

---

[23] Serbs, around 40 per cent of the population, made up 78.9 per cent of personnel in the federal administration (Norman Cigar, *Genocide in Bosnia: The Policy of "Ethnic Cleansing"*, College Station: Texas A&M University Press, 1995, p. 212, citing *Ekonomska Politika*, Belgrade, January 27, 1969) and 60–70 per cent of military officers (Iraj Hashi, "The Disintegration of Yugoslavia", *Capital and Class* 48 (Autumn 1992), pp. 73–74).

[24] Hashi, op. cit., p. 63. This was partly due to global economic trends in the 1970s–1980s: prices rose for manufactured goods, produced in the developed north, and fell for primary products, produced in the south.

[25] "The grip which the IMF now exercises over the country's economy needed a fulcrum and found it in the increased power of the federal state, not only over the republican and provincial centres, but also over the main levers of the economy," (Branka Magaš, *The Destruction of Yugoslavia*, London: Verso, 1995, p. 97).

[26] Nationalism could also divert the Yugoslav working class from multi-national class struggle: in 1987 there were 1700 strikes by workers from all Yugoslav nations, often cross-ethnic strikes, against the IMF/federal government austerity regime.

spoils (Croatia under Franjo Tudjman).[27] The groundwork of the Croatian and Bosnian wars of 1991–95 had been laid, as rival bourgeois nations re-emerged from the corpse of socialist federation.

Current frozen conflicts: Bosnia

The first frozen conflict we will look at is Bosnia, a republic populated by Serbs, Croats and Bosnian Muslims (Bosniaks). In March 1992, when Bosnia applied for recognition, the European Commission (EC) pushed the Carrington-Cultheiro ethnic partition plan, which had been drawn up by Bosnian Serb and Croat nationalists – the Serb Democratic Party (SDS) and the Croatian Democratic Union (HDZ) – backed by Serbia and Croatia.[28] Despite their own 1991 conflict, these two countries joined forces to divide Bosnia, conquering regardless of ethnic composition, expelling 2,000,000 people and leaving 100,000 dead – overwhelmingly Muslims. Throughout the war, the EC and US continually pushed partition plans dressed as "peace" plans, rewarding ethnic cleansing.

The US-imposed Dayton Accord of November 1995 ended the war via the partition of Bosnia. An ethnically-defined Serb Republic (Republika Srpska, RS) was established on 49 per cent of Bosnia (Serbs were 30 per cent of the population), with its own army, police, parliament, education system and flag, in territory from which 1.5 million non-Serbs had been expelled.

The government-controlled half of Bosnia was transformed into a "Muslim-Croat federation". While Milošević and his Bosnian Serb allies had gained RS, Tudjman had to give up the Croat republic he had conquered in Bosnia, but this federation agreement put Croatia in a position to exert effective control over this half of Bosnia, while also preventing a poor, landlocked Muslim state full of refugees to emerge as a "Gaza in Europe".[29]

---

[27] The same Milošević who cultivated rising Serbian nationalism also gathered Belgrade's liberal economists into the "Milošević Commission" in 1988 to further "liberalize" the economy; see Lenard J. Cohen, *Broken Bonds: The Disintegration of Yugoslavia*, Boulder: Westview Press, 1993, pp. 55-56.

[28] *Statement of Principles for New Constitutional Arrangement for Bosnia and Herzegovina*, Lisbon 23 February 1992, from *Yugoslavia Through Documents*, ed. Snežana Trifunovska, Dordrecht: Martinus Nijhoff, 1994, pp. 517–519.

[29] This was a commonly expressed anxiety in Europe; e.g., according to Chris Hedges, "In the Truce Line, a Vast New Divide", *The New York Times*, 11 February 1996, p. E3: "The possibility there would be an overtly Islamic state in Europe, allied with Iran, is one of the main reasons the French opposed the establishment of Bosnia in the first place."

Multi-ethnic Bosnia was smashed. A quarter of a century later, there has been considerable, though not outstanding, success in terms of refugee return. However, the situation remains frozen due to the unjust nature of the peace.

First, we need to understand why the Dayton arrangement – and the previous partition plans and Serbo-Croatian conquests – cannot be considered a case of "self-determination" of the Bosnian Serbs or Croats.

Even within the Yugoslav federation, the Republic of Bosnia-Herzegovina was exceptional. Orthodox Serbs, Catholic Croats, and Bosnian Muslims lived either in mixed communities in cities, or in an interspersed patchwork of localities. While officially a republic of all three nations – a highly progressive concept – as industry developed and an urban working class grew, these "three nations", living in the same apartment blocks, working in the same factories, intermarrying and producing mixed children, were becoming one nation: Bosnian, or "Yugoslav". The multi-ethnic heartlands of Bosnia – cities such as Sarajevo, Tuzla, Zenica – were an embryonic "post-capitalist" nation formed via this real working-class unity.

However, the fact that significant numbers of Serbs and Croats (though far from all) sided with their "fatherland" nationalist regimes during the war indicates that this process was incomplete. In theory Serbs and Croats had the right to self-determination, including to join their "fatherlands". However, Bosnian Serbs and Croats were names of interspersed ethnic groups, not of geographical regions. Separate states could only be forged via ethnic cleansing.

In the 1991 census, Muslims (43 per cent of the population) formed an absolute majority in 31 of Bosnia's 100 districts, Serbs (31 per cent) were a majority in another 31 districts, and Croats (17 per cent) were a majority in 13 districts. That leaves 25 districts with no majority, and even districts with majorities were interspersed rather than contiguous, and often non-contiguous with neighbouring "fatherlands".[30] Where should these 25 districts, and the 9 per cent of mixed Bosnians identifying as "Yugoslav", fit in an ethnic partition?

Dayton therefore is both based on injustice and inherently unstable. On the one hand, the leaders of RS, already effectively independent,

---

[30] Stjepko and Thomas Golubic and Susan Campbell, "How Not to Divide the Indivisible", in Rabia Ali and Lawrence Lufschultz (ed.), *Why Bosnia? Writings on the Balkan War*, Stony Creek, Connecticut: The Pamphleteer's Press, 1993.

continually threaten to take it further, secede, and join Serbia. On the other, the Bosnian Croat HDZ leaders resent their lesser status compared to RS, and demand revision of Dayton to split the federation to create a third, Croat, entity. Therefore, the strategic wartime alignment between Serb and Croat nationalists has continued, and both play the "anti-Islamist" card with their own and western audiences.[31]

From the point of view of the Bosniak leaders, Dayton partition meant defeat; being the weakest and most geographically scattered ethnic group, with no "fatherland", their interests coalesced with those of the mixed Bosnian population around the multi-ethnic principle. However, if partition were taken further, the Bosniak-nationalist Party for Democratic Action (SDA) would be forced to change tack. The current size and shape of RS is only valid as part of Dayton, part of a tenuous sovereign state, with no historic, geographic or ethnic basis, so if it secedes, or the Croats split the federation, everything is up for grabs. As early as 1997, the SDA put forward a claim for 60 per cent of Bosnia if it were to break up.[32]

Meanwhile, multi-ethnic social-democratic parties continue to garner a large proportion of votes, in opposition to all nationalist scenarios.[33] Their advocacy of a civil state certainly accords with the reality of a partially mixed population and with the most advanced aspects of Bosnian tradition and is far superior to the excessive and unequal decentralization of Dayton. At its 7th Congress in 2019, the SDA also advocated a civil state.[34] However, this in itself may raise suspicion among Bosnian Serbs and Croats that, pushed too far, a purely "civil" state without any ethnic reference or autonomy could be a colour-blind "mask" for "majoritarian" Bosniak control, which would also not accord with Bosnian reality.

One consequence of Dayton is a lack of Bosnian voice in world affairs. When the UN voted on recognition of Palestine in 2011, the

---

[31] Mersiha Gadzo, "Large Increase in Anti-Bosnian, Anti-Muslim Bigotry", *Al Jazeera*, 19 September 2019, https://www.aljazeera.com/indepth/features/increase-anti-bosnian-anti-muslim-bigotry-report-190923053105055.html.

[32] Senad Pecanin, "Planning for Partition", Institute for War and Peace Reporting, *War Report*, May 1997.

[33] V. Hopkins, "Sarajevo Leader Sweeps Nationalism Aside in Bosnia", *Financial Times*, 14 August 2017, https://www.ft.com/content/68419cb0-8836-11e9-a028-86cea8523dc2.

[34] "Bosnian Croat Leader: Civic State Model Inapplicable in Bosnia", *N1 News*, 14 September 2019, http://ba.n1info.com/English/NEWS/a378112/Bosnian-Croat-leader-Civic-state-model-inapplicable-in-Bosnia.html.

Bosniak and Croat representatives in the tripartite government were in favour, but the Serb delegates vetoed it, due to the strong ties between Israel and RS, so Bosnia was forced to abstain.[35]

The internal consequences are more severe; with everything determined by ethnicity, all three ethnic elites use this to feather their nests. This can take the form either of permanent internal division, or at other times, cooperation among the rival ethnic elites in running this clientelist state.[36] In 2014, this led to a magnificent working-class uprising against all the elites, projecting multi-ethnic and non-ethnic slogans.[37] Ultimately, however, the inbuilt division proved stronger than that round of popular struggle, and today, with a moribund economy, and 400,000 unemployed, the main response of the population is emigration – 170,000–200,000 have left over the last few years.[38]

Current frozen conflicts: Kosovo

The second frozen conflict is Kosovo, with its 90 per cent Albanian population. Western governments had long opposed Kosovar independence, concerned it would encourage other minorities (e.g. Basques in Spain). When 99 per cent of Albanians voted for independence in December 1990, they were ignored; when the EC recognized Slovenia and Croatia in January 1992, other Yugoslav states also applied, but Kosovo was again ignored. This flowed from Kosovo's status under the Yugoslav federation as an autonomous region within Serbia, rather than a republic, signifying the status of its Albanian majority as a "national minority", whose "fatherland" was Albania, rather than a "nation".

---

[35] Michael Freund, "Fundamentally Freund: Israel's Best Friend in Europe", *The Jerusalem Post*, 5 March 2014, http://www.jpost.com/Opinion/Op-Ed-Contributors/Fundamentally-Freund-Israels-best-friend-in-Europe-351233.

[36] For example, in August 2019, the three main ethno-nationalist parties put out a plan to form a new Council of Ministers (a kind of governing cabinet), that is, the Serb nationalist SNSD, the Croat nationalist HDZ and the Bosniak nationalist SDA: Peter Lippman, "Bosnia-Herzegovina Report 2019, #4: Political Charades and Hot Rhetoric; Militarization of Police", September 2019, on http://balkanwitness.glypx.com/PL2019/report2019-4.htm.

[37] Michael Karadjis, "Bosnia's Magnificent Uprising: Heralding a New Era of Class Politics?" *Mihalis Balkan Analysis*, 12 February 2014, https://mihalisk.blogspot.com/2014_02_09_archive.html.

[38] Peter Lippman, "Bosnia-Herzegovina 2019, Report #1: Why Bosnia; Exodus; Protests; Scandal", July 2019. on website http://balkanwitness.glypx.com/PL2019/report2019-1.htm.

However, the Albanians were more numerous than many Yugoslav "nations", and this legal inequality was combined with Kosovo's *drastically* poorer economy. Following a mass civil movement, Tito's 1974 constitution upgraded Kosovo's status to "high-level" autonomy, sharing many features of a republic.[39]

Milošević's first attack on the Yugoslav federation was to abolish this autonomy in 1990; resistance was crushed, Albanian workers were sacked en masse, and a state of virtual apartheid was imposed on Kosovo.

Albanians resisted peacefully, but US recognition of RS in Bosnia in 1995 – achieved via horrific violence – while ignoring Kosovo's plea to be included at Dayton, led to an armed uprising for independence led by the Kosovo Liberation Army (KLA) in 1998. The US denounced the KLA as "terrorists",[40] fearing the insurgency could destabilize weak governments in Albania and former Yugoslav Macedonia (with its Albanian minority) and the southern Balkans more generally, involving NATO members Greece and Türkiye, the "nightmare scenario".[41]

Following a year of Albanian resistance and Serbian counterinsurgency, NATO introduced the Rambouillet Accord in early 1999 – allowing only a return to autonomy within Serbia – as a compromise to quell the instability. When Milošević rejected it, NATO began bombing to force acceptance, but Milošević's response – expelling 850,000 Albanians, who formed massive refugee camps across borders – meant Albanians would no longer accept the autonomy they had reluctantly accepted at Rambouillet. NATO reacted by stepping up its bombing of civilian infrastructure in Serbia, while ignoring the Serbian tanks "cleansing" Kosovo, further driving the populations apart.[42]

Following Serbia's defeat in mid-1999, half the Serb population fled Kosovo, fearing revenge attacks by returning Albanian refugees. But in the north, Serb paramilitaries prevented the return of Albanians. The Ibar river dividing north and south Mitrovica became a physical barrier dividing Kosovo, with the region north to Serbia's border declared a

---

[39] For example, Kosovo was represented directly in the federal presidency, rather than through Serbia, and had its own high court, central bank, territorial defense forces etc., features of a republic.

[40] Peter Gowan, "The NATO Powers and the Balkan Tragedy", *New Left Review* 234 (March–April 1999).

[41] Chris Hedges, "Kosovo's Next Masters", *Foreign Affairs*, May–June 1999.

[42] Of 400 Serbian tanks in Kosovo, NATO destroyed only 14 – mostly in the last 10 days of the war: M. Evans, *The Times*, London, June 24 1999.

Serb zone,⁴³ which contains Trepca, the largest mining and metallurgy complex in the Balkans.⁴⁴ Northern Mitrovica became Kosovo's Serb centre, with its university, hospital, school system and police. This situation – unofficial partition, NATO occupation, a UN-controlled government – lasted a decade, and this legal limbo denied Kosovo development credits and investment, leaving half the population unemployed, a recipe for permanent instability.

Eventually, this led to recognition of "supervised" independence by most EU states and the US in 2008, based on the Ahtissari Plan.⁴⁵ Kosovo's "supervision" is symbolized in its flag, the map of Kosovo surrounded by six stars, representing six ethnic groups, in the EU blue and white, with no symbolism or colours from the Albanian or Serbian flags – an attempt to mask the national divide by imposing a "civil" constitution.

The exception to this is the enhanced autonomous status of the Serb minority, with dual citizenship with Serbia, control over their education, health and most income from their areas, financial links with Serbia, and significant governmental representation for Serbs and minorities. Over time, a pragmatic coexistence has come into being, with Serb parties in parliament sometimes even in coalition with Albanian parties. The last violent anti-Serb outbreak occurred in March 2004.⁴⁶

However, Serbia, five EU states, Russia and many other countries do not recognize Kosovo, preventing its EU and UN membership and stalling economic progress. Serbia says it will never recognize Kosovo, while Kosovo has imposed 100 per cent tariffs on Serbian imports.⁴⁷

EU and US negotiators demand Kosovo activate the autonomous Community of Serbian Municipalities (ZSO), since Serbia and Kosovo agreed to it in the 2013 Brussels Agreement, at the time considered

---

⁴³ S. Erlanger, "Fears Grow over the De Facto Partition of Kosovo," *New York Times*, November 14 1999.

⁴⁴ Chris Hedges, "Kosovo War's Glittering Prize Rests Underground," *New York Times*, July 8 1998.

⁴⁵ "Comprehensive Proposal for the Kosovo Status Settlement", March 26 2007, https://reliefweb.int/sites/reliefweb.int/files/resources/1DC6B184D02567D1852572AA00716AF7-Full_Report.pdf.

⁴⁶ For example, Serbeze Haxhiaj, "Serbs, Albanians Learn Each Other's Languages in Kosovo Town", *Balkan Insight*, 5 February 2019, http://www.balkaninsight.com/en/article/serbs-albanians-learn-each-other-s-languages-in-kosovo-town-02-04-2019.

⁴⁷ Some tariff protection may be understandable given Serbia's early post-conflict absolute domination of Kosovo's market, but this level is aimed at political pressure.

a landmark which could unfreeze the conflict; Kosovo has dragged its feet.[48]

Kosovar Albanians certainly have the right to self-determination, but so do Serbs. Despite their high legal status, most Serbs oppose independence. Kosovo consists of parts of two nations with no common national consciousness, sharing the same geography; unlike Bosnia, it was never even partially a multi-ethnic society, but a Serbian colony, and once the tables were turned, the Serbs feel oppressed.

Albanian-majority regions – most of Kosovo – should have the right to join Albania, and Serb-majority regions to join Serbia, if they wish. In similar vein, Serbian president Aleksandar Vučić and former Kosovo president Hashim Thaci have jointly proposed the exchange of Serb-dominated northern Kosovo for the Albanian-majority Preševo region of southeast Serbia.[49]

This is rejected by the EU; any ethnic-based border changes pose the question of the Albanian minority in North Macedonia or of the Bosnian Croat demand for republic status, and are thus considered highly destabilizing. While partition would allow Serbia to keep the north's economic assets, it would be the worst outcome for Kosovar Serbs, only 40 per cent of whom live in the north. Its secession would abandon the majority of Serbs, living in smaller, more vulnerable enclaves surrounded by Albanians, and they would lose northern Mitrovica as a Serb centre inside Kosovo.

Therefore, many Serb leaders oppose partition. However, Rada Trajković, president of Kosovo's Serbian National Council, suggested an arrangement "according to the Cyprus model" – the UN's Annan plan for reunification based on a Greek Cypriot entity and a Turkish Cypriot entity forming a bi-zonal, bi-communal federation.[50]

Such a bi-national federation – more than mere Serb autonomy, less than full partition – accords with the reality of a society divided

---

[48] Michael Rossi, "Brussels Agreement Remains Kosovo's and Serbia's Best Hope", *Balkan Insight*, April 19 2018, https://www.academia.edu/36444118/Brussels_Agreement_Remains_Kosovos_and_Serbias_Best_Hope_ Balkan_Insight.

[49] Michael Rossi, "A Land Swap between Kosovo and Serbia Would be Deeply Problematic – and Potentially Dangerous", *European Politics and Policy*, 17 August 2018, http://blogs.lse.ac.uk/europpblog/2018/08/17/a-land-swap-between-kosovo-and-serbia-would-be-deeply-problematic-and-potentially-dangerous/.

[50] "Serbia Cannot be Kosovo's Hostage", *B92*, 27 February 2008, https://www.b92.net/eng/news/politics.php?yyyy=2008&mm=02&dd=27&nav_id=48003.

between two nations, allowing Albanians and Serbs to run their own affairs and represent themselves however they choose. The rationale for denying Albanians full independence – that their treatment of Serbs requires western "supervision" – would thereby have less credence.

Current frozen conflicts: North Macedonia

The third frozen conflict is in the former Yugoslav Republic of Macedonia, whose recognition was blocked by Greece following EC recognition of Slovenia and Croatia in January 1992.

On 17 June 2018, the Prespa agreement was signed, in which Greece agreed to recognize its northern neighbour as "North Macedonia".[51] For the sake of expediency, this essay will simply use the new agreed-upon name for all reference to this state.[52]

The people consider their ethnicity and language "Macedonian" and their government long rejected any name other than simply "Macedonia" for their state, while the Greek government rejected any name that included the word Macedonia. "North Macedonia" was therefore ruled out for 27 years, until this decision by Greece's leftist Syriza government and North Macedonia's Social-Democratic Union (SDSM) government, which is rejected by right-wing nationalists in both countries.

The issue is complicated by the presence of an ethnic "Macedonian" minority in northern Greece (and Bulgaria), whose very existence is not recognized, and whose language and cultural rights have been suppressed for decades.[53]

Greece has asserted that calling itself "Macedonia", and any interest in the minority in Greece, implied territorial claims on Greece, whose northern region is also named Macedonia, though the state's constitution rules out any such claims.[54]

---

[51] Helena Smith, "Macedonia Changes Name, Ending Bitter Dispute with Greece", *The Guardian*, 18 June 2018, https://www.theguardian.com/world/2018/jun/17/macedonia-greece-dispute-name-accord-prespa.

[52] For the purposes *solely* of expediency, the now internationally accepted title will be used for the state's name *but also for its people*, aware that this will still be considered unacceptable to many on both sides.

[53] Human Rights Watch/Helsinki, 1994, *Denying Ethnic Identity: The Macedonians of Greece*, New York.

[54] "The Republic of Macedonia has No Territorial Pretensions Towards any Neighboring State," Article 3, The Constitution of the Republic Of Macedonia, Published in *The Official Gazette of the Republic of Macedonia*, no. 52/91.

Macedonia is a geographical region, covering northern Greece, southwest Bulgaria and North Macedonia, encompassing numerous ethnicities, allowing nationalists on all sides to obfuscate. Greek nationalists cite the Hellenic culture of ancient Macedonia to claim that non-Greeks are not entitled to use that name. Ethnic Greeks living in Greece's Macedonian region call themselves "Macedonian", not as an ethnic signifier, but to identify with ancient Macedonia's Greek heritage, and claim that use of the name by non-Greeks is "insulting".

The ethnic "Macedonian" people speak a South-Slavic language which entered the Balkans around 600 AD. Just as today's Egyptians speak Arabic rather than ancient Egyptian but see themselves as Egyptian, both ethnic Greek and ethnic North Macedonian peoples living in Macedonia today should be entitled to claim connection to the region. However, ethnic Macedonian ultra-nationalists are equally good at obfuscation, drawing maps that show *their* "Macedonia" encompassing entire geographic Macedonia, including heavily Greek regions near the Aegean.

This essay does not take a side on the "name" issues. However, the Prespa agreement recognizes the reality that *a nation exists*. The historical record demonstrates that the North Macedonian people underwent a normal process of national development, self-identifying as "Macedonian" – regardless of one's view of this, contradicting claims that Tito's Yugoslavia foisted "Macedonian" consciousness on them to make territorial claims on Greece.

Let's compare two quotes from the time. In 1906, John Foster-Fraser claimed:

> *You will find Bulgarians and Turks who call themselves Macedonians, you will find Greek Macedonians and it is possible to find Romanian Macedonians. You will not, however, find a single Christian Macedonian who is not a Servian, a Bulgarian, a Greek or a Romanian.*[55]

However, Greek author Stratis Myrivilis wrote in 1924:

> *... their language is understood by Bulgarians and Serbs. They dislike the Bulgarians because they take their children to the army. They hate the Serbs for mistreating them...They do not want to be called "Bulgari" (Bulgarians), nor "Srrp" (Serbs), nor "Gkrrts" (Greeks). Only Macedonians.*[56]

---

[55] John Foster-Fraser, *Pictures from the Balkans*, London: Cassel, 1906, p. 5.
[56] Stratis Myrivilis, *Η ζωή εν τάφω* (*Life in the Tomb*), Athens, 1991 (first published in book form 1924), p.104–105.

Others found no concept of nationality at all[57] or multiple nationalities within one family.[58] One writer was told a village "is Bulgarian now, but four years ago it was Greek", because the Bulgarians offered a cheaper priest and teacher.[59] Clearly, none of this has much to do with real Bulgarian or Greek national identities.

National development is an uneven process; most likely, neither "Macedonian" nor "Bulgarian" was a fully developed consciousness in 19th century Macedonia. Authorities often designated Slavic-speaking people in Macedonia as Greek if adhering to the Greek Orthodox "Patriarchate" and as Bulgarian if adhering to the Bulgarian Orthodox "Exarchate". As they struggled against Ottoman oppression, many Exarchate Slavs identified as Bulgarians, whose language was similar; some Patriarchate Slavs developed a Greek consciousness despite language. Yet neither process was absolute or inevitable.

Geographic distance from Bulgaria and Serbia was one factor. Economic traffic along the Vardar river, connecting the central Balkans to Thessaloniki, was early dominated by urban Greek and Jewish traders. However, economic growth and resulting migration of the Slavic peasants to the towns led to the belated growth of a Slav-Macedonian middle class in the Vardar region, distant from the Bulgarian bourgeoisie based on the Black Sea coast.[60] Like elsewhere, these new middle-class elements in central Macedonia would come to see themselves belonging to a separate nation defined by the region they inhabit.

Such incipient "Macedonian" nationalism was facilitated by existing "proto-nationalism". Edmond Bouchie de Belle claimed that "in nine

---

[57] According to English author Henry Brailsford (*Macedonia: Its Races and Their Future*, London, 1906, p. 121) the Macedonians had "no highly-developed consciousness of race, and what little they possess is of recent growth. Their passion is not for their race but for their country. They are a people of the soil fixed in their immemorial villages..."

[58] For example, George F. Abbott (*The Tale of a Tour in Macedonia*, London, 1903, pp. 80–81) describes one family where there may be a "Servian" father, a "Bulgarian" son and "Greek" daughters. "If they are caught young by the Bulgarian propaganda, and reared in its schools, they are imbued with the idea that they are Bulgarians. If the Servians are first in the field, they become Servians." Meanwhile, "the old mother is generally content to embody her national convictions in the declaration that she is a Christian."

[59] "...if a father cannot contrive to place all his sons in a secondary school belonging to the race which he himself affects, the prospect of a bursary will often induce him to plant them out in rival establishments...a boy who is educated at the expense of one or other of these peoples must himself adopt its language and its nationality" (Brailsford, op. cit., p. 102).

[60] *Encyclopedia Britannica*, 15th Edition, 1974, Volume 2, p. 628.

instances out of ten" the peasants called themselves "Macedonians", which "does not have the character of a patriotic declaration, but simply that the villager lives in Macedonia", falling neatly into Hobsbawm's concept.[61] Given the nation's belated development, this vague identity was less likely to reach the ears of official circles.

It is not surprising that "proto-nationalist" peasants would refer to themselves by their geographic region, or even identify with figures from both Macedonia's Hellenic past such as Alexander the Great and its Slavic past, such as Marko Kralevich.[62]

The Internal Macedonian Revolutionary Organization was split from its formation in 1893 between those pushing for an independent Macedonia and those advocating Bulgarian annexation. Why fight for independence rather than join Bulgaria – the opposite choice to that made by ethnic Greeks in Crete and later Cyprus – if there was no incipient national consciousness? Finally, the very experience of taking part in the 1903 Illinden uprising was itself a further step in national development, as was the ravaging of Macedonia by armed bands from the three neighbouring countries following its crushing.[63]

Returning to today, the most charged period was the early 1990s, when enormous Greek nationalist rallies rocked Greece and many western cities. But already by 1995 the two countries adopted a pragmatic Interim Accord whereby Greece ended its economic blockade of its neighbour, which agreed to change its flag, which had displayed an ancient Macedonian symbol, allowing trade ties and Greek investment.[64]

---

[61] Edmond Bouchie de Belle, *La Macédoine et les Macédoniens*, Paris: Colin, 1922, p. 303.

[62] A 14th century Slavic ruler of a Macedonian principality based in Prilep. Russian researcher V. Grigorovich observed in 1844–45, "In every place that I have seen, I heard of no other names than those of Alexander G and King Marko. They live in the memory of the people in quite general imagery" (Mitko Panov, *The Blinded State: Historiographic Debates about Samuel Cometopoulos and His State*, Leiden: Brill, 2019, p. 221).

[63] "This explains why IMRO attracted so much popular support with its slogan 'Macedonia for the Macedonians'. The miserable peasants were torn this way and that, and retribution was sure to follow whatever decision they made. If they declared for the Exarchate they could expect a visit from the Greek bands. If they remained under the Patriarchate they were hounded by the Bulgarians as traitors." See Stavrianos, *The Balkans Since 1453* (note 15 above), p. 521. Dobre Daskalov, a participant in the uprising, similarly stated "now that we have been abandoned by them all to our fate, we feel ourselves one. We are no longer Bulgarians or Serbs, Romanians or Greeks, exarchists or patriarchists, but Macedonians condemned to death" (E. J. Dillon, "Macedonia and the Powers", *The Contemporary Review* 79 (1903), p. 741).

[64] *Greece and the Former Yugoslav Republic of Macedonia: Interim Accord,* Signed at New

Today's Prespa agreement is an inevitable, extremely belated, follow-on from that earlier agreement. If territorial claims do not exist (and the North Macedonian army is too small to be a threat), and if Greece can make progress with minority rights, then continuing the "name" conflict was not in either country's interests. Indeed, Greek investment there would seem in the interests of Greek capital, as would good relations with a weak neighbouring state, given its more powerful rivals in the region.[65]

The question then is why Greece was so uncompromising in the early 1990s, and why it took decades to agree on the current name. Part of this may have been fear that the new state's independence would encourage activism among the minority in Greece; another may be simply exploitation of genuine nationalist feelings among Greek-Macedonians by populist politicians; while nationalist mobilization was also a useful diversion for the neo-liberal Mitsotakis government of the time to push through its austerity program. But further aspects will be touched on in the final section.

Yet while this conflict is now unfrozen, about 25 per cent of North Macedonia's population, bordering on Albania and Kosovo, are another part of the divided Albanian nation. Compared to Kosovo, their position may have seemed relatively benign, but this hid marked disadvantages; for instance, ethnic North Macedonians accounted for 97 per cent of police and army officers, and no Albanian university existed, combined with grinding poverty.

Following mass Albanian demonstrations in 1997, the election of the Macedonian ultra-nationalist VMRO government brought this crisis to a head, and in 2001 an armed insurgency erupted. Following EU and US intervention, the main Macedonian and Albanian parties signed the Ohrid Agreement in August 2001, ending the insurgency.[66]

The agreement rejected the Albanian demand that North Macedonia become a state of two peoples. While valid in Bosnia, Cyprus and Kosovo, such a framework would not work where this is the only state

---

York on 13 September 1995,. https://peacemaker.un.org/sites/peacemaker.un.org/files/MK_950913_Interim%20Accord%20between%20the%20Hellenic%20Republic%20and%20the%20FYROM.pdf Google, or search in un-library.org.

[65] Türkiye and Bulgaria were the first countries to recognize Macedonia, hence gaining early entry into its economy, though Bulgaria refuses to recognize Macedonian language or ethnicity, viewing them as Bulgarians.

[66] Ohrid Framework Agreement, August 13 2001, https://www.osce.org/files/f/documents/2/8/100622.pdf.

the North Macedonians have.[67] Ohrid aims for a "civil" state, with strong devolution of authority to municipalities, effectively giving local power to minorities. There is no specific mention of Albanians; Macedonian is the official language, but in any region where 20 per cent of the population are non-Macedonian (which only applies to Albanians), the minority language is co-official; an Albanian university was opened; and minority representation increased in state organs.

The Ohrid Agreement has been hailed as a highly successful model, compared either with the extreme – and unequal – ethnic-based territorial decentralization in Bosnia, or a more centralized model. However, the colour-blind "civil" state may still mask real issues, as shown by sporadic ethnic clashes in recent years. When another VMRO government was defeated in 2017, the Macedonian SDSM formed a coalition with Albanian parties, accepting their "Albanian Platform",[68] whose main plank was making Albanian the second language throughout the country.[69] On January 11, 2018, the new parliament passed this law.

On the one hand, unofficial alliances between the two ethnic groups via political parties in coalition governments in Macedonia, as in Bosnia, have the tendency to encourage a "clientelist state", whereby the alliances are maintained by each side allowing the other to feather its nest.[70] On the other, the relative ethnic peace brought about a mass civic movement across ethnic groups against all corrupt ethnic elites and their neoliberal politics in 2016, again as it had in Bosnia.[71]

---

[67] Greeks and Turks in Cyprus, Serbs and Albanians in Kosovo, Serbs and Croats in Bosnia, are all smaller parts of other nations. It is true that the Bosniaks have no other state; but they are merely the largest group (44%), rather than the majority, in Bosnia, hence being officially a state of three nations is workable; whereas Macedonians are a two-thirds majority in North Macedonia.

[68] "Ivanov's Actions Unite Macedonia Albanians in Outrage", *Balkan Insight*, 3 March 2017, http://www.balkaninsight.com/en/article/ivanov-s-actions-unite-macedonia-albanians-in-outrage-03-03-2017.

[69] "The Platform for Albanians in Macedonia, June 28, 2017", https://www.aacl.com/the-albanian-platform.

[70] Harald Schenker, "Patronage Politics Push Macedonia to a Precipice", *Balkan Insight*, 28 December 2012, http://www.balkaninsight.com/en/article/patronage-politics-push-macedonia-to-a-precipice?utm_source=Balkan +Insight+ Newsletters&utm_campaign=a3964c5b14-RSS_EMAIL_CAMPAIGN&utm_medium=email.

[71] Adela Gjorgjioska, "Social Upheaval in Times of Neoliberalism: The Deep Roots of Macedonia's Protest Wave", *LeftEast*, 22 April 2016, http://www.criticatac.ro/lefteast/social-upheaval-in-times-of-neoliberalism-the-deep-roots-of-macedonias-protest-wave/.

Current frozen conflicts: Cyprus

While not part of the Balkans, Cyprus's close connection to the region is reflected in its similar nation-based frozen conflict. The 1974 catastrophe was essentially the final act of the Asia Minor catastrophe.

As in Bosnia, Kosovo and Macedonia, the Cyprus issue is rooted in the presence of more than one nation in the same geographic area, the 80 per cent Greek majority and the 18 per cent Turkish minority. While today we sometimes hear "we are all Cypriots", such a consciousness was absent during the struggle against British rule in the 1950s.

Greek-Cypriots are essentially Greek and Turkish-Cypriots Turkish, regardless of cultural peculiarities; a Greek-Cypriot child receives a Greek education, for example. Therefore, despite stories of genuine bi-communal coexistence, any kind of oppression, injustice or fear drove the two communities apart.

In the struggle against British rule, the Greek Orthodox Church and the right-wing Greek nationalist EOKA, who led the struggle, raised the slogan of "Enosis", or "union" with Greece, rather than independence. This cannot simply be attributed to the right-wing nature of this leadership; it reflected widespread Greek consciousness among the people.

This meant, however, that Turkish Cypriots felt no stake in this struggle, whereas a struggle for bi-communal independence could have involved them. Worse, they had good reason to fear EOKA and its leader, General Grivas. Meanwhile, the British divide-and-rule strategy had involved stuffing their colonial authority and police with disproportionate numbers of Turkish-Cypriots. While this use of the minority was pure exploitation, the Greek struggle for Enosis led many Turkish-Cypriots to desire this British "protection".

Türkiye also stepped in to offer "protection", facilitating the rise of the mirror-image right-wing Turkish-nationalist TMT, led by Rauf Denktash, a former colonial functionary. To the slogan "Enosis", they responded with "Taksim", or partition. Meanwhile, both EOKA and TMT persecuted Greek and Turkish Cypriot leftists who attempted to maintain bridges between their communities, especially members of the Communist Party, AKEL.

The acceptance by Archbishop Makarios of independence in 1960 was a pragmatic rather than ideological decision but nonetheless an opportunity. Right-wing nationalists in both communities undermined the arrangement from the outset, but ultimately it was Makarios himself who in 1963 pushed his 13 amendments to the constitution to reduce the proportional representation of the Turkish community.

One amendment called for abolition of the two communities' separate local councils. While theoretically aimed at fostering inter-communal unity, this ignores the existence of two nations with significant mutual distrust; real unity could only develop organically after prolonged coexistence, rather than being unilaterally imposed. The mistake is viewing "minority" issues from a "majoritarian" perspective, i.e. the idea that a purely "civil" state with "minority rights" suffices in a multi-national state.

Turkish-Cypriots withdrew from state organs and set up their rival administration, the nucleus for Taksim; as with other partitionist scenarios, the problem was the two populations living interspersed. Inter-communal clashes erupted over 1964–67. Despite his ongoing commitment to Enosis, Grivas was appointed head of the Cypriot National Guard, which attacked Turkish communities. Meanwhile, in backing the TMT's own violence, Türkiye's intervention reached the scale of aerial bombing of Greek Cypriot forces.

The 1967 coup in Greece, and the violent campaign by Grivas' EOKA-B to overthrow Makarios and bring about Enosis, led Makarios to change tack, opening talks with Turkish Cypriot leaders. Little headway was made given Türkiye's control over the minority, and the ironic alliance between NATO members Greece and Türkiye, backed by the US, against Makarios, due to his independence, and the power of AKEL as the largest party in Cyprus.

The Greek junta/EOKA-B coup against Makarios in 1974 precipitated Türkiye's invasion to "protect the Turkish-Cypriots". However, the Cypriot junta was overthrown six days later, and its Greek sponsor the next day, yet Türkiye deepened its invasion, seizing 38 per cent of Cyprus and ethnically cleansing 200,000 Greek-Cypriots, who have never been able to return to their homes in the north.

In 1983, the Turkish-Cypriot Denktash regime declared the occupied north an independent "Turkish Republic of Northern Cyprus" (TRNK), despite Turkish-Cypriots being only 18 per cent of the total population, and the expulsion of the Greek-Cypriot majority from the region. This non-solution – recognized by no country except Türkiye – resembles Bosnia's "solution", RS a copy of TRNK. Türkiye's 35,000 troops and its colonization of northern Cyprus with non-Cypriot Turks further invalidate its "independence".

Yet UN-led inter-communal talks have continued for decades, and the basics have long been accepted by all sides – the reconstitution of Cyprus as a bi-zonal, bi-communal federation of the two peoples, with freedom of movement and refugee return, yet details block agreement.

The UN's Annan Plan, based on this model, aimed to achieve agreement in time for a united Cyprus to enter the EU in 2004.[72] Turkish-Cypriots – tired of the poverty and international isolation – erupted into huge demonstrations, representing virtually their entire population, in support of the plan.[73] While the Denktash regime rejected the plan, its leftist opposition supported it; and the new soft-Islamist AKP government in Türkiye, aiming for EU accession, and rejecting the Turkish-nationalist basis of Kemalist military rule, also welcomed the plan, though the military rejected it.

In the 2004 referendum, 64 per cent of Turkish-Cypriots voted "Yes", rejecting their leaders' advice.[74] Yet 75 per cent of Greek-Cypriots voted "No". One reason was the limitations on the right of refugee return. Both component states would have been allowed to limit the numbers from the other community within their entity for a period, a measure requested by the Turkish minority for fear of being swamped by the larger numbers of Greek-Cypriots.

From the standpoint of international human rights law, rejection of this aspect was indisputably correct. Pragmatically, however, the choice was between this plan and no plan; after decades of separation, accepting some plan may be seen as an essential step towards getting a better one in future, by allowing the two communities to interact to eliminate fears from the past.

Voting "Yes" may also have allowed a dynamic unity to be forged with the Turkish-Cypriot mobilization; rejection led instead to demoralization, as the Republic of Cyprus joined the EU while the TRNK remains Türkiye's colony. On the other hand, the plan maintained the

---

[72] The Annan Plan for Cyprus, http://www.hri.org/docs/annan/ (last updated 6 April 2004).
[73] Michael Karadjis, "Cyprus: Myth of 'Turkish Cyprus' Collapses", *Green Left Weekly*, 29 January 2003, https://www.greenleft.org.au/content/cyprus-myth-turkish-cyprus-collapses.
[74] Considering that non-Cypriot Turkish colonists also voted and are largely under the influence of the ruling power, the 64 per cent likely represented close to 100% of actual Turkish Cypriot votes.

neo-colonial role of Türkiye, Greece and Britain as "guarantors" – established in 1960 and the basis for Türkiye's invasion – including the presence of foreign troops.

The issue here, however, is not evaluating the decision, but rather, understanding that the extraordinary difficulty of reaching any solution remains rooted in the reality of two nations existing in Cyprus, influenced by rival "fatherlands". An extended period of coexistence following some solution remains the minimal condition for any future concept of Cypriot nationhood to emerge.

***

The Dayton plan, the Ahtissari plan and the Brussels agreement, the Prespa agreement, the Ohrid agreement and the Albanian Platform, and the Annan Plan, represent differing arrangements designed to incorporate sovereign states consisting of parts of different nations. While none are perfect (and some far from it), the consensus today is that proposals to redraw Balkan borders along ethnic lines would be a recipe for disaster, further war and ethnic cleansing.[75] But the status quo has also left unstable, weak economies, left out of the EU, leading to mass emigration.[76]

Greece, Türkiye and rivalry on Europe's semi-periphery

The Cyprus case brings us to the region's dominant nations, Greece and Türkiye. Greece underwent extraordinarily rapid growth from 1960 onwards.[77] Greek companies rushed in with the collapse of the East bloc in 1991, acquiring important holdings throughout Serbia, Bulgaria, Romania, North Macedonia and Albania.[78] Greece had clearly emerged as

---

[75] See Timothy Less, "Multi-ethnic States Have Failed in the Balkans", *Balkan Insight*, 16 January 2017, http://www.balkaninsight.com/en/article/multi-ethnic-states-have-failed-in-the-balkans-01-16-2017 and Jasmin Mujanovic, "New Partitions are the Last Thing the Balkans Need", *Balkan Insight*, 10 January 2017, http://www.balkaninsight.com/en/article/new-partitions-are-the-last-thing-the-balkans-need-01-10-2017.

[76] "53,500 Nationals of Bosnia and Herzegovina Left their Country for the EU", *Sarajevo Times*, 16 August 2019, http://www.sarajevotimes.com/53500-nationals-of-bosnia-and-herzegovina-left-their-country-for-the-eu/.

[77] Between 1960 and 1973, Greece's 8.8 per cent annual increase in labour productivity was second only to Japan (9.4 per cent) in the OECD, D. Livieratos, "Productivity in Greece" (in Greek), *Spartakos,* no. 30 (June-August 1991), p. 17.

[78] "Business in the Balkans. Key Players. Major Regional Investors", *Greece Now*, viewed 19 September 2000, https://web.archive.org/web/20000919224748/http://www.greece.gr/BUSINESS/BusinessInTheBalkans/KeyPlayersInBalkans.stm.

a poorer part of developed European capitalism rather than a developed part of the "Global South", a status often accorded to Türkiye.

Yet Türkiye's also rapid growth since the 1980s challenges such schematic classifications; both are better seen as rivals on Europe's semi-periphery. Türkiye made similar inroads into the Balkans, utilizing Muslim connections in the region, just as the pattern of Greek investment reflected its cultural connections. Political alliances tended to reflect this: Greek support for Serbia,[79] German support for Croatia and Turkish support for Bosnia, for example.

It was in this triumphalist, ethno-maximalist early 1990s that a confident Greek capitalism imposed its blockade on Northern Macedonia. As an Orthodox people, at odds with the mostly Muslim Albanian minority, this contradicted Greece's exploitation of "cultural" connection. Yet with Milošević proposing partition of North Macedonia to Mitsotakis,[80] Bulgaria rejecting "Macedonian" ethnicity and Albania connected to the minority, Greece was in a position to fully assert itself against the weak state, whether to offer itself as protector, or to take part in its dismemberment.[81]

Meanwhile, unlike Türkiye, Greece is now a full member of the EU "club". Is this about Türkiye's non-compliance with EU principles, or about European imperialism having a Christian border? The answer is not straightforward. The EU is entirely justified in demanding Türkiye comply with its standards: occupation of Cyprus, violation of freedom of movement and residence in Cyprus, anti-Kurdish repression and restrictions on internal democracy are incompatible with EU membership.

---

[79] Greek-nationalist fighters were even present in Srebrenica during the 1995 genocide; see this call for a Greek apology for the role of some Greek nationals, signed by 163 academics, journalists and other citizens, "Δέκα χρόνια από τη μεγάλη σφαγή της Σρεμπρένιτσα" (Ten Years since the Great Massacre in Srebrenica), 2005, https://web.archive.org/web/20160330010513/http://cm.greekhelsinki.gr/uploads/2005_files/ghm713_on_greek_appeal_on_srebrenica_greek.doc. See also https://mihalisk.blogspot.com/2005/09/call-for-greek-apology-for-srebrenica.html.

[80] Howard LaFranchi, "Greeks Unite in Opposition to Independent Macedonia", *Christian Science Monitor* 24 June 1992, https://www.csmonitor.com/1992/0624/24013.html. To his credit, Mitsotakis rejected this proposal. However, there were many politicians, including in his own party, who were riding the nationalist-populist wave more fully than Mitsotakis.

[81] The broader fears were outlined by Greek diplomat Dimitri Germidis: "What we fear is a civil war where the Slavs, mostly of Bulgarian origin, might try to crush the minorities. Albania would quickly enter the fighting, so would Bulgaria, and where would that leave Greece?" (LaFranchi, op. cit.).

However, Turkish leaders have little incentive to comply if they believe this will still not earn them accession. Statements by European leaders in France, Germany, and elsewhere that Europe is Christian may lead Türkiye to keep the Cyprus issue as a bargaining chip.[82] With EU "expansion fatigue" apparent, the prospect of 70 million people, mostly Muslim, a great many rural or poor, entering the EU labour force with citizenship and social security rights, is not attractive to EU leaders.

Rejection of its EU aspirations has led Turkish geopolitics to turn to the Middle East, especially following the Arab Spring and the Syrian catastrophe, which drove 3.6 million refugees into Türkiye.[83] Türkiye's geopolitical rivalry with Saudi Arabia and Iran now eclipses that with Greece. This means Türkiye has even less interest in dealing with Cyprus.

However, the discovery of large-scale gas deposits in the East Mediterranean means Greece and Cyprus remain on Türkiye's radar, with unconventional new alliances developing. As AKP-ruled Türkiye turned towards support for populist Islamist forces in the region, including the Palestinian Islamist movement Hamas, its decades-long US-sponsored alliance with Israel under the Kemalist military broke down.

Therefore, a Greece-Cyprus-Israel-Egypt partnership has emerged to exploit the gas reserves as Türkiye tries to block Cyprus and pushes rival claims.[84] If in the past, progressive Greek opinion favoured Palestinian rights, the new alliance – *strengthened* under the leftist Syriza government – reflects not only changing geopolitics, but the weakening of Greece's position.

---

[82] For example, former French president Valery Giscard d'Estaing stated in November 2002: "Turkey is not a European country", it is part of "another culture, another way of life" and its accession would mark "the end of Europe" (Ian Black, "Turkey Must be Kept out of the Union, Giscard Says", *The Guardian*, 10 November 2002), https://www.theguardian.com/world/2002/nov/09/turkey.eu. On 4 March 1997, representatives of the Europe-wide Christian Democratic Party declared that "...within this civilization project [i.e. the European Union] Turkey has no place", while German Chancellor Kohl stated that "the European Union is based on Christian principles and cannot accommodate countries that do not share this identity" (M. Müftüler-Bac, "The Never-Ending Story: Turkey and the European Union", *Middle Eastern Studies* 34.4 (1998), p. 240.

[83] UNHCR, *Syria Regional Refugee Response: Turkey*, 20 September 2019, https://data2.unhcr.org/en/situations/syria/location/113).

[84] Nour Samaha, "US-Russia Rivalry in the Middle East is now Spilling Over into the Mediterranean Sea", *EinNews*, 19 August 2019, https://www.einnews.com/article/493945832?lcf=ZX9dkeSQfK-5FADPuwjBkQ==.

Comparing the confident Greek capitalism of the early 1990s with today's post-crisis reality, the fragility of semi-peripheral capitalism is laid bare. While massive corruption, a non-tax-paying oligarchy, exorbitant NATO-directed arms purchases and the inflexibility of the European Troika (the European Commission, the European Central Bank and the International Monetary Fund) are important issues, the underlying problem was the fundamental weakness of the southern European semi-periphery; trying to join the northern "core" via entering the Eurozone could only lead to disaster.[85]

Greece's "integration into the German-led European industrial and monetary sphere of influence" led to "industrial stagnation and de-industrialization", which, however, was temporarily cushioned by "incorporation into a credit-induced growth model"; but this was ultimately caught in the "global scissors movement, between a technology-intensive Germany and a labor-intensive China", and so collapsed.[86]

For the Greek people the disaster has been catastrophic; and phenomena such as alliance with Israel, selling the port of Piraeus to China and the humiliating collapse of Greece's short-lived, heroic resistance to the Troika, highlight the weakness of the semi-periphery. However, the North Macedonia decision may represent a humbled Greek capitalism looking more pragmatically at its weaker neighbours than in the triumphalist early 1990s. Ultimately, the peoples of the Balkans still need to find the best way to work together in their common interests, beyond Greek-Turkish rivalry and the range of differing plans for ethnic power sharing in the region.

---

[85] Stavros Mavroudeas & Stergios Seretis, "Imperialist Exploitation and the Greek Crisis", *East-West Journal of Economics and Business* 21.1-2 (2018), pp. 43-64, https://www.u-picardie.fr/eastwest/fichiers/art222.pdf.

[86] Christos Papatheodorou, Spyros Sakellaropoulos & Paris Yeros, "Greece at a Crossroads: Crisis and Radicalization in the Southern European Semi-periphery", *Monthly Review Online*, posted 30 May 2012, http://mrzine.monthlyreview.org/2012/psy300512.html. The exact figure given is 3,666,059.

Jorge Sotirios

Fortress Europe[1]

For all the antipathy between Christian and Muslim, sixteenth-century Europeans respected and feared the power, reach and efficiency of the Turks. The "Gran Signore" as the Ottoman Sultan was commonly known, was regarded as perhaps the most powerful ruler in the known world. Renaissance observers described him as the successor to Alexander the Great and the Roman emperors.

Mark Mazower, *The Balkans*

It's the Balkans here. Ain't no mucking about!

Dionysis Savvopoulos, composer

May 2013

The sight of a grey sky over the densely wired rooftops provided the perfect motivation – it was time to head out of the dreary, overcrowded city and embark on a road trip. After downing a strong Greek coffee, I barrelled down the stairs with luggage bouncing off each step. I managed to get into the passenger side after heaving Mina's shoulder bag to the back seat. She screeched away, turning right at the dumpster on the corner of Grigoris Lambrakis Avenue, and then headed towards the freeway which tore past Schisto.

The passage between Xerxes' throne and Mount Egaleo – the land surrounding Schisto freeway – remained a wretched sight. Concrete housing frames were left incomplete on arid parcels of land. Spiral staircases connecting floor to floor were easily visible. Scrapyards and garbage dumps predominated on either side of the road. The people

---

[1] Extract from the book by Jorje Sotirios, *Graffiti over Marble. A Portrait of Greece in Crisis*, Underwood, Queensland: InHouse, 2020.

that survived here were without doubt hard-as-nails. Pontians, Roma, former Soviets – they made this hostile area their home. I wonder if the Greek crisis with all its drama was merely a melodrama to these hardy outsiders? Surely their bare-as-bones lifestyle would hold them in good stead? The Greek middle class by contrast would have felt the drop in living standards, lacking a resilience the marginalized possessed.

Once we had driven past the first toll-booth at Elefsina, Mina swerved off the highway to grab a *frappé*. Although she was bleary-eyed first thing in the morning, she would rev up considerably, charged with her fix of caffeine. Along our route an overhead road sign directing motorists to THERMOPYLAE whizzed past. Mina mentioned that the legend of Thermopylae had been commemorated decades ago by the planting of three hundred trees in Kamena Vourla. These cypresses resembled upright spears, but alarmingly they had been reduced by my count to a few dozen. Leaf blight was said to have caused the rot. The Greek economy had shrunk since cutbacks were implemented in 2010, but had the Greek landscape and the symbolism of its illustrious history been decimated too?

Some hours into our journey, the craggy peak of Mount Olympus emerged over the horizon. Clouds scrolled in a steady procession over the pinnacle. I had scaled Schisto's peak the previous year, but the majestic Olympus was issuing a greater challenge. If the gods could lure me away, as sirens are said to do at sea, I wanted desperately to hear them whistling through the forests on the way up.

The road signs suddenly changed. The Balkans loomed large. The exits to BULGARIA and TURKEY appeared on our right. "Look at how far we have come!" Mina blurted out, stating the obvious but also the metaphorical – our journey was taking us to places we'd never been to before. After a demanding six-hour drive we entered Thessaloniki along the main boulevard. What immediately impressed me was Thessaloniki's urban charm. After the Great Fire of 1917, which had destroyed the city centre, wide boulevards reminiscent of European capitals were constructed, leaving little trace of the city's congested Ottoman past. Fortunately, historical remnants survived in hidden pockets of the city. Thessaloniki still maintained a Turkish quarter called *Ano Poli* – Upper Town – Ottoman houses loomed beside a number of lodgings clumsily built after the Smyrna catastrophe in 1922, to cater for the influx of Greek refugees from Asia Minor. The ornate and the grunge existed side by side. There were traditional dwellings containing courtyards under trellises of grapes beside rough-and-tumble shacks, many with their windows boarded up.

After the Balkan wars of the early 20th century, Thessaloniki was transformed into a classical Greek city which wrestled with its Balkan past – yet it's a dialectic that continues to give the city cachet. When it was known as "Salonica" the city evoked an atmosphere of diverse races, religions and tongues. The Sephardic Jews who had taken up residence ever since 1492, when they were expelled from Spain, spoke a variant of Spanish called Ladino. Thessaloniki was "a city of ghosts" (to quote the title of Mark Mazower's book) that had left traces of its past everywhere you peered into.

The cultured bourgeoisie and their tastes could be traced in Art Nouveau hotels which had wrought-iron balconies and plush interiors. Corridors wider than some of their elegant rooms often hung chandeliers bursting with light. The hotel we located was situated across from a handful of vacant warehouses, formerly used to press olives transported from the plains of Thessaly. In the Ladadika, a hotchpotch of architectural styles with bistros and bars were enclosed within densely-packed apartments. Across these cobblestone streets, poky music joints echoed with American rap. The Aristotelian University of Thessaloniki, in close proximity to the Ladadika, pumped new blood into tired urban veins.

At times Thessaloniki looks like a proper European city, leaving in the shade certain Athenian suburbs which appeared better suited to dull Balkan provinces. In the media rush to document Athenian turmoil during the crisis, Thessaloniki received little coverage, as if it didn't possess anything of merit to radically alter the nation's future. If Athens is Sydney then Thessaloniki matches Melbourne, albeit on a smaller scale. Thessaloniki and Melbourne compare themselves to an adversary, perhaps out of insecurity, whereas Athens and Sydney couldn't care less about any perceived rivalry, certain of their innate superiority.

Throughout the streets of Thessaloniki buildings of modernist design, with their clean lines and sharp edges, were looking neglected. There were dozens of defunct shops too, suggesting the economic crisis had impacted far and wide. The businesses surviving were sandwich outlets and Byzantine icon sellers. Mina stated that the moment the crisis hit Greece, cheques first began bouncing in Thessaloniki, and even today local courts were tied up with the fall-out of bankruptcies. The queues of blue cabs outside the railway station were even longer than the queues of yellow ones in Athens. Drivers were often out of pocket having completed a gruelling 12-hour shift, or so they claimed. They drove in the hope that there'd be a small profit, with tourists' tips a significant percentage of daily takings. Cleaners who worked at swank hotels had similar tales of doing it tough. Artemis had migrated from Odessa a decade ago, as had her brothers. Her siblings though had recently departed for Germany to escape wage exploitation, in which a paltry €2.50 was the hourly rate working in hotels. Not only were Greece's workers leaving Greece for abroad to survive, so too were Greece's foreign workers.

During the crisis, hard-luck stories were a drachma a dozen in Greece's second largest city. Factories had closed down, their production outsourced to Bulgaria, a low-tax haven, which meant Coca Cola had ceased operating as a production plant, its premises now used solely as storage. Greek businesses meanwhile relocated to Bulgaria (primarily retail and property investment). As many as 700,000 Bulgarian holiday-makers arrived in Greece each summer. Industry was being phased out, but tourism was booming. Was this the template for 21st-century Greece? A tourist destination, but little else?

By far the most intriguing graffiti was the number **381**, scratched and spray painted at strategic spots. I saw it engraved on the brick veneer of the Roman rotunda in the heart of the city. What could it possibly refer to? I had a fanciful theory. 381, as any Greek will tell you, was approximately the number of years Greece was enslaved under Atatürk (otherwise known as the Ottoman Empire). To be exact: from 1453, which was the year Constantinople fell to the Turks, up to 1821, which marked the start of the Greek War of Independence, comes to 368 years under foreign rule, but as some regions and islands were not liberated till the 20th century, 381 stands as the number of years under foreign occupation.[2]

Was the graffiti a conscious reminder to younger Greeks never to forget the past? Suspicion of "the Turk" is a constant warning in Greek education, army and political life regardless of the rhetoric which defangs the neighbour from foe to "friend". In a highly symbolic gesture

---

[2] Correction: I got carried away! "381" referred to the fan base of one of Thessaloniki's teams. Graffiti projects a message, but likewise the viewer projects his understanding onto the graffiti, and the two may not correlate.

to never forget, there are approximately 381 pleats in the kilt of the national costume, the *foustanella*, to signify each year Greece was under Ottoman rule.

It was interesting times for Greek-Turk relations with trade pacts preferable to war. Türkiye's emerging middle class spent their holidays on the Greek isles, contributing to the local economies. The yachting set dropped anchor in the Aegean, whilst Turkish youth hitch-hiked all over Ikaria. Exerting soft power on Greek TV too, Turkish soap operas like *Fatmagul* captivated Greek viewers such as Mina with their exotic settings perfect for cheesy romance. Interestingly, Mina's preference wasn't for the Italian *bello,* who she deemed too effeminate, but rather the Turk she regarded as "a real man". "The Turk" carried an air of excitement and mischief. The Oriental legacy was kept well and truly alive in Mina's over-heated imagination.

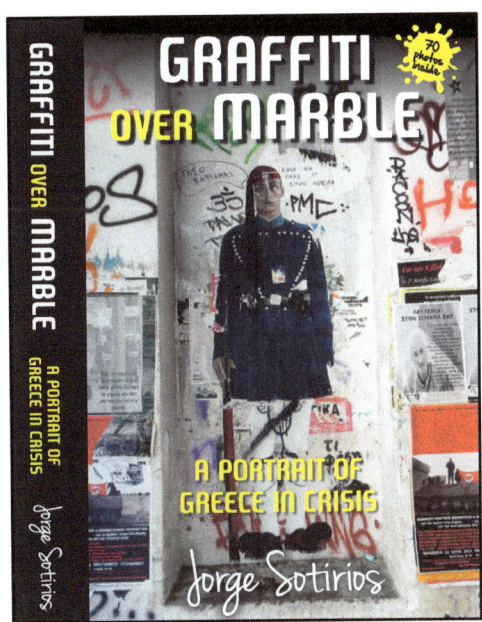
Graffiti over Marble by Jorge Sotirios, front cover

Perhaps it's fitting and somewhat karmic that Atatürk's birthplace was actually Salonica. The father of Türkiye, Mustafa Kemal, was not born within the borders of modern Türkiye, but next door in his nemesis, Greece, in 1881. Atatürk once described Salonica as beautiful, and hated losing this citadel after the First Balkan War of 1912. He grew up in a stately mansion in the heart of the city, a formidable dwelling possessing ornate wooden shutters and a doorway so low in height you'd bump your head against it, if you didn't bow upon entry. The building had been transformed into the Turkish consulate and it was heavily patrolled by the Greek police, stationed in vans in a security cordon.

Violence and suspicion were associated with the Turks in the Orientalist literature of the West, especially in the 19th century. Türkiye often appeared as a danger to European identity. A notorious saying in Greece resonated as an existential reminder of the threat to nationhood: "Omer Vrioni's horse continues to trample us." This saying refers to a legendary warrior who defeated the Greeks in a crucial battle in 1821. Greeks were trampled underfoot by Omer Vrioni's horse, literally and metaphorically. "The Turk" is therefore a concept not only seared in the mind, but equally on the broken backs of every Greek.

There are significant reminders of the Turk in the Greek vernacular. "I'll turn into a Turk" is an expression uttered when any Greek is pushed to the breaking point and ready to explode. Yet another interesting saying is "A Greek will always beat a Turk, but put two Greeks together and...", with the implication that Greeks will squabble endlessly, and shoot themselves in the foot, allowing the dreaded Turk to claim victory by default. Byron despaired of this negative trait on his ill-fated mission in Messolonghi in 1824, watching the Greek Resistance feud, when its energy could have been better spent focused on the War of Independence.

One bright economic sign in Thessaloniki was the role religious tourism was playing – which may be confusing for those who prefer to view Greece as the cradle of western philosophy. The 1000 years of the eastern Roman Empire that ended with the Fall of Constantinople in 1453 entraps Greece to its memory to this day. Byzantium lingers well into the 21st century. Religion continues to play a significant role in the Greek economy. The Russian middle class were regularly visiting Orthodox sites on package tours, but initiatives to re-open mosques had been explored by the mayor of Thessaloniki, Yannis Boutaris. His commercial *nous* led to the opening up of traditional mosques and synagogues for tourism after his election in 2011, only to be vilified by the Church for doing so. His entrepreneurial flair was deemed as despicable as the Maniates, who supposedly loved money more than they hated the Ottoman Turks. During a protracted economic slump, the attempt to exploit Greece's vast cultural capital (short of selling off monuments) was considered *poniria*, cunning, in other words. For Boutaris, whether tourists came from Türkiye, Israel or Russia was irrelevant since they all came with their pockets full.

The Orthodox hierarchy loathed Boutaris, despising his progressive politics. They were annoyed at his persistence in separating church from state, an issue which continued to be a thorn in the side of Greek democracy. The Church's hard-line attitude masked their unwillingness to cede ground to any religious or secular authority. The opening of Parliament, for instance, was a religious ritual where elected MPs swore fealty to the Orthodox faith embedded in the Constitution. Whilst synagogues were tolerated as they were few, it was the mosque that had the Orthodox clergy alarmed. The hierarchy would blatantly stall attempts for a grand mosque in Athens. Plans, permits, safeguards, architectural design – it seems there is nothing the Church would not do to hinder the necessary approval.

I was given a tour of a mosque tucked away on the first floor of a reclaimed building in Ladadika. James, a Ghanaian immigrant, guided me. This was an unofficial mosque like those often found in basements in the grungier parts of Kerameikos and Metaxourgeio in Athens. Once I exited the elevator I observed a large carpeted space with racks for shoes and slippers upon entry – that was it. If I termed it Spartan, you'd get the drift. Islam had become the *bête noire* of Orthodoxy, which made new immigrants to Greece from Islamic nations vulnerable. The type of makeshift mosque I visited with James appealed to him, but it remained a sore point for certain Muslims in Greece who wanted a place of worship to be proud of. Hussein Almomani, the President of the Jordanian community in Athens, was one such figure pushing for the construction of a formidable mosque, which led to outrage by Orthodox fanatics, nationalists, and Golden Dawn rank-and-file. He persisted nonetheless. Almomani highlighted the contributions by Jordanian, Iraqi and Egyptian immigrants to Greece over the preceding decades. Chemistry, medicine and dentistry were professions that benefitted by their presence. A mosque would simply acknowledge their foothold in Greek society.

"Just because we are Muslim shouldn't make us the enemy", stressed Almomani. "During the Ottoman Empire, we too suffered under the Turks." The mosque served as a hot-button issue and in a time of economic upheaval was regarded as an existential threat to Greek identity, which seeped into European narratives of being culturally contaminated by "the Other".

Thessaloniki's synagogue by contrast did not need to be built from scratch, only restored to its original condition. Elderly men from Israel were a visible presence in Thessaloniki, revisiting their childhood city, once esteemed as "The Flower of the Balkans", with grandchildren in tow. The presence of Sephardic Jews dated from the 15th century and amounted to about 70,000 Greek Jews living in Thessaloniki in the early 20th century. A sizeable proportion of them were marble carvers or builders. Many fought in the Greek army when World War II broke out.

In 1943 the Nazi occupation rounded up Jewish families and transferred them to the Haidari camp, before deporting them to Auschwitz-Birkenau on a packed train. The journey took five days to reach the Polish zone annexed by the Third Reich. The Chief Rabbi's submission to German commands made Thessaloniki's Jews easy pickings. Thessaloniki's Archbishop failed to lift a finger, although the Archbishop of Athens courageously denounced the deportation of Jews when he caught wind of the evil in 1943, taunting the German high command to execute him without a blindfold if they had a problem.

In 2013, the City of Thessaloniki was commemorating the 70th anniversary of the roundup of its Jewish compatriots. The deportation of Greek Jews was just one small fragment of the European twentieth-century nightmare. Some forty-five thousand Jews were used as slave labour in Auschwitz or met their death in the gas chambers. A significant component of Greek history had been excised from the city, leaving traces in cultural memory.

In the Byzantine quarter of Komotini, a small city east of Thessaloniki, Islam and ancient Greece rubbed shoulders. The mosque in Orpheus Street made for a surprising juxtaposition. But it shouldn't have. Komotini had a significant Muslim community. Since the atmosphere had been fraught with hostility since the crisis began, Muslims generally kept a low profile. The Muslims of Komotini were descendants of Muslim inhabitants from the Ottoman period. I'd almost forgotten the inter-twining of Greek-Turk relations within families. Albanian Muslims like Ali Pasha had Greek Christian wives, whilst numerous Turks throughout Ottoman Greece had Christian mothers.

Mina had never been inside a traditional mosque before but was curious to visit one. We located Komotini's main mosque within the *agora*. We noticed the big wooden doors weren't locked, but slightly ajar. Once inside Mina commended the interior. Koranic inscriptions on the wall, a marble pulpit from where the Imam would preach to the faithful, and a vast blue carpet as bright as the sky and as soft as feathers. Stained glass windows refracted light indoors.

The Far Right were active near the mosque. Golden Dawn had set up a branch in Komotini's main square, on the fifth floor of a commercial apartment block. From that height they could easily pick out the three minarets silhouetted against the skyline. Neo-Nazi flags were fluttering, with a banner that stretched across the balcony proclaiming:

RID THE LAND OF FILTH. They don't mince their words in the Balkans. Notions of purity were embedded in fascist ideology. Golden Dawn therefore projected themselves as a cleansing agent.

In interviews conducted with Golden Dawn operatives, mostly over the phone (as they refused to meet), they claimed they got along well with Komotini's Muslim community, but believed Islam was a virtual Fifth Column. Golden Dawn claimed adherents accepted €500 a year per family to maintain the wearing of the headscarf as decreed by Turkish authorities. Golden Dawn maintained that there were provocateurs who were deliberately stirring up trouble. When I asked for evidence (receipts, invoices, electronic transfers, names and a rap sheet) I was met with stonewalling and the interview was abruptly terminated.

Church and mosque, the cross and the crescent, the belltower and the minaret, whilst not commonly seen together in Türkiye, are often pictured side-by-side in Greece. Between Komotini and Xanthi I spotted up to a dozen minarets in tiny villages off the Egnatia highway. Why should such a sight therefore be so offensive to the nationalists, when Islam was never a new idea in Greece, but part of its historical fabric? Islam became the scapegoat for frustrations at the unravelling of Greece, of living in a ruined economy that had fallen beneath the Great Depression. The Orthodox church, sensing an opportunity, played with fire by not denouncing the anti-Islamic extremists in their congregations. A dangerous tactic that backfired, gifting Golden Dawn a portion of the Church's base.

It struck me that religion played a big role in Greece because Greece has never been truly secular. Rather Greece has evolved into a quasi-theocratic State. The Orthodox Church played a significant role in Greek life (evidenced by the official opening of Parliament), one that has shadowed Greek politics and enmeshed itself in everyday reality. Islam became the *bête noire* of twenty-first century Europe and the West, putting religion once again in the crosshairs of modernity.

The drive to the north of Greece was significantly different from the drive south into the Peloponnese. Heading north, you enter a different zone altogether with the appearance of non-Greek destinations imprinted on road signs. BULGARIA and TURKEY become concepts that penetrate the mind. There is a sense of adventure for travellers, but for some with long memories, it's a zone to fear and dread. I could imagine that reality. The freeway will suddenly stop. The boom gate approaches.

Europe comes to an abrupt end at the Turkish border. Customs officials will greet you with hardened Balkan features, whilst army personnel will give your vehicle the once-over. Your identity now needs verification. Your papers must be in proper order. The atmosphere changes. As does the car radio, which starts to receive frequencies that no land border can hold back. Turkish melodies and Bulgarian bagpipes inundate the sound waves, luring you to the other side. You must rethink the ground under your feet, as well as readjust the tunes filtering into your ears.

We were now in Thrace, a region where Mina's rumour mill went into overdrive. She claimed that somewhere up here a Fifth Column had the Turkish flag hoisted high as an act of defiance to the Greek state. Thrace was a tinderbox ready to explode, of this she was certain. Considering the Balkans was historically associated with savagery and bloodshed, an area filled with "brigands, robbers and sheep-stealers", Mina and I took our chances.

At Xanthi, the Nestos River was flowing under stone bridges. Tourism in this area focused on the carnival held before Lent when costumes and masks are brought out of storage. As we arrived a fashion shoot for a bridal catalogue had been underway. The "groom" was immaculately attired in his three-piece suit, whilst the "bride" tugged at his cravat like an owner dragging a dog to the kennel. With the cuffs of his pantaloons upturned, the couple posed barefooted, as is no doubt the norm in traditional Greek weddings.

Xanthi preserved the old and the new, the traditional and the modern. Student life was pumping energy into this regional locale known for agriculture. A plethora of bars took up space in serpentine fashion in the heart of the old town, whilst trucks packed with produce (potatoes, wheat) roared noisily along the freeway, on a ring-road by-passing the town. Xanthi was once prosperous. Peer into any of its mansions and you'd notice the ceilings were higher, the staircases were wider and the chandeliers brighter than anything experienced in Thessaloniki, which was hardly short of grandeur.

A yo-yo best describes the geopolitics of this region. The Balkan Wars of 1912-13 saw the area go from Ottoman rule to Bulgarian to Greek, back to Bulgaria, only to go back to Greek after World War I. Turkiye lost significant territory it had gained with the dissolution of the Ottoman empire. What was in effect a victory for Greece is regarded as a trauma in the Turkish psyche, serving to exacerbate the longstanding mistrust between the two nations. Greece regained past Greek lands and Türkiye lost the last of its territories on the European continent. Little wonder Atatürk was saddened at the loss of Salonica: not only was it a treasured childhood memory, it was more importantly a foothold in Europe.

After the Great War (1914-18) there was a concentrated effort to Hellenize the north since it only became part of the modern Greek state in 1912. With villages re-named Kentavros, Gorgona and Medusa I was perplexed at the ancient references so far from the Peloponnese. The Peloponnese clearly evokes the classical period with the Olympic Games (Olympia) and Herakles' Labours (Nemea, Stimfalia). In the north of Greece, classical names appeared impulsively planted, a security measure by the state to erase the Ottoman legacy. The invention of tradition, so cogently described by Eric Hobsbawm, can be seen here occurring in the simple Greek village.

Thrace had been annexed by Bulgaria from 1941 to 1944. I was intrigued that the hatred of the Bulgar remained, especially in Xanthi. An aristocratic grandmother imparted many stories of living in Xanthi's *haute bourgeoisie* society, and her dislike of Bulgaria became evident. *Kyria* Eleni peppered her speech with Turkish and French. Growing up during the interwar period, she recalled attending the synagogue before the Jews were forcibly removed in 1941. The genocide in the town of Drama, where "rivers of blood" flowed, especially traumatized her. She spoke with respect of the Jews and the Turks, but of the Bulgarian, not at all.

"They wanted to extinguish Greek identity and were worse than the Germans", she had stated with undisguised contempt. I found her animosity revealing. The hatred of the Turk is no doubt predominant, but Greek-Bulgar relations have been equally poisonous. "Never make the Turk or Bulgar your friend" was one saying. I found it unnerving to hear such hostility. But it had a long tradition with children's books stating that just as dogs hate cats, "Greeks hate Bulgarians".

The trip continued towards the border. On the way to Alexandroupolis the landscape broadened out. Slopes beside the road were carved with fire trails between sections of forest. The trails appeared as though Zeus had shorn a Mohawk upon the skull of the earth using a cut-throat razor. Agricultural land stretched across lush valleys. Cherries were the prime produce up here – roadside stalls were empty though, waiting for the first batch of stone fruits to arrive.

Alexandroupolis was a stop-over, nothing more. Our car followed a convoy of army trucks heading to Orestiada, a bleak town near the borders of Bulgaria and Türkiye. We were soon entering the Evros zone. The region possessed a chain of Greek towns acting as a buffer that allowed a strong military build-up to maintain a presence. The Evros river threaded through the region acting as a major crossing point for refugees, using Türkiye as a corridor to Europe. The river used to be a deterrent to border crossings when it concerned Greek or Turkish nationals. In a time of global upheaval, it had become an incentive for anyone fleeing the Middle East or Africa.

We meandered into the town of Soufli, the type of town where heads at the local *kafenio* swivel in unison to inspect new arrivals. Soufli had once been a renowned centre of silk production, but that industry stood in the way of progress once synthetics conquered the market. Traditional marble has been caught in a similar plight, undercut by synthetics of less quality.

Mina and I continued onwards. Yet another convoy of army trucks was packed with recruits benched morosely under flapping camouflage covers. Training camps, army regiments, and air-force patrols were concealed behind vegetation or checkpoints. With an economy in free-fall, the elephant in the room had to be military spending. A significant percentage of the Greek budget went to maintaining a hi-tech military. Greece spent its money on the procurement of weapons, ballistics, naval ships, submarines and surveillance systems, with Germany and Israel the major recipients of the largesse. Although the austerity measures bit into health and education budgets, defence spending had increased without pause.

In this fraught military zone of Greece, conscripts from every inch of the land were often posted. Winter in this sparse region was deemed hell on earth. Recruits were squished inside freezing foxholes to guard Greek territory bordering Türkiye and Bulgaria. A cousin had been stationed at Didymoteicho ("Twin Walls") and remembered hating every moment in this wilderness. He had been regularly locked up for back-chatting his military superiors, but karma paid him back nicely – his teenage daughters regularly flouted his curfews.

Orestiada – a modern town named after ancient Orestias, once located across the border in Türkiye and which legend claimed was founded by the mythical Orestes – was our next stop. The town grew to become a hotspot after 1923 when the Treaty of Lausanne exchanged populations between Greece and Türkiye. Orestiada was the last station in Greece on the eastbound railway line, and with many R&R hotels, the town catered for military personnel. Everywhere you looked appeared to be camouflaged in military hues. Not only did the uniforms and trucks exhibit a blend of green-yellow-brown, so did the people on the street with sickly complexions. The town seemed to be permanently shrouded in dust.

After spending an evening in Orestiada we resumed the journey before dawn. The dirt roads were intermittently pierced by random streetlights of piss-weak intensity. When the sun broke out the land came alive, resonating with birdsong. Bales of hay were clustered in large piles on endless plains. We passed farmers dragging on cigarettes at the local *kafenio*. Their muddied tractors, parked by the kerb, suggested industrious folk. Mina and I would diverge for the day. She intended crossing the Greek border, to embark on a shopping spree in Türkiye, whilst I would continue on to Fylakio, a remote village which housed refugees in a detention centre, formerly a police station.

Once I drove there I observed the following: Euro cargo loads distributing provisions parked outside, barbed wire fencing enclosing housing blocks, a demountable next to a basketball field and a flagpole at the entrance with a torn Greek flag. The image that touched me most was that of garments hung out to dry from barred windows. Cotton dresses, woollen socks, underwear. Mundane items gave a human face to the hidden reality. They were not just numbers, nor anonymous hordes. They were as real as I was, without any of my privileges.

I had learnt from former guards deployed to Xanthi that many within the Fylakio complex (up to 200 men, women and children claiming to be Yazidis who had fled ISIS-controlled Iraq) were kept inside small cells. Unwashed bedding was not uncommon. So bad were the sanitary conditions (flea-infested mattresses) that earlier in the year detainees had set fire to their furnishings to protest these squalid conditions.

The Evros region was dotted with detention centres: Soufli, Tychero, Feres and Fylakio were the towns singled out by human rights organizations that had documented refugee accommodation in graphic detail. Testimonies described hellish conditions: beds the size of a grave, polluted drinking water, atrocious food. Add to that the lack of legal access, sexual harassment and psychological abuse and these centres were a recipe for disaster. Europe was not at all the safe haven the refugees had assumed when they fled their war-torn countries. I wondered if Europeans, including Greeks, really cared. Ever since WWII, Europeans sought to aim up to high ideals to rectify their wretched past. In the 21st century, however, Europe was not what it claimed to be; there was an existential deficit that fine-sounding words could not conceal.

The refugee intake in Greece was phenomenal. A staggering 80% of illegal entries into the EU were through Greece. Greek resources were woefully insufficient. The Dublin II Regulation of 2003 provided for the treatment of asylum seekers in the country of entry. Northern Europe maintained southern Europe as a buffer zone, with the EU allocating a budget of €2 billion for border patrol. Italy and Spain as well as Greece were the intermediaries in a human migration from North Africa and the Middle East. The land border in Greece was highly porous until the Evros fence blocked access, leading to a rerouting of the migrant trail. Spain and Italy had effectively guarded their littoral on the Mediterranean Sea. Greece, with its many islands, became the preferred route into Europe. Lesbos, Kos and Samos bore the brunt on account of their proximity to Türkiye. Invariably the rafts, dinghies, fishing vessels were overloaded with Iraqis, Afghanis and Syrians fleeing one or more of the four horsemen of the modern apocalypse: war, famine, persecution and drought.

From Fylakio I drove to a smaller village bordering Bulgaria called Neo Ormonio. I dropped into the local pub. Stavros the barman was a guy straight out of the Teamsters Union. Braces slung over his paunch kept his trousers from falling down. A few strands of hair were combed over a large dome. He had a grouchy expression moulded permanently into his features. I asked for directions to the Evros river but he was less than forthcoming, polishing his counter with a cloth that it obviously didn't need. Stavros probably eked out a living in this hardscrabble land with a minimum of fuss and no doubt regarded my queries a thorough nuisance. With great reluctance, he ultimately led me outside and pointed to a long row of trees straddling the embankment in the near distance. I'd find the Evros over there, he curtly advised, beyond the wheat silos. That was his way of getting rid of me. It worked.

I headed towards the river I'd heard so much about. Men with short hair and stubble were wearing unfashionable leather jackets, casting stern glances in my direction – or towards the itinerants who'd crossed the border in their clapped-out utilities. The Evros River is the last stage before entering Europe for the refugee, yet for Greeks like Stavros it was a *skatodromos* to find. The river was obscured by forest. Tree after tree acted as a barrier along the embankment. Across the river in the far distance an electrified fence that had been erected by FRONTEX, the European border agency, and covering 12.5 kilometres of the 200-kilometre Greek-Turk land border.

I later read the fence (so miniscule to the naked eye) was four metres high, with barbed wire ringed on top. There were also unconfirmed land mines as well as camera surveillance and heat sensors. Berlin got rid of its wall in the twentieth century, but Greece now had its own in the twenty-first. A fence acting as a formidable wall to deter intruders. "Fortress Europe" had been constructed in reality.

Costas Vertsayias

Balkans So Close Yet So Far

Balkans?

What does that word conjure up in the minds of non-Balkan people? Backward, tribal, petty, suspicious, always at each other's throats, unable to get on with their neighbours, chaotic politics and disorderly finances – and one could easily add many more pejoratives. Why? In a word: history!

It was not always the case. For many of the region's inhabitants, that great Balkan river, the Danube, was for a thousand years the divide between civilization – their civilization – and barbarism. Even more importantly, where did European civilization begin? Where did Europe get its name from? Until the thirteenth century where would you find the largest and most opulent city of Europe? Yes, in each case the answer is the Balkans! What happened? To answer this question and to understand the Balkan peoples one must understand their turbulent history and how it has shaped (and continues to shape) their widely misunderstood behavior and attitudes.

Definitions almost always fail to provide the full picture on even a simple question, such as: Where are the Balkans? If you say they are located in the most eastern of the three European peninsulas that jut into the Mediterranean Sea you would be correct. Which countries comprise the Balkans? This is more difficult, as at times all territory coextensive with the Ottoman Empire in Europe was considered as the Balkans. This would include much of today's Hungary – though the inhabitants would vehemently deny any such association.

Today the countries commonly regarded as part of the Balkans are Albania, Bosnia and Herzegovina, Bulgaria, Croatia, Greece, Montenegro, North Macedonia (the Former Yugoslav Republic of Macedonia, or FYROM), Romania and Serbia. Moldova could be added to this list as it was part of Romania until the Soviets established it as a new country. Kosovo must also be included after its declaration of independence from Serbia (2008), although it is not universally recognized. Finally, Türkiye in Europe (Eastern Thrace), which contains Istanbul, one of the greatest cities of history, is obviously part of the Balkans. Twelve countries in an area a little larger than New South Wales. Granted, six of these are the result of the breakup of Yugoslavia. Slovenia is omitted as historically, geographically and by religion it has been aligned to central Europe, as against Croatia, which, although fiercely Catholic and part of the former Austro-Hungarian Empire, could not escape the Balkan fate imposed upon it by history and geography.

However, the concept of the Balkans itself is relatively new in historical terms. "Balkan" is a Turkish word meaning "a chain of wooded mountains". The term "Balkan Peninsula" was apparently coined by a German scholar in 1808, while the Greek term "Χερσόνησος του Αίμου" is based on the ancient name of this mountain range. In Greek mythology Haemus (Αίμος), King of Thrace and son of Boreas, was so haughty that Zeus changed him into a mountain; it is an apt description of Balkan peoples, who have an exaggerated opinion of their historical importance.

Historical evidence records the Greeks, Illyrians, Thracians and Phrygians as inhabitants of the region in the distant past. Of these people, the Greeks are the only ethnic group that have a continuous documented presence. The Albanians claim to be the descendants of the Illyrians, but there is no linguistic or other evidence to support their claim. However, it is true that the Albanians, whether descended from Illyrians, Thracians or Pelasgians (a generic name for pre-Greek inhabitants of Greece and neighbouring areas) are an ancient people and the other Balkan nations of today are relative newcomers. The Slavic tribes crossed the Danube in the 6th century and over the centuries settled extensively throughout the Balkans as far south as the Peloponnese. The Bulgarians were a Turkic tribe that became dominant in its area but was linguistically assimilated by the numerous Slavs. The Romanians claim descent from the Ancient Dacians, a Thracian tribe, although their language is derived largely from the Latin of Roman garrisons and settlers. The reality is that the Thracians (a very large nation according to Herodotus), Illyrians and

Phrygians were first Hellenized, then Romanized and then assimilated by the newer peoples of the Balkans.

But whatever may have happened in distant antiquity, the Hellenistic age and the Roman Empire, it is the Byzantine era and the subsequent Ottoman Empire that left indelible marks on the Balkans and which contributed to the present character of the "Balkan" peoples. Byzantium gave Greeks, Bulgarians, Serbs, Romanians, Slav Macedonians and some Albanians their religion, which became deeply entrenched in their culture and way of life. The Byzantine-style churches and monasteries dotting the landscape in all these countries are a constant reminder.

But it is the long Ottoman dominion that is the cause of the present turmoil. Why? Many reasons but let's isolate two:

1. The absence of frontiers meant people moved around, and over a five-hundred-year period different ethnic groups settled in areas distant from the majority of their compatriots, so that when the new Balkan states were created large numbers remained outside their respective national homes. The result was a national policy in the new states to liberate their unredeemed countrymen.

2. The Ottoman authorities did little to develop institutions or the rule of law during their long overlordship, and so these new states, with their largely illiterate population, were left in the hands of a small privileged class who took control of the government and the economy. This led to ineffective governments, marked by revolution and dictatorship, corrupt public life and interference of the major powers in their affairs.

So all of this gave rise to the negative connotations associated with "Balkan".

However, all the fault cannot be laid at the Ottoman door. The Great Powers of the day had such a deprecatory attitude to the Balkan states that they thought they could interfere whenever it suited their interests. Twice the Anglo-French landed troops in Greece to prevent Greece from taking its own course of action (Crimean War) or to force it to do their will (World War I); the Russians' insistence on the creation of a greater Bulgaria (San Stefano Treaty of 1878) created an unrealistic expectation in that country which led it to turn on its allies in the second Balkan War and fight on the German side in both World Wars; German influence in the Ottoman army (Liman von Sanders was commander-in-chief of the

Turkish armed forces during World War I) led to Türkiye fighting on the German side and perhaps contributed to the mass expulsion of the Christians in Asia Minor; and Austria's involvement in Bosnia led to World War 1. So, it is not entirely the Balkan peoples' fault that the Balkans were known as the powder-keg of Europe. It should not be forgotten that Australia's baptism of fire and arrival on the international scene also occurred in the Balkans (Gallipoli campaign).

There is a personality and an event that must be noted in any history of the Balkans. The man is Rigas Velestinlis or Pheraios, and the event is the Balkan Wars. Rigas had a dream of what could have been achieved in the Balkans. The first Balkan War is an extraordinary example of what was achieved by Balkan collaboration.

Rigas Velestinlis (Pheraios) (1757-1798)

Rigas was born and schooled in Thessaly. His vision was developed whilst living in what is today Romania – a Greek-ruled region of the Ottoman Empire open to western ideas. His message was to all the Balkan peoples (although Greeks were to have a leadership role). He wanted to create a democratic, multinational, multicultural state with equal rights for all its citizens, modelled on the ideas of the European Enlightenment and the French Revolution. He wanted not only to overthrow the Ottoman rulers but also their Christian lackeys – so his vision had both a political and a social aspect. At the time wealthy Greeks, Serbs, Vlachs (or Aromanians) and Armenians lived in the Austro-Hungarian and Russian Empires and had established prosperous communities. Among them, national movements were gradually emerging.

Rigas, for his part, began to work on how to reach agreement on common action to overthrow the oppressive and backward Ottoman Empire, where Christian subjects for the most part, irrespective of nationality, lived in wretched circumstances. He set about to create a simultaneous uprising throughout the Balkans. As he wrote in his famous war-song, the *Thourios*:

> *Βουλγάροι κι Αρβανίτες, Αρμένοι και Ρωμιοί,*
> *αράπηδες και άσπροι, με μια κοινήν ορμή,*
> *για την ελευθερίαν, να ζώσομεν σπαθί!*

The Austrians captured him and he was murdered in Belgrade in 1798. He had an enduring influence throughout the Balkans and is honoured to this day.

In 1866 the Belgrade newspaper *Radnik* (*Worker*) promoted the idea of a Balkan federation. The baton was taken up by socialist activists; the idea of a democratic Balkan federation was proclaimed in Belgrade in 1910 and at the inaugural conference of the Greek Communist party

Rigas Velestinlis (Pheraios), 1757-1798, by Damianos Kyriazis, Benaki Museum

in 1918. (COMINTERN's insistence in 1924 on a Macedonian state in the framework of such a federation had disastrous results for Greece.)

Rigas' message was truly visionary, progressive and well before his time. It might have been implemented but for the second Balkan War and World War I.

Balkan Wars

The first Balkan War of 1912 marks a historical high mark for the Balkan states. It established more or less their current borders (until the breakup of Yugoslavia in the 1990s), doubling their territories at the expense of the Ottoman Empire, whose territory in Europe was reduced to Türkiye's present frontiers. The successful outcome was based on a concerted and effective collaboration that would have made Rigas proud.

In February and May 1912 the Bulgarians and Serbians signed treaties which provided for their mutual defence, an offensive strike on the Ottoman Empire, the number of troops each country would make available and how any captured territory would be divided. When Greek Prime Minister Eleftherios Venizelos became aware of this he managed after much travail to sign a similar treaty with Bulgaria just days before the commencement of hostilities. It was the fact that Greece had the only Balkan navy that persuaded the Bulgarians to sign the treaty. The agreement, significantly, did not provide for how the liberated territory would be divided. Further treaties were signed between Serbia and Montenegro and Bulgaria and Montenegro, while Greece conducted separate negotiations with Montenegro and Serbia. The so-called Balkan Alliance was in fact created by these bilateral agreements, rather than a single treaty.

It should be noted that Greece was regarded somewhat contemptuously, as a result of its defeat in the Greco-Turkish War of 1897, its subsequent bankruptcy and the forced stewardship of the Greek economy by its European creditors. Sounds familiar? This worked in Greece's favour as the Bulgarians (the most powerful military state of the Balkans) did not believe that the Greeks could do anything more than pin down a few Turkish divisions whilst the Bulgarian army advanced on Adrianople. This underestimation allowed Greece to capture Thessaloniki.

The Balkan Alliance, or rather alliances, had as their purpose the liberation of all Ottoman territory in the Balkans. Russia supported the Serbo-Bulgarian alliance as it was perceived as anti-Austrian, but was against it being broadened to include Greece and Montenegro. The alliance from its outset contained the seeds of division, as the Serbo-Bulgarian arrangement provided for Thrace to be taken by Bulgaria, Macedonia to be divided between Serbia and Bulgaria, and Serbia to extend to the Adriatic at the expense of the Albanian population. The intervention of Austria and Italy to create an Albanian state thwarted Serbia's western expansion and brought it into collision with Bulgaria, which was unhappy with the territory it received in Macedonia.

Nevertheless, the first Balkan War was the first successful collaboration of the four Balkan states with well co-ordinated action at the military, strategic and diplomatic levels. Bulgaria provided 180,000 men, Greece 110,000 and Serbia 80,000. All four states greatly increased their territory, but Bulgaria's dissatisfaction led to its attack on Serbia in June 1913, with disastrous consequences. Serbia, Greece and Romania joined together and occupied new territory and Bulgarians committed atrocities in the territories they were forced to abandon. Bulgaria would try again to take Macedonia by siding with the central powers in WWI and Nazi Germany in WWII, and once again committing atrocities in the occupied territory of Greece delivered to it by the Nazis.

The vision of a united Balkans

The Greek PM Venizelos believed fervently in Rigas' vision of a united Balkans and declared the following in the Greek Parliament on 13 August 1917: "...I tried to avoid a second Balkan War...I was prepared to agree to our territory being reduced by 8 to 10,000 square kilometres in order to conclude a peaceful agreement with Bulgaria so as to establish a Balkan Federation...a great power that would be able to protect the interests of its constituent states...".

The Asia Minor catastrophe followed WWI with all its tragic consequences for Greece. In 1930, however, Venizelos embarked on a campaign to bring the Balkan states and Türkiye together. He convened the first Balkan Conference in Athens in that year. This was followed by the Second Balkan Conference in Constantinople in 1931, the third in Bucharest in 1932 and the fourth (and last) in Thessaloniki in 1933. The Balkan Conference adopted a constitution, whose first article provided for the rapprochement and cooperation of the Balkan peoples in their economic, social, cultural and political relations, with the final objective being the union of Albania, Bulgaria, Greece, Romania, Türkiye and Yugoslavia (which had been formed by the union of Serbia, Croatia and Slovenia in 1918). Once again, it was Bulgaria that prevented any progress due to its insistence that the inhabitants of southern Serbia (today's North Macedonia) and northern Greece be recognised as a Bulgarian minority. The Great Depression, WWII and the Soviet domination of the Balkans except Greece and Türkiye ended these precursory attempts at Balkan reconciliation and cooperation.

The fall of Communism and the EU

History never stagnates. Communism collapsed unexpectedly in 1989 and Greece found itself in an advantageous position as the only EU and NATO member in the Balkans. Greece provided humanitarian aid and Greek business invested quickly and heavily in Albania, Bulgaria, FYROM (as it was then), Romania and Serbia, while migrants from these countries poured into Greece. It looked like Thessaloniki would become the *de facto* capital of the Balkans. The Greek city became the centre of various activities, such as the Inter-Balkan Medical Centre, the "AIMOS" Universities Network, comprising the rectors of 25 Balkan institutions, and the union of Balkan law societies with its permanent seat in Thessaloniki. However, there were no visionary leaders such as Rigas or Venizelos in the Greek governments, not to mention that Athens inexplicably boycotted Thessaloniki's new role. Inevitably that enormous opportunity was soon lost.

In 2003, at Thessaloniki, the Heads of States at the EU-Western Balkan Summit declared: "The future of the Balkans is with the European Union". Bulgaria, Slovenia and Romania became members of the EU in 2004 and Croatia joined in 2013. FYROM became a candidate country in 2005, Montenegro in 2010 (negotiations began in 2012), Serbia in 2012 (negotiations began in 2014) and Albania in 2014. Bosnia-Herzegovina and Kosovo are both potential candidate states.

The EU is anxious to impede the overt political interference and economic influence of Russia, China and Türkiye in the central Balkans. It has set an ambitious target for Serbia and Montenegro to join by 2025. It has promised membership to all the candidates provided that they meet EU standards in human and civic rights. There is, however, an important rider. The EU will only accept a new member state if it has resolved its conflicts with its neighbours. For the first time in centuries the EU is presenting an opportunity and an incentive for the Balkan states to look forward and not be hostages of the historical past. Greece and Bulgaria, two countries which went through wars, occupations, ethnic cleansing and every kind of violence and abuse of human rights, now enjoy peaceful co-existence and good neighbourly relations within the EU – a model for the other Balkan states. Bulgaria's insistent claims on South Serbia (which led to the creation of a new state and ethnic identity to unhook that population from any Bulgarian connection) have mellowed with the historic signing of a peace treaty with FYROM in August 2017. The Bulgarian parliament unanimously voted in its favour; even the Bulgarian nationalists, who still proclaim that "Macedonian" is a Bulgarian dialect, voted in favour of the treaty. In FYROM the fear of implosion arising from its Albanian minority forced its leaders to negotiate a settlement with Greece over the name issue, as they were aware that FYROM would not gain membership of NATO and the EU without a compromise; finally in June 2018 the leaders of both countries agreed on the name "North Macedonia". North Macedonia started to dismantle monuments linking the modern nation with the ancient Macedonia of Philip and Alexander, and to change street names that implied this link. Meanwhile, the US has established a military presence in North Macedonia and Albania.

However, elsewhere in the central Balkans solutions may not come that easy. Bosnia and Herzegovina, which is a federation of Croats, Serbs and Bosniaks (the Balkans' newest nationality) is a mini version of Yugoslavia and will probably go the same way as the former Yugoslavia. Only the Bosniaks are committed to Bosnia and Herzegovina, as both the Serbs and Croats want to be united with their respective motherlands. There is a Bosniak minority in Serbia and it has been suggested that there be territory swapping. The EU, UN and USA oppose such a proposal as Kosovo's recognition has not been finalized and there is a similar suggestion on the table for that region. Serbia knows that it will not gain entry to the EU without it renouncing claims to Kosovo. Albania is the Balkans' most aggressive state. It has secured Kosovo's independence and is looking to its union in the future. It makes claims on North Macedonia, Montenegro and occasionally on Greece. There is a Greek minority in Southern Albania. There are Turkish and Muslim minorities in Bulgaria and Greece. There is a large Hungarian minority in Romania and in Serbia. Moldova is an independent state only because Russia is preventing its union with Romania. So there are potentially five or six flash points where another Balkan War could erupt. It would be good for Albania to remember that Greece's *Megali Idea* (The Great Idea) was consumed in the flames of Smyrna, Bulgaria's in the creation of North Macedonia, Serbia's in the break-up of Yugoslavia and the loss of Kosovo. Now Albania is pursuing its own *Megali Idea*. Where will it end?

Commonalities, differences, bridges and barriers

Many people in the Balkans, apart from Greece, still set their sights on changing borders and liberating unredeemed "historic" territories. The breakup of Yugoslavia into seven states in our time is an example of that mentality. There is a deliberate effort to accentuate differences. For example, the Bosnians, Croats and Serbs all speak variants of what used to be called Serbo-Croatian and can understand each other without difficulty, yet their policy makers are at work trying to prove that they are separate languages! FYROM's academia was directed to establish a standard written language that would be distinctly different from standard Bulgarian. Albanian and Bulgarian history books emphasize unsubstantiated and/or erroneous claims on an Illyrian and Thracian past and monuments. FYROM completely usurped the history of its neighbours. Romania makes incongruous claims about its history.

All Balkan states look back to a glorious past – Serbia to the empire of Stefan Dušan, Croatia to its medieval kingdom, Bulgaria to Tsar Simeon, Romania to Rome and the Dacians. And the Greeks, of course, look back to the Second Rome, Byzantium.

Instead of looking to the past, appropriating neighbours' heritage or manipulating history, the Balkan states should consider their shared heritage. It is substantial: Orthodoxy, a history of Byzantine rule and/or cultural influence, a struggle for liberation from Ottoman oppression. Their bandits/freedom fighters are called *hajduk* in Serbia and Bulgaria, *panduri* in Romania and *kleftes/armatoli* in Greece. They share much in common in music (the Byzantine lyra has survived as the Bulgarian *gadulka*, the Pontian and Cretan *lyra*, while the Byzantine *tambouras* may be an ancestor of the *gusle* played in the Yugoslav successor states). The *gaida* (bagpipes) are played in Bulgaria, Greece and the former Yugoslavia. They share common dances called the *horo* or *oro* in most Balkan states. Some Greek and Turkish songs and dances are virtually indistinguishable aside from language.

Balkan foods – *baklava, burek, giouvetsi, kaimak, kefte, lukaniko, pastourma, patsa, skara, soutzouk, toursia, tzatziki,* and many more – are to be found under similar names in Bulgaria, North Macedonia, Serbia, Greece and Türkiye. Traditional forms of dress, the so-called "national" costumes, are often similar across borders.

There has been a regular friendly sporting competition: the Balkan Games (officially the Balkan Athletics Championships) were first held in Athens in 1929, when Greece, Bulgaria, Romania and Yugoslavia competed. Türkiye competed in 1931 and by 2017 all twelve Balkan states (including Kosovo) took part.

Even geneticists have shown that Albanians, (mainland) Greeks, Romanians and Southern Slavs are closely related. How could it be otherwise with at least 1500 years of continuous contact and intermarriage.

Linguistically, the Balkan languages belong to at least five different branches of the Indo-European family – Albanian, Greek, Latin, Slavic, and Indic – one member of the Uralic family (Hungarian), and two members of the Turkic, Gagauz and standard Turkish. Due to the proximity of the different groups to each other, Orthodoxy, Byzantine domination, movement of peoples and the historical prestige of the Greek language, the latter has had a considerable influence on other Balkan languages.

However, it has not all been one way traffic Greek contains many everyday Turkish, Albanian and Slavic words, and Slavic toponyms are found everywhere on the Greek mainland as far south as the Peloponnese. Not to mention that Albanian dialects (known as Arvanitika) were widely spoken in Greece until recent times and Vlach (Aromanian) is still spoken in some areas. There are also some Slavophones, and the Muslims of Thrace speak their own languages. The truth is that most people in the Balkans during the Byzantine and Ottoman empires were bilingual or multilingual.

Minorities are bridges between nations. They facilitate cultural exchange and good neighbourly relations. In the Balkans they are perceived as a threat and an excuse the neighbour may use to intervene and take your territory. There are some minorities peculiar to the Balkans that may overcome these psychological barriers – the Pomaks, Sarakatsani, Vlachs, Gagauz, Yörüks.

The Pomaks straddle the Greco-Bulgarian border, speak a Bulgarian dialect and perhaps have the best claim to be the only true descendants of the Thracians. Many have fair hair and blue eyes. Originally Christian, they converted to Islam during the Ottoman period. The Pomaks are a peaceful people who resent being reminded of their Christian past, have opposed Bulgarian attempts to make them Bulgarians, and now face the prospect of being Turkified. They wish to be left alone and be Pomaks.

The Muslims of Greece and Bulgaria should not be exploited by Türkiye to create fear and suspicion between neighbours. They are the best bridge of friendship between those three countries. The few Greeks left in Istanbul and the Ecumenical Patriarchate make that city and Türkiye a magnet for the world's 300 million Orthodox and a boon for Turkish tourism. They should not be persecuted but encouraged.

The Sarakatatsni were Greek transhumant stockbreeders living mostly near the northern Greek border areas. Some were trapped in Southern Serbia (now North Macedonia) and Bulgaria when the new Balkan frontiers were established in 1912-13. Most were forced to leave, or to change their names in order to stay, and it is only after the fall of communism that Bulgaria has given them the freedom of expression they lacked for seventy years. They have become a bridge of friendship between Greece and Bulgaria.

The Vlachs are found in large numbers in Albania, North Macedonia, Serbia and Greece. They speak a language akin to Romanian, are devout Orthodox and, in Greece, have a fervent Greek national consciousness. They have been successful merchants, generous benefactors and great patriots (Rigas was probably a Vlach). The Vlachs are a bridge between Greece, Albania, FYROM, Serbia and Romania.

The Yörüks are or were nomadic shepherds with a similar lifestyle to the Sarakatsani, to whom they are not related. They are a Turkic people originally from central Asia Minor who were settled in southern and central Macedonia.

The Gagauz are a Turkish speaking Greek Orthodox people of Moldova. They are a bridge between Romania, Greece and Türkiye.

All these peoples have unique traits, are relatively small in population, and as they do not form a cluster in a particular area they do not pose a threat as a minority that could challenge a state's territorial integrity. Their uniqueness and diversity transcend borders and they are the perfect bridges to overcome the barriers of hatred and fear built up over the centuries.

Can the Balkan states overcome their past? Can they overcome their preoccupation with yesterday's atrocities and injustices? (Yes, they happened, we can't forget that.) Can they break the chains that prevent them from moving forward, the need to avenge past grievances dictating what must happen next?

Do they really want to gain some square kilometres of territory, at the cost of their place in a Europe where human and civil rights guarantee the citizens' existence, in a world where neighbours do not fear or suspect each other, but share and learn that life and freedom is every human's right?

The Balkan peoples are more than neighbours. They have lived together, worshipped together, suffered together. This is what they must remember, not that they have fought each other. There are many similarities in their culture and way of life. Indeed, apart from language little sets them apart. Their shared experiences should bring them together.

Will Rigas' dream be implemented by the EU?

Billy Cotsis

Absorbing Greece: Its Historic Impact On The Balkans And Near Neighbours

Not in my wildest dreams growing up could I have imagined that around the world there are pockets of Greek civilizations with a connection to the past. Ukraine, Magna Graecia in Italy, Egypt and the Black Sea are just some of the places where Greek speakers can still be located. Their language is inherited from the colonies of archaic and classical Greece, from the Hellenistic states or the Byzantine empire.

Throughout my travels to dozens of Greek communities as an adult in places that were once dominated by the Hellenes, I have met and immersed myself with the people as I learnt about their history and customs. I am no longer surprised by what I find, as Greeks are seemingly everywhere, though in smaller numbers than in ancient and medieval times. After years of travelling and research, I have come to the conclusion that Greek "speakers" in the older communities seem to fall into one of these three categories:

- Eventual absorption into the host country
- Keeping the Greek language and other cultural identifiers
- Partially keeping cultural identifiers but with reduced ability to speak Greek.

South Italy as Magna Graecia, the best example of Greek and local culture mixing

Imagine a place where time stands still. Then think about an eerie feeling, a sensation. Stop and admire the tranquillity, listen to the peace. Think about a true living connection with an ancient and Byzantine past.

This is probably the best way that I can describe to you a magical place that exists in southern Italy, a real example of the crossover between Greeks and other cultures, that survives to this day. Magna Graecia is where the remnants of an ancient Greek minority continue to speak and live like a Greek in a foreign, at times difficult, environment. This is due to the Catholic church having forced the Christian Orthodox churches to change to the Latin rite over the centuries and to a series of natural disasters in the *Greko* heartland in Calabria which has impacted the population.

Magna Graecia, or "Greater Greece", is a vast area of southern Italy that was once dominated by ancient Greek colonies. There remain perhaps 35,000 Greek-speakers, living monuments of a glorious past. Though this number is tenuous, and includes people who have some knowledge of the language and identify as *Greko* (Calabria) or *Griko* (Apulia). There are some counts that place the figure above 80,000 people.

What intrigues me the most about the people of Magna Graecia is that they have a connection with Greece dating back over 2,700 years. The Greeks of the area once dominated the economy, social and political life through their large numbers, commercial dominance and achievements in mathematics, science and philosophy.

I have visited the region twice, once in 2002 and again in 2018, to make documentaries about the Greko and Griko speakers. A great example of the Greko spirit can be found in a town called Bova Marina; I was overwhelmed by this town with a population of 4,000. Although there are very few Greek speakers remaining in Bova Marina, I could not but help being charmed by street names that appear in both Italian and Greek, a Modern Greek school, a Greek restaurant with a library upstairs owned by Salvatore Dieni and numerous, strong Greek cultural organizations, which include young people in leadership roles.

In 2002 I met with Carmelo Nucera, or rather word filtered around town that some foreigners had got lost, missed Rome and somehow ended up in Bova Marina, not exactly known as a tourist haven. Oh, and word got around that I was looking for Greeks. Within an hour Carmelo came and found us. He was a former Mayor of a smaller Greko town with 800 people, but significantly, half are Greko speakers or descendants. Another person who met with me was local teacher Filippo Violi.

One town that will always stand out above all the towns that I visited, perhaps all the places I have ever been to, is Gallicianò. Driving up the mountain, along the new paved road you could see a magnificent dried riverbed, which runs through the mountains and was once a vital natural resource linking the Greek towns. You could feel the moment. Stopping by the signpost that welcomes visitors, you could read the "Welcome" message in Italian and *Greko*.

Greko and the other dialects of Greek in Magna Graecia are at times difficult to comprehend and many times I had to ask for the villagers to repeat what they were saying. They in turn would ask me to slow down when speaking modern Greek.

This beautiful village greeted us with its charm, friendliness and authenticity, as if it had been expecting us. When we arrived and walked into the main square, I had to do a double take: I could hear the men talking *Greko*. Without trying to be impolite to our guide or hosts, I quickly made my way to the gathering of men and introduced myself and began to ask them just about every question you could imagine.

Gallicianò has a population of less than 100. It is located in the heart of the mountains and, like the overwhelming majority of *Greko* towns, few of the young people speak *Greko* fluently. However, the work of inspirational people such as Maria-Olimpia Squillaci, Danilo Pandilis Brancati, Eleonora Petrulli and other young people, is helping keep the language going.

If ever there was a town which represents the ancient Greek spirit, then surely Gallicianò embodies that spirit. It is a town that has survived everything that fate has thrown at it, such as poor economic development, and is still there, proud, resilient and independent. I take great heart to learn that the town has a Greek church and is teaching the Greek Orthodox religion.

The Greek language, as the main language of the region, began to die out only as recently as the 16th century. It is hoped that those who have remained remarkably committed to the preservation of the *Greko* language, can obtain resources and support from the Italian government, Greece and elsewhere to preserve the *Greko* culture.

What made me very proud was driving through the countryside of areas that are defined as being "Greek", even though the majority of the population is Italian, and seeing signs that say welcome to the Greek area, in Italian, modern Greek and *Greko* in Calabria and *Griko* in Salentine Apulia. It warms the heart to see images of the Greek and Italian flags linked together and seeing the pride of place that the Italians reserve for the Greek heritage of these areas.

I should mention a grand or rather royal welcome that we received in the picturesque town of Bova, otherwise known as Vua, in the hills above Bova Marina. After arriving in the main square, we were greeted by the Mayor, mobbed by interested villagers of both Italian and *Greko* descent and were met by the late Agostino Siviglia, who spoke to us in *Greko* and read to us his beautiful poems.

It was with Agostino's son that I had the funniest conversation in my life — a "little bit" conversation. This consisted of speaking to him in a "little" bit of *Greko*, a "little" bit of modern Greek, a "little" bit of Italian, a "little" bit of English and a "little" bit of sign language and this went on for a whole night!!

When I was taken to see the local *Greko* dancing, I was told that Italians had embraced Greek dancing for centuries. Indeed, as mentioned earlier, the Romans and Hellenes, the Italians and Hellenes, all have a history that has intersected over the millennia. The south certainly has many characteristics seen in the Greek republic, and why would it not, for Greek culture was dominant until recent centuries.

I should note that the coastline of Calabria, especially around the Bova Marina area, is wonderful, there are no tourists, it has the best gelato in all of Italy and of course it is a place to have a relaxing and quiet holiday. But you may struggle to locate any of these places on the map, although if you look up Aspromonte, you will come across the Greek towns of Amendolea, Bova or Vua, Chorio, Condofuri, Gallicianò, Roccaforte, Roghudi, all places worth visiting.

From Calabria, the region of Apulia is not far off, an area that has more towns of Greek origin that maintain a significant level of *Griko*-speakers. This area features eleven large *Griko*-speaking towns and is known as Grecia Salentina.

In Sternatia, a town of 2,800, over 50% of the people speak the *Griko* dialect; however, these are mainly the older residents. On the day I choose to trek out to the town the heavens opened up and the rain or rather flooding reminiscent of Noah's day took hold. Looking for an ark or a sanctuary, I chose to shelter in what appeared to be a school or church. Once inside, I could hear a group of people talking a kind of Greek far easier to understand than the Calabrian dialect. We soon became friends with those also seeking refuge and found out that the people of this town, like many of the surrounding towns, were passionate about preserving their Greek identity.

Once the rain stopped, we walked around the town and, just like our visit to Bova Marina, word got around that we were looking for Greeks. A carload of teenagers drove past and offered a lift to the Greek town of Calimera!

When the ancient Greeks colonized the Mediterranean, from Egypt to Spain, I doubt they could have imagined how the colonies would turn out. For hundreds of years the Mediterranean was a Greek lake and there was considerable trade and connectivity between Magna Graecia and what we now call the Balkans on the coast. The Romans would take the Greek culture along with their own and spread it across the Balkans. In more modern times, Italy has influenced the Balkans via Venice, Genoa and its proximity to Albania and to Croatia and other former Yugoslav countries.

Bulgaria

For the uninitiated, Bulgaria is one of the newest members of the European Union. Sofia, which was known in Roman times as Serdica (Σερδική), is the capital of this former communist country. Whilst we weren't overwhelmed by the aesthetics of the city, it has an amazing array of churches. The most important are the Byzantine churches of Saint Sofia and Saint George.

If you enjoy the tranquillity and spirituality of sitting in old churches, there are few that can compete with Saint George. This small church was built about 1600 years ago when Bulgaria was under Byzantine rule and is the oldest church in Sofia. The murals on the interior are from the tenth century CE.

Another impressive church is Saint Sofia (the city is named after the church), dedicated to the "Holy Wisdom" of the Judeo-Christian God.

St George Rotunda church, Sofia (formerly Roman baths, 4th century)

This is a rather large church and was built during the reign of Justinian during the sixth century CE, on the site of an earlier building. It is estimated that there were once dozens more Byzantine churches; however, few have survived the number of foreign occupations and the passing centuries. Nonetheless, the Bulgarians have built some impressive modern churches that take in the traditional Byzantine style. The majestic Alexander Nevski Cathedral, which is located near the daily collectors' markets, and the Saint Nikolai Church are both worth a visit.

Across Bulgaria, you will find Byzantine churches and a number of Thracian and Hellenistic sites. The country has an array of former Greek cities and towns. Almost all the one-time Hellenes either gradually left or were absorbed into the rich Bulgarian culture. It is estimated by the Greek government that there are almost 30,000 Greeks in Bulgaria and most are from modern times, including the Sarakatsani, descended from transhumant stockbreeders. This is a figure that includes business-people who have moved there and descendants of Greek communists who fled the civil war. By contrast, a recent Bulgarian census has the number of Greeks at 1,379 and a further 2,556 Sarakatsani.

It is worth noting that Plovdiv has an estimated population of approximately 700 Greeks and is the second biggest city in Bulgaria. It was founded by Philip II of Macedonia as Philippopolis and was a well-known Hellenic city during ancient and Byzantine times. As a major city, the Bulgarian settlers here would certainly gain a fair amount of Hellenic culture and religion upon arrival. As the balance changed in later medieval times, the Greek culture left an indelible mark on Bulgarians through cities such as Philippopolis and Varna.

Flying to Varna should be easy, but nothing is ever easy in Bulgaria when it comes to transport. There's nothing like planes flying close to the mountain peaks or taxi drivers who believe it's their duty to increase the tourist levy by more than a few dollars. However, during my visit to Bulgaria we met an array of friendly people. Varna was founded as Odessos and is typical of the ancient Greek colonies on the Black Sea. They were built as outposts for trade and as places for the growing population of ancient Greece to migrate. The Black Sea therefore is a special place for all Hellenes and it was with a deep sense of nostalgia that we made our way to the deck chairs and café bars on the sand. It may not be crystal clear, but the Black Sea was rather nice. You could imagine the ancient and medieval Greek ships trading throughout the *Mavri Thalassa*.

After a few days of relaxation, iced coffee, Bulgarians speaking broken Greek and enjoying the delicious and inexpensive food of Varna, including the Shopska salad that is similar to that found in Greece, I hired a car and set our course for Nesebur, which is 90 km from Varna on the Black Sea coast and near the city of Burgas, a former Byzantine stronghold.

Nesebur is a World Heritage listed town and arguably the best place in Bulgaria for medieval architecture and a brilliant sea backdrop. It is a tourist haven and has a rich blend of architecture from medieval Bulgaria as well as the Byzantine influences. This includes the ancient Greek and Byzantine walls surrounding the town and numerous churches. The ruins of the city known as Mesembria that date back to the Thracians and ancient Greeks are now lying below sea level; however, the Archaeological Museum of Nesebur houses a number of finds from these periods, as well as Byzantine artefacts and icons. This was one of the major towns of the Byzantine Empire and became a melting pot of Byzantines and Bulgarians.

There is an abundance of Greek Orthodox churches in Nesebur and the real highlights are Saint Stefan (twelfth century), Saint John the Baptist (tenth century), Saint John Aliturgetos (could be eleventh century), and the Pantokrator Church (ninth century). Despite the church of Saint John Aliturgetos having been ruined by an earthquake, you can feel the character and atmosphere of the area (this can be argued with all the churches) and it has a great view of the sea.

As I made my way through the picturesque lanes of the town, I came across a sign. This time rather than an advertisement for a Greek business, it read: Βουλγαρο-Ελληνικός Σύλλογος Μεσημβρίας (Voulgaro-Ellinikos Syllogos Mesimvrias).

In ancient times much of Bulgaria, as well as some areas of the modern Greek region of Thrace, was inhabited by a people known as the Thracians. The ancient Hellenes who built towns in what is now Eastern Macedonia and Thrace, as well as colonizing the Black Sea coast and the interior through Philip II and his successors, had an enormous linguistic and cultural impact on the Thracian towns. The Thracians returned the favour with their arts and music (just think of the mythical Orpheus). Thracians were eventually absorbed by the Greeks and the medieval Bulgarians.

Later, of course, the whole area was part of the Byzantine Empire until the rise of the Bulgarians and finally the coming of the Ottomans. This ensured a significant interaction among peoples of the region in commerce, in music and other arts, and in food culture.

There are dozens of towns and cities in Bulgaria whose place names were originally Greek, although many names have been changed over the centuries. Sozopol (Σωζόπολις, the earlier Apollonia) is one example.

Albania

Since Albania came into existence in 1913, the territory of southern Albania has been disputed by Greeks and Albanians. Like most countries that share borders with Greece, boundary lines are often in dispute courtesy of the strange interpretations by the foreign powers that drew up all Balkan boundaries in the twentieth century. The region sent Greek-speaking deputies to the Greek parliament from 1914 until 1925. In 1940–41, after Mussolini sent his troops to attack Greece from Italian-occupied Albania, the Greek military repelled them and advanced well into the region.

In the 90s, as the Albanian economy collapsed, hundreds of thousands found their way into Greece. Many in Greece did not understand the extent of, or perhaps were not interested enough to know, the influence of the Greeks on Albania. The Greeks have of course shared the territory of Albania with Illyrians, Romans, and in modern times the people known as Albanians, for millennia, as Greek colonies and empires dominated the landscape.

One of the best examples is the town near Corfu, Sarandë or Saranda. This is an interesting port and reminds me of the pretty Aegean port of Kuşadası in Türkiye (Asia Minor), as there is so much to do in a relatively small place. Its population is approximately 35,000, and there is a beautiful Greek church, Ayios Nikolaos, and a number of Greek taverns and shops. In fact, even the shops that are not owned by Greeks usually speak Greek or play Greek music. I really felt like I was in mainland Greece, not in another country. I even tried my best to find Albanian cuisine, but ended up eating Greek food every day. Saranda of course means forty, standing for Άγιοι Σαράντα (Forty Saints), in Greek!

For a country with an oppressive, totalitarian past and a reputation for a negative attitude towards its ethnic minorities, I was pleasantly surprised by what I came across in the south: Muslims and Christians working together, socializing and interacting. I spent many an afternoon at the coffee shops talking with Greeks and Albanians.

I met Lucas Mosakos at a cafe bar. Tall and well dressed, I expected him to be a model. Instead he was an artist, having decorated the shop with his own work, drawing on influences from Greece as well as Albania. His young Albanian colleague was adding the colour to the Greek frescoes.

It was at my daily afternoon discussions that I soon learned that despite the occasional tension and animosity in Greece towards Albanians, southern Albania, or Northern Epirus, is filled with people trying to get on with their lives. Under the dictatorship of Enver Hoxha, which ended with his death in 1985 after decades of rule, minorities were given limited rights. Schools that taught Greek were closed down and those who advocated their cultural beliefs were persecuted. Conversely, Tirana University actually taught Modern Greek. Albania was in effect closed to the outside world until the collapse of the communist regime in 1991. Probably the most bizarre contribution to Albania is Hoxha's bunkers. Virtually the entire countryside is littered by thousands of UFO-like steel bunkers that were built in the belief that Albania might enter into a nuclear conflict. While Albanians starved and people were persecuted, the communist regime felt it necessary to build bunkers!

Getting from place to place in Albania can be tricky at the best of times if you do not have a vehicle or bike. I met Dimitris Fotis at his kiosk (περίπτερο) on the beach. Playing Greek music and wearing his Euro 2004 jersey, it was not hard to figure out his culture. Dimitris told me that there are 100 villages in Northern Epirus that speak Greek. Dimitris and his father Christos became my tour guides of the Greek villages. These villages were small, pretty, inspiring and at times full of life. The larger towns that I visited include Delvinë, Finiki, Butrint – where we had to catch a swing bridge to cross the river and which is also the site of ancient Greek ruins – and Gjirokastër. I am extremely grateful for their assistance, allowing me to travel to my desired destinations.

Gjirokastër (Αργυρόκαστρο) is not only an amazing town of 40,000 people, it has become a World Heritage listed site. The town is a former Byzantine stronghold. The architecture and religion of the Byzantines have been imposed on the city and the surrounds. The day I visited this historic town, clouds gathered and rain threatened. It was overcast and, combined with the dark features of the buildings, highlighted by a Byzantine castle at the highest point of the town, this made me think I was in a Gothic movie. This is a must-see destination. It's romantic, Gothic, historical and very lively, all at the same time.

Having previously visited ancient and Byzantine villages in the Ukraine, Asia Minor (Türkiye) and Magna Graecia (southern Italy), I have seen how proud the people of the Greek-speaking villages outside of Greece are of their culture and the past. Some of the proud villages, including Dervitsiani and Kakavia, display banners in the town centre that read "Καλώς Ἤρθατε" ("Kalos Irthate", meaning "Welcome") in Greek and it is also translated into Albanian; any traveller will indeed feel welcome when they visit. Also on the main highways, the government has posted signage in the Albanian and Greek languages.

In this region, the people certainly have kept their culture and language stronger than any other region in the Balkans except Greece. They have not drawn too much on Albanian culture, it does however appear that non-Greeks have been influenced to an extent by Hellenic art, music and theatre. Though in Albania the Italian, Serbian, Croatian and other influences are arguably meshed in with this young nation, ensuring a diverse and rich culture.

I met Konstantina Beziani, who was the Director of Minorities in the Office of the Prime Minister and a Deputy Minister. Her role was to work with ethnic (Greek, Serbian, Montenegrin and other Slavic) and cultural (Vlach and Roma) minorities. She told me that the Greeks are the largest of all the minorities in Albania. The last five years had seen a real improvement in the political environment for minorities. Konstantina Beziani's father Theodhoros Vezianis was a founding member of OMONIA, the Democratic Union of the Greek Ethnic Minority in Albania. OMONIA has for many years been at the forefront of lobbying on behalf of the Greek minority and promoting Greek culture in Albania. He was the organizer of the renowned Festival of Pogoni on August 15 every year, featuring polyphonic singing, a feature of music on both sides of the border.

As opposed to the communities of Southern Italy, who are struggling to keep their identity, the young people in Northern Epirus will maintain their culture. They in turn have not necessarily absorbed the Albanian culture, and it can be argued that Greeks through sheer weight of numbers and history have of course influenced Albanians in the south.

In October 2004, Kostis Stephanopoulos, who was the Greek President at the time, told the Albanian government that despite the questions over Northern Epirus, Greece and Albania will be working strongly for a better future. Since then new schools for Greeks have been funded and established by the Greek government. In 2005, the Greek elementary school Omiros in Korçë (Κορυτσά) and the Computer Science Department in the University of Korçë were financed by the Greek Foreign Ministry International Development Cooperation Agency. It is also worth mentioning that Albania is a very important trading partner for Greece and trading relations continue to grow and flourish. During 2013, the number of Greek-descent representatives in the Albanian parliament was six.

In keeping with the spirit of being Greek and all things bizarre, I came across a remote village where the locals were building a Greek church, and what amazed me was the use of authentic ancient Hellenic columns that had been dug up and used to support the structure of the church. In many respects, this is a metaphor for the Greeks in Northern

Epirus – a very old civilization drawing upon their past to help build a long-lasting future.

Albania has many ancient and Byzantine sites that are well preserved, such as the Butrint National Park. Hopefully there will come a time when more organized tours are coordinated and tourist numbers increase. The friendliness of the people (I was driven around by Dimitris's father for hours on a very hot day is a typical example) is exceptional and the potential for economic growth is evident. It's hard to believe that as recently as the 1990s there were major problems between ethnic Hellenes and the government. Whilst various problems remain, Albania has certainly come a long way in recent years from the persecution of minorities and the building of bunkers.

Croatia

What is now Croatia was part of the Roman Empire from an early date and generally came under the sphere of western Christianity. Croatian traditions and culture have similarities to some of the other Slavic areas, and the language differences were not always as pronounced as they are now. The contact with and influence of the Greeks in later medieval and modern times is not as great as in, say, Serbia, Albania and Bulgaria.

Standing at the customs counter I was falling asleep when I realized I had been standing in front of the customs officer for about five minutes. I thought: "Why hasn't she stamped my passport?" I peered at her computer and as I suspected she was checking Interpol and other databases. As has become my custom at airports, I politely asked why was I being held up and how do I know that she herself is not a double agent. Her supervisor explained: "But, sir, we have to do a check on you, as you do not look British"!!

On a visit to Zadar you can't fail to notice some Orthodox Christian influence, for example in the Byzantine-style basilica, St Donatus (Sveti Donat). This large church is said to have been built in the ninth century CE in what was once the Roman forum. The church is the highlight of the town and it is fair to say the most impressive attraction. You can sit in the church and escape from the heat of the day and have a good think about where to get your next beer from.

Zadar itself was founded by the Illyrians rather than Greeks but was known to the Greek traders who settled there as Ἴδασσα (Idassa).

The whole area of Zadar City is a traveller's delight. The old town is built on a little island connected to the mainland. You can see the old fortifications, no cars are allowed inside the old town. It reminds me of Old Rhodes town – it is visually stunning and rather romantic, surrounded as it is by the sea and numerous boats.

Another interesting point is that the ancient Greeks of Corcyra (Kerkyra) and Sicily founded perhaps a dozen colonies on the Croatian (Dalmatian) coast and nearby islands. This includes Issa (Vis), Pharos (Hvar, Lesina), Corcyra Melaina (Korčula), Epidauros (Cavtat), Narona (Vid), Tragurion (Trogir), Epetion (Stobreč), Salona (Solin), Asseria (near Benkovac) and Heracleia (whose modern site has not been located).

The forces of the great Byzantine general Belisarius conquered Dalmatia in 535 AD and by the eighth century Zadar was the capital of this Byzantine province. Byzantine control of most or parts of Dalmatia lasted until 1102 AD. Furthermore, the small Greek independent state known as the Despotate of Epirus (founded by Michael Komnenos Doukas) controlled some sections of Dalmatia and its islands in the thirteenth century before being overrun by the Greeks of Constantinople and then the Venetians. By that stage, the Venetians controlled most of Dalmatia.

The spread of Greeks across the ancient and medieval world was a phenomenon that is hard to imagine will occur again. Certainly, the British, Spanish and French came close, but none had the longevity of the Greeks; from the early colonies of the eighth century BCE to the last of the Hellenic empires over two thousand years later, the Greek speakers were almost everywhere in the known world. Greeks tended to leave their mark with their culture, arts, education, science and language, especially across the Balkans and Mediterranean. It brings to mind how much the Greeks have influenced the region culturally and artistically, as well as in religion and language. With the advent of European and eastern empires and the rise of nationalism, elements of these were absorbed across the Balkans and Mediterranean. Conversely, the Greeks of Greece and Cyprus naturally absorbed some of the influences that they came across, affecting their language and elements of their culture.

ELENI ELEFTERIAS KOSTAKIDIS

Afterword: The Inspiration For This Book

It would be an omission not to say a little more about the three outstanding documentary films mentioned in the Introduction to this book, in addition to Peeva's *Whose Is This Song?*

Lode Desmet is an award-winning international filmmaker, whose documentary *Blind Man's Brexit* was shortlisted for the 2019 European Journalist of the Year award. His documentary *The Majority Starts Here* follows six young people who are brought together twenty years after the break-up of Yugoslavia and who experienced the Yugoslav wars between 1991 and 2001 when they were children. When Magda from North (former Yugoslav) Macedonia, Simona from Serbia, Vanja from Bosnia-Herzegovina, Bardh from Kosovo, Djordje from Montenegro and Zvonimir from Croatia meet for the first time, they share their experiences of the war from their individual perspectives while visiting their respective countries. They all enjoy similar music and pastimes.

The documentary includes a re-enactment of life in a shelter during the bombings, which some of them experienced as very young children. They spend two nights with no electricity or internet, eating only "shelter food" and using candlelight. The re-enactment brings back suppressed memories.

In Kosovo they encounter the hostility between the Chetniks and the Partisans. In former Yugoslav Macedonia they notice the giant monuments to various "national heroes", including an enormous statue of the much-contested Alexander the Great. When they ask a museum representative about "the waste of money on monuments when people have no housing and no work", he replies: "It is a matter of preserving the history of Macedonia", dismissing the sensitivities of the ethnic Albanian minority who find the whole project offensive.

In Belgrade, a Serbian war veteran states: "The country comes before the individual". He is willing to sacrifice his fifteen-year-old son for the good of the state – to which Zvonimir replies: "I think the state should serve the people, not the people the state". Simona from Serbia adds: "People like this are starting to become the minority. The problem with these kinds of people is that they are always the loudest ones." A Serbian refugee, expelled from Croatia during the 1991-95 war, says: "You cannot defeat hatred with hatred".

Desmet shows that, until recently, it has been a minority of vocal right-wingers and racists that have influenced the susceptible and created these ugly wars. He doesn't need to articulate this, as in each country the nationalists expose themselves well enough. By the end of the film the young people have been able to understand "the Other", to identify the commonalities in their experiences, and acknowledge the trauma that they all endured in the name of nationalism.

They all agree that they do not want that kind of hostility, those futile wars, ever to recur. The only way to remove the racial hatreds of the past is to affect the present, and they agree that they can do this. As Magda says: "I think that we are the majority". So they resolve to stay friends and encourage peace between their countries.

In *Mother Europe* Petra Seliškar creates a landscape seen through the eyes of a five-year-old child, her daughter Terra (meaning Planet Earth), who hasn't lived through any ugly wars but questions the concept of borders as they travel from one country to another in search of identity and shared culture. The child's innocent drawings, juxtaposed with the comments of the various personalities they meet, tell a story of innocence lost in the Balkans but also of hope for the future.

They ask one man about his identity and he doesn't know what to answer. Branko lives in present-day Montenegro, his mother was Italian and his father from Croatia. When he goes to enlist in the army giving his surname, Barich, he is told that "no such name exists in Montenegro". So he asks his aunt what his nationality is and she answers: "We are Croatian". When he travels back home he asks his father: "What is my nationality?" "Ask your mother", his father replies, to which his mother answers: "Are you stupid or what? You are

Yugoslavian, you dumbass." "That was the end of my nationality", he concludes.

One scene is at the "Old Yugoslavia" theme park, where visitors from all over the Balkans come to relive and enjoy a time in the past when the people were united and shared their dances, music and food. It is very popular, especially with the older generations who grew up in the Tito-created state of Yugoslavia in a time of peace and harmony. They long for the past, nostalgic for the peace and security it afforded them – something the next generation missed out on, with many misguidedly embracing the nationalism that led to racism, war and ethnic cleansing during the break-up of Yugoslavia.

Towards the end of the film they journey to Greece, where they attend a politicized concert in which one performer claims they are "singing to build a different international relationship that doesn't recognize a nation as a concept". This probably sums up Seliškar's philosophy as expressed in the film.

Both of these films are travel documentaries, like Peeva's *Whose Is This Song?*, in which the camera is used as an onlooker while the filmmakers meet people and ask pertinent questions. Both challenge perceived ideas of borders and identity.

Twice a Stranger, by Andreas Apostolidis and Yuri Averof, is also a documentary, though more traditional in style. Here the directors speak to experts from Greece, Türkiye and England, as well as to witnesses affected by the events and to children of the dispossessed. The documentary includes audio and subtitles in all three languages and some original newsreel footage. It deals with events leading up to the refugee crisis of 1922 on and the exchange of populations between Greece and Türkiye, which was sanctioned by the Great Powers of the time in the Treaty of Lausanne in 1923. In this legalized "ethnic cleansing" over 1.5 million Christians from the former Ottoman Empire were forced to settle in Greece, and approximately 600,000 Muslims from Greece were removed to Türkiye. "The criterion used was religion and did not depend on consciousness, identity and way of life or the desires of the people involved."

The pain and loss felt by these refugees is still felt generations later when their children and grandchildren speak of the devastation, their confused identities and their yearning for lost homelands. "Whoever wants to leave their homeland? No-one!"

One shock these populations had to endure was rejection from the indigenous people in their new homeland. Some locals used the abusive term "Turk-seed" (Τουρκόσποροι) for the Christians from Türkiye, while a similar term was used by Turks for the Muslims from Greece. As a refugee from Asia Minor now living in Mytilini, Angeliki Papamakariou, says: "We were once kings and here we are trash". As Renée Hirschon puts it: "This was not repatriation. This was uprooting people from their homelands from both sides". "[The Greeks from the Ottoman Empire] felt a sense of superiority coming from a conviction that Ottoman society was sophisticated, was multi-ethnic and had a level of civilization which they found lacking in the modern Greek state. A cultural finesse."

On the other side, the Muslim "brothers" from Greece were needed in Türkiye to re-populate the villages now empty of Christians. "The brothers were drinking ouzo and raki in coffee-houses. Their women did not wear the headscarf! ... The brothers came but the brothers were speaking Greek." Referring in the film to the music and shared melodies of Greeks and Turks in Asia Minor prior to the Greeks' expulsion, Ayhan Aktar says: "Culturally [the Greeks] were Anatolian". Even the early *rebetika* was "similar to Turkish classical music".

All three films have influenced the direction of this book. They may be a good starting point for readers who would like to explore further the world of Balkan documentary film.

Alfred Vincent

The Balkans: Reference Notes

These notes provide very basic information on the countries of the region, focusing on the main stages in each country's formation as an independent state with its present borders. The statistics below are based on Wikipedia, last consulted in the early months of 2023. For additional detail or updates, the Wikipedia articles are a convenient source.

Because of the negative connotations often associated with the term "Balkan(s)", many writers prefer the alternative, "southeastern Europe". The present writer has not followed that trend as he believes these prejudices need to be overcome. The Balkans should be recognized as an area with great cultural wealth and diversity, a rich historical heritage and unparalleled natural beauty.

PRESENT-DAY STATES

ALBANIA (SQIPËRIA)

Area: 28,748 km². Population: approx. 2,793,592 (January 2022 estimate). Capital: Tirana. Main language: Albanian, with Greek as the second most-spoken language. Religions: Sunni Muslim (59% at 2020), with important minorities of Catholic and Orthodox Christians.

In medieval times Albanian communities were dominated by local lords and princes, while some areas were controlled at different times by the Byzantine Empire, the Serbian kingdom and the Republic of Venice. The country was gradually taken over by the Ottomans from the late 14th century, despite the vigorous rebellion of Skanderbeg (Gjergj Kastrioti) from 1443 to 1468. From 1788 to 1820 Albania was ruled by Ali Pasha Tepelena, from his capital at Ioannina in northern Greece. After his fall it was recovered by the Ottoman sultan. Albanians declared independence in 1912 and its borders were defined by the major European powers in the Treaty of London (1913).

Albania was occupied by Italy from 1939 to 1943, and then by Germany. Civil war erupted between nationalists and communists, with the latter prevailing. Albania under Enver Hozha was allied with the Soviet Union and then, from the mid-1950s, with the People's Republic of China. After Hozha's death in 1985, liberalization led to multi-party elections in 1991. Economic emigration, especially to Greece, caused a decline in the population from its peak of about 3.1 million. The collapse of government-backed pyramid investment schemes in 1997 led to the breakdown of public order and intervention by UN peacekeeping forces; since then, the economy has recovered somewhat, with increased foreign investment, tourism and emigrant remittances. Albania joined NATO in 2009.

BOSNIA AND HERZEGOVINA (BOSNA I HERCEGOVINA, abbreviated BiH or B&H)

Area: 51,129 km². Herzegovina is the southern and southwestern region. Total population (2020 estimate): 3,475,000. Capital: Sarajevo. Main languages: Bosnian, Croatian, Serbian (all formerly considered variants of Serbocroatian). Religions: Muslim (50.7% in 2013 census), (Serbian) Orthodox Christian (30.7%), Roman Catholic (15.2%). In general Muslims identify as Bosnians or Bosniaks, Orthodox Christians as Serbs, and Catholics as Croats.

In medieval times the Byzantine Empire, Serbia and Hungary vied for control of the B&H lands, which were dominated by powerful feudal families, imperfectly controlled by Bans (Princes). Ban Stefan Tvrtko conquered several neighbouring regions and was crowned king of Bosnia and Serbia in 1377. After Tvrtko's death in 1391 royal authority was weakened and infighting between Bosnian nobles helped the Ottomans to gain control, ending with the kingdom's abolition in 1463. Under Ottoman rule much of the population adopted Islam.

After the Russo-Turkish War of 1877-78, B&H was occupied by Austria-Hungary, and was formally annexed in 1908. After World War I, B&H joined the Kingdom of Croats and Slovenes, which later became Yugoslavia (see separate article on Yugoslavia, below).

In 1990 Bosnia and Herzegovina declared independence. Nationalist uprisings led to civil war from 1992 to 1995, ending with the establishment of a federal republic with two main units: the Federation of Bosnia and Herzegovina (i.e. Bosniak- and Croat-dominated areas) and the Republika Srpska.

BULGARIA (БЪЛГАРИЯ/BĂLGARIYA)

Area: 110,993 km². Population (2021 estimate): 6,520,314. Capital: Sofia. Official language: Bulgarian. Religion: Orthodox Christian, with Islamic minority (approx. 10%).

From the 7th century CE the region was conquered by the Turkic-speaking Bulgars, who were later assimilated by the Slav-speaking majority. Around 679 the Bulgars established the First Bulgarian Empire, which became a rival to Byzantium until defeated by Emperor Basil I in 1014. After a period of revival (the Second Bulgarian Empire, 1186-1396), the country was conquered by the Ottomans.

After the Russo-Turkish War of 1877-78 Bulgaria became an autonomous principality under Ottoman overlordship. It annexed the province of Eastern Rumelia (now southern Bulgaria) in 1885 and declared independence under King (Tsar) Ferdinand in 1908. After the Balkan Wars (1912-13) Bulgaria occupied much of western Thrace down to the Aegean coast. In World War I it became an ally of Germany, and upon Germany's defeat it was forced to give up its Thracian territory to Greece.

In World War II Bulgaria again allied itself with Germany and occupied much of northern Greece. In 1944 it was invaded by the Soviet army; in 1946 the monarchy was abolished and Bulgaria became a single-party communist state, part of the "Eastern Bloc" of countries aligned with the Soviet Union.

With one-party rule ending in 1989, Bulgaria adopted its present constitution as a parliamentary republic in 1991. It joined NATO in 2004 and the EU in 2007.

CROATIA (HRVATSKA)

Area: 56,594 km². Population: (2021 estimate): 3,888,529. Capital: Zagreb. Official language: Croatian (formerly considered a variant of Serbocroatian). Religion: Roman Catholic, with a Serbian Orthodox minority (4.4% in 2011).

The medieval duchy of Croatia was recognized as a kingdom by 925, under Tomislav. The Croatian kingdom was united with Hungary in 1102. It had its own parliament and a viceroy appointed by the Hungarian king. The southern region of Dalmatia had been controlled by the Byzantine Empire and parts of it, including the towns of Zadar, Split and Šibenik, and the islands of Korčula and Hvar, later became domains of the Venetian Republic. Dubrovnik (Ragusa) and its hinterland formed an independent city-state which became a major economic power in the region, though paying tribute to the Ottoman Empire

From 1527 Hungary and Croatia were amalgamated with the Habsburg monarchy of Austria, whose ruler usually held the title of Holy Roman Empire. Slavonia, the northeastern region, was conquered by the Ottomans between 1536 and 1552, but was restored to the Habsburgs in 1699. With the fall of the Venetian Republic in 1797 Dalmatia eventually became part of the Austrian Empire in 1815 and hence later of Austria-Hungary. After the break-up of the Holy Roman Empire in 1806 Croatia and Slavonia remained attached to that Empire's successor states, first the Austrian Empire and then Austria-Hungary from 1867.

In 1918, after the defeat of Austria-Hungary in World War I, Croatia (including Dalmatia and Slavonia) became part of the Kingdom of Serbs, Croats and Slovenes, renamed Yugoslavia in 1929. In World War II Croatia was occupied by the Axis powers and a fascist puppet government was established. After the war it became a federated state within the Socialist Federal Republic of Yugoslavia (see below for article on Yugoslavia).

Croatia declared independence in 1991, and after a conflict in which many resident Serbs were forced to flee, it was recognized with its present borders in 1995. Croatia joined NATO in 2009 and became a member of the European Union in 2013.

GREECE (ELLADA/ΕΛΛΑΔΑ)

Area: 131,957 km². Population (2021 census): 10,432,481. Capital: Athens (Athina/Αθήνα). Language: Greek. Religion: Greek Orthodox Christian, with small Islamic (2%) and other minorities.

The area of modern Greece was part of the Roman Empire, whose eastern half formed what is now known as the Byzantine Empire or Byzantium (see below). In 1204, when the capital Constantinople was captured by the army of the Fourth Crusade, most of Greece was distributed among crusader chiefs (i.e. westerners) and the Venetians. A local Byzantine dynasty established its independence in Epirus, and the Byzantine emperors of the Palaeologos dynasty, who reconquered Constantinople from their base in Asia Minor in 1261, gradually regained control of much of the Peloponnese. By the mid-fifteenth century most of what is now Greece had been annexed by the Ottoman Empire (see below), except for some areas under the Republic of Venice, including Crete (to 1669) and the Ionian Islands (to 1797).

After the Greek Revolution of 1821, southern and central Greece, with nearby islands, was established by treaty as a kingdom in 1831, with its independence guaranteed by Britain, France and Russia. Borders expanded with the addition of the Ionian Islands (1864), Thessaly (1881), southern Epirus, Greek Macedonia and the northern Aegean islands (1912).

Greece's occupation of the Smyrna district of western Asia Minor in 1919, with its large Greek population, was opposed by the forces of the Turkish nationalists under Mustafa Kemal, leading to the Greek defeat of 1922 (the Asia Minor Catastrophe). The Greeks (Orthodox Christians) of Asia Minor, including Pontus, fled as refugees, as did a smaller number of Muslims from Greek territory. This exchange of populations was ratified by the Treaty of Lausanne in 1923. The country was occupied by Germany and its allies from 1941 to 1944. In 1947 it gained the Dodecanese, previously under Italian occupation.

Greece's post-war history was marked by a Civil War between right- and left-wing forces from 1946 to 1949 and by a right-wing military regime from 1967 to 1974. After an attempted countercoup in December 1967 the king fled, and a referendum in 1975 decided not to restore the monarchy. Greece joined NATO in 1952 and has been a member of the EU since 1981.

KOSOVO (KOSOVA)

Area: 10,887 km². Population (2022 estimate) 1,806,279. Capital: Prishtina. Language: Albanian, with Serbian as a second official language. Religion: Sunni Muslim, with a Serbian Orthodox minority.

Kosovo Polje, the Plain of Blackbirds, was part of the medieval Serbian kingdom, and was the scene of the Serbs' defeat by the Ottomans in 1389. From 1455 to 1912 it was part of the Ottoman Empire, although, like Bosnia and Herzegovina, from 1878 to 1909 it was occupied by Austria-Hungary. After World War I it was incorporated into the Kingdom of Serbs, Croats and Slovenes, which became the Kingdom of Yugoslavia (see below). After World War II Kosovo and Metohija formed an autonomous region of the federated state of Serbia within Yugoslavia – Metohija being the western half.

From 1989 the Yugoslav government restricted the rights of the Albanian Muslim majority, which had grown to over 90%, provoking Kosovar leaders to declare independence. Open war with Serbia broke out in 1998, leading to NATO's bombing of Belgrade in 1999, which forced Serbia to withdraw from Kosovo. The United Nations resolved that Kosovo should be autonomous within the Federal Republic of Yugoslavia, and sent a mission to secure peace. In 2008, after the final break-up of Yugoslavia, Kosovo declared independence from Serbia. It has been recognized by many but not all member-states of the United Nations.

MOLDOVA

Area (including Transnistria): 33,851 km². Population (Worldometer 2022 estimate, including Transnistria): 4,012,637. Capital: Chișinău. Language: Romanian (also called locally Moldovan). Religion: 91.8% Eastern Orthodox. Moldova is also the Romanian name of the Romanian region known in English as Moldavia (see below under Romania); the two should not be confused.

Although Moldova does not belong geographically to the Balkans, it is included here because of its historical association with Romania. It includes most of the historical region of Bessarabia, and was part of the principality of Moldavia (see under Romania) until 1812, when it was ceded to Russia. After alternating between Russian and Romanian rule, in 1940 it was established as the Moldavian Soviet Socialist Republic within the USSR. It has been an independent republic since 1991.

Moldova includes the autonomous territorial unit of Gagauzia, established in 1994, whose predominant ethic group, the Gagauz, are Orthodox Christians speaking a Turkic language.

In 1991, upon the dissolution of the USSR, a territory on the eastern bank of the Dniester river broke away to form the republic of Transnistria, with Tiraspol as its capital. Armed conflict with Moldova ended with a ceasefire in 1992; however, Transnistria has not received international recognition. Its population was 475,373 according to the 2014 census, which Russians representing 29.1%, Moldovans 28.6% and Ukrainians 22.9%. Russia maintains a military presence, nominally as a peacekeeping force.

MONTENEGRO (CRNA GORA/ЦРНА ГОРА)

Area: 13,812 km². Population (2021 estimate): 620,739. Capital: Podgorica (formerly Titograd). Official language: Montenegrin (formerly considered a variant of Serbocroatian). Religion: 72.1% Eastern Orthodox Christians, 19.1 Muslims. Ethnicity: in 2011 45.0% identified as Montenegrins, 28.7% as Serbs, 8.6% as Bosniaks (Muslims), 4.9% as Albanians.

In medieval times the rugged land now called Montenegro (the Black Mountain) was divided between Serbian principalities, but incorporated into the main Serbian kingdom by 1186. Independent again after the fall of Serbia to the Ottomans, the region was annexed by them in 1496. Coastal regions, including the towns of Budva and Kotor, were controlled by Venice. In practice the core parts of Montenegro remained autonomous under their prince-bishop (*vladika*), an office passed down from uncle to nephew. One of these, Petar II Petrović-Njegoš (reigned 1830-1851), is also Montenegro's national poet.

Montenegro was recognized internationally as an independent principality in 1878 and as a kingdom in 1910. In 1922 it became part of the Kingdom of Serbs, Croats and Slovenes (subsequently Yugoslavia, see below), and after World War II it became a federated republic within the Yugoslav federation.

When the other federated states declared independence in 1991-92, Montenegro was included with Serbia in the reduced Federal Republic of Yugoslavia. When this was dissolved in 2006, Montenegro declared its independence. It joined NATO in 2017 and is negotiating accession to the EU. Although still a republic, in 2011 Montenegro legislated to allow descendants of the Petrović-Njegoš dynasty to perform certain non-political official functions.

NORTH MACEDONIA (СЕВЕРНА МАКЕДОНИЈА/SEVERNA MAKEDONIJA)

Area: 25,713 km². Population (2021): 1,836,713. Capital: Skopje. Main languages: Macedonian (see below) and Albanian (first language of about 25% of the population). Religions: Eastern Orthodox Christianity (about 46.1% in 2021), Islam (32.2%).

In medieval times the Byzantine, Bulgarian and Serbian empires vied for control over the area, until its conquest by the Ottomans from the fourteenth century. In 1913 after the Balkan Wars most of it was assigned to Serbia, but was occupied by Bulgaria during World War I. After the war it became part of the Kingdom of Serbs, Croats and Slovenes and hence of Yugoslavia. After World War II it was constituted as the Federated Socialist Republic of Macedonia within the Yugoslav federation. Its official language was codified for the first time in the 1950s. The republic declared independence in 1991.

The name of the country and its majority language were finalized by the Prespa Agreement of 2018 between Greece and the former Yugoslav Republic of Macedonia (FYROM), after a long dispute arising from the fact that Macedonia is also the name of the neighbouring Greek region. The Agreement clarified that the name North Macedonia has no territorial implications, that this state is not a successor to the ancient Greek kingdom of Macedon, and that "Macedonian", in the context of the modern state, denotes the main language of that state, not that of the ancient kingdom. The modern language belongs to the South Slav family and is related to both Bulgarian and Serbian.

North Macedonia joined NATO in 2020 and is negotiating entry to the EU.

ROMANIA (ROMÂNIA)

Area: 238,397 km². Population (2022 estimate): 19,038,098. Capital: Bucharest (București). Language: Romanian (with recognized minority languages, including Hungarian and Romani). Religion: Romanian Orthodox (81 %) with Catholic and Protestant minorities.

Modern Romania was formed by the joining of several medieval and early modern entities, in particular Wallachia, Moldavia and Transylvania. From the mid-14th century Wallachia and Moldavia were established as autonomous principalities. Although eventually forced to recognize Ottoman overlordship, for centuries they were the only self-governing, predominantly Orthodox Christian polities in the Balkans. A large and influential Greek community developed in both. In the 18th century the two states were governed by Greek princes, appointed by the Sultan from the elite group known as Phanariots (from the Phanari district of Constantinople). In 1859 they united under the same prince, and adopted the name Romania in 1862.

In medieval Transylvania, Orthodox Romanian-speakers were the largest community, together with Hungarians and Germans, although they had no political rights. After being part of the Hungarian kingdom since 1002, Transylvania become a semi-independent principality in 1570, under princes from the local Hungarian nobility, with the Ottomans and later the Habsburg Empire as their overlords. After 1711 the princes were replaced by Habsburg governors, and in 1867 Transylvania became part of the Austro-Hungarian Empire. After the defeat of this Empire in World War I, Transylvania and other smaller areas were awarded to Romania.

In World War II Romania initially allied itself with the Axis powers (Germany, Italy and their allies), but changed sides in 1944. After occupation by the Red Army, it became a one-party state, part of the East European socialist bloc. The socialist government was overthrown in 1989. Romania joined NATO in 2004 and became a full member of the EU in 2007.

SERBIA (SRBIJA/СРБИЈА)

Area: excluding Kosovo (see above): 77,474 km²; including Kosovo 88,499 km². Population (2022 estimate, excluding Kosovo) 6,797,105. Capital: Belgrade (Beograd/Београд). Religion: Eastern (Serbian) Orthodox, with small Catholic, Islamic and other minorities. Main language: Serbian (formerly regarded as a variant of Serbocroatian).

From 1211 the Serbian regions were established as a kingdom under the Nemanjić dynasty and as an Empire under Tsar Stefan Dušan (reigned 1331-55). Dušan's empire became a rival to Byzantium, although soon after his death it was split into principalities. These were conquered piecemeal by the Ottomans and remained part of the Ottoman Empire until the nineteenth century.

The First and Second Serbian Uprisings (1804-13, 1815-17) led to the creation of an autonomous principality under nominal Ottoman overlordship. Serbia became fully independent in 1867 and was established as a kingdom in 1882.

In the Balkan Wars of 1912-13, Serbia acquired new territories, including present-day Kosovo and North Macedonia. After World War I it formed part of the Kingdom of Serbs, Croats and Slovenes, which was renamed as the Kingdom of Yugoslavia in 1929 (see below). After World War II Serbia became a federated republic in the Socialist Federal Republic of Yugoslavia. In 1991-92 the other republics (Croatia, Slovenia, Bosnia and Herzegovina, and (North) Macedonia declared independence, and a new Federal Republic of Yugoslavia was formed, comprising Serbia and Montenegro. After a peaceful dissolution of its union with Montenegro, Serbia (with Kosovo) was established as a separate republic in 2006. In 2014 Serbia commenced negotiations to join the EU.

Within the former Yugoslav federation Serbia included the autonomous regions of Kosovo (see above), and Vojvodina (north and west of Belgrade, bordering on Hungary). While Kosovo is now *de facto* independent though not recognized by Serbia, Vojvodina remains an autonomous province within Serbia, with Novi Sad as its capital. Its population includes Hungarian and other minorities, and five languages as well as Serbian are used in administration.

SLOVENIA (SLOVENIJA)

Area: 20,271 km². Population (2021 estimate): 2,108,708. Capital: Ljubljana. Language: Slovenian (also called Slovene). Religion: mainly Catholic.

Geographically Slovenia is marginal to the Balkans, but is included here because of its inclusion in the former Yugoslavia. In contrast to Serbia, for example, Byzantine influence in Slovenia was minimal and it was never part of the Ottoman Empire. Slovene, however, is a South Slav language, related to Croatian and Serbian.

The Slovene lands were for centuries part of the domain of the Austrian Habsburgs, except for coastal areas that belonged to Venice until 1797. After the dissolution of the Austrian Empire in 1918, Slovenia joined the new kingdom of Serbs, Croats and Slovenes, later Yugoslavia. It became independent in 1991 and joined the EU in 2004.

TURKEY (TÜRKIYE)

A request by the Turkish government for the Turkish-language form *Türkiye* to be used in English instead of *Turkey* was accepted by the United Nations in 2022.

The Republic of Türkiye comprises the Asian part (Asia Minor) and European Türkiye, or eastern Thrace, to the North and West of the Bosporus and the Sea of Marmara. The following details refer to European Türkiye, the only part that belongs geographically to the Balkan region. Its main city, Istanbul (formerly Constantinople/Κωνσταντινούπολις), extends to both sides of the Bosporus, and is Türkiye's largest urban area, although the national capital is Ankara. Türkiye was established as a republic with its present borders in 1923, after the dissolution of the Ottoman Empire.

Area: 23,764 km². Population (2019 estimate): 11,961,338. Language: Turkish. Religion: Islam. There is a small Greek community in Istanbul, which remains the home of the Ecumenical (Orthodox) Patriarchate.

FORMER STATES

THE BYZANTINE EMPIRE (also known as BYZANTIUM or THE EASTERN ROMAN EMPIRE)

The Byzantine Empire was initially the eastern portion of the Roman Empire, which was ruled separately from 395 CE, with its capital at Constantinople and with Greek as its dominant language. Its people used the term Romania (not to be confused with the modern state of that name) and called themselves Romaioi. "Romans". Byzantine culture can be said to have three foundations: the Greek language, Orthodox Christianity and Roman law.

Around 1000 CE, the Empire included Asia Minor, Greece, and large parts of the Balkans and southern Italy. Constantinople was the seat of the dominant patriarchate in Eastern Orthodox Christianity. Even in areas where Byzantium was not politically in control, its religious and general cultural influence was profound.

From around 1071, with the Seljuk Turkish conquest of Asia Minor, Byzantium began to decline. After the sack of Constantinople by Crusaders in 1204, many of its Greek territories were divided among western warlords and the Venetian Republic. Although a Greek dynasty recaptured the capital in 1261, the Empire never regained its former power and wealth. With the capture of Constantinople by the Ottoman Sultan Mehmed IV in 1453, it finally came to an end.

HOLY ROMAN (HABSBURG) EMPIRE, AUSTRIA and AUSTRIA-HUNGARY

The Holy Roman or German Empire was considered to be the successor of the Roman Empire in central, western and southern Europe. It is also known as the Habsburg Empire because it was ruled by the Habsburg dynasty of Austria almost without a break from 1438. It was dissolved in 1806 and replaced by the Austrian Empire, which merged with Hungary in a dual monarchy in 1867.

Although most of its territory lay outside the Balkan area, the Empire controlled parts of the modern Balkan countries for some periods. The nobility of Croatia elected a Habsburg archduke to be their king in 1527, hence aligning the country with the Empire. Bosnia and Herzegovina were administered by the Austro-Hungarian Empire in 1878 and annexed in 1908.

The assassination of Austrian Archduke Franz Ferdinand in 1914 by a Serbian nationalist led to the Austrian invasion of Serbia and hence to World War I. After the war the Austro-Hungarian Empire was dissolved.

OTTOMAN EMPIRE

Named after its founder Osman, the Ottoman dynasty began as local rulers in northwestern Asia Minor, but rapidly expanded through conquest into the Balkan area, culminating with the capture of Constantinople in 1453. The conqueror, Sultan Mehmed IV, regarded himself as the successor to the Byzantine emperors. At its height, around 1600, the Ottoman Empire controlled most of the Balkans, Asia Minor, Syria, Palestine, Egypt and much of North Africa. In the Empire, Islam was the dominant religion. However, other religious communities, including the Orthodox Church, continued to exist, though with

Ottoman oversight and certain restrictions. The Ottoman Empire was formally abolished in 1923 and replaced by the Republic of Türkiye.

VENICE

From being a Byzantine province, Venice gained its independence as a republic around 900 CE and developed into a major economic power, trading with the Middle East. After the Fourth Crusade (1204), Venice acquired towns, coastal areas and islands in what is now Slovenia, Croatia, Albania and Greece as a reward for providing transport for the crusaders.

Hence Venice controlled the Peloponnesian ports of Koroni and Methoni from 1209 to 1500, Crete from 1211 to 1645/69, and the Ionian Islands (Kerkyra/Corfu, Paxoi, Lefkada, Kefalonia, Ithaki, Zakynthos, Kythera) from various dates in the 14th – 16th centuries down to the dissolution of the Republic in 1797. After a long struggle over Dalmatia (the islands and coastal parts of Croatia) Venice held this area from 1420 to the end of the Republic. Over this period it also controlled Kotor and its gulf, regarded as part of Albania despite its Slavic language. For shorter periods Venice also held coastal areas of modern Albania.

Venice's cultural influence is still noticeable in many of its former dominions.

YUGOSLAVIA (JUGOSLAVIJA)

The Kingdom of Serbs, Croats and Slovenes, founded in 1918, was renamed Yugoslavia in 1929. It represented an attempt to unite all the South Slav peoples (*jug* = "south"), except the Bulgarians, in a single state. During World War II Yugoslavia was occupied by Nazi Germany and its Axis allies. Powerful communist and other resistance movements arose but were opposed by local fascist organizations. After the war Yugoslavia was reconstituted as a federal republic, consisting of the six state entities of Bosnia and Herzegovina, Croatia, Macedonia (present-day North Macedonia), Montenegro, Serbia (with the autonomous regions of Kosovo-Metohija and Vojvodina) and Slovenia.

In 1991-92 all except Serbia and Montenegro declared independence from Yugoslavia. Fierce fighting broke out in various regions, with some "ethnic cleansing" of minorities. Since 2006, with the dissolution of the reduced Federal Republic of Yugoslavia (see above under Serbia and Montenegro), there has been no state named Yugoslavia.

LANGUAGES

SLOVENIAN, CROATIAN, SERBIAN, BOSNIAN, MONTENEGRIN, (NORTH) MACEDONIAN AND BULGARIAN are all members of the South Slav group within the Slavic sub-family of languages, which also include Russian, Ukrainian, Polish, Czech and Slovak. The Slavic languages form a branch of the Indo-European family, which also includes the Germanic and the Romance (or Neo-Latin) languages.

Croatian, Serbian, Bosnian and Montenegrin are official languages of their respective states. Before the break-up of Yugoslavia they were regarded as variants of the language known then as SERBOCROATIAN. This could be written in either the Latin alphabet or a version of the Cyrillic. Linguistically, it could be divided into dialects, classified traditionally according to linguistic features which do not necessarily coincide with national borders. OLD or CHURCH SLAVONIC is also a member of the South Slav group.

GREEK forms a separate branch of the Indo-European family. Modern forms of Greek are derived from the *koine*, the "common" language of post-classical times, which was based mainly on the dialect of Athens and became an international language after the conquests of Alexander the Great. An exception is Tsakonian, an old dialect, now endangered, once spoken widely in southern mainland Greece, which derives from the local Doric form of Ancient Greek. Pontian Greek, formally spoken in northeastern Asia Minor, is also very different from the standard modern language.

For much of the history of independent Greece the language of official business, academic writing and most of the press and education was some form of *katharevousa*, "purist" Greek, in which foreign loan-words were avoided and elements of Ancient Greek were preserved in morphology and syntax. However, varieties of *demotic*, vernacular Greek, were adopted by literary writers and became the almost universal language of literature from the earlier twentieth century. Its users have borrowed vocabulary from katharevousa wherever they found this useful. Demotic was adopted by law as the language of education in 1976 and was soon established as the only official language, what we can now call standard Modern Greek. Archaizing forms of Greek, similar to that of the New Testament, are still use in church services.

ALBANIAN, like Greek, forms a separate branch of the family. It is divided into two main groups of local dialects, Tosk in the south and Gheg in the north, with a modern standard language based on Tosk. The Albanian dialects spoken or formerly spoken in parts of Greece are known as Arvanitika and are basically varieties of Tosk.

ROMANIAN is one of the Romance languages, i.e. descended from Latin, which was brought to the Balkans by Roman soldiers and settlers in the early centuries CE. Hence it is closely related to languages such as Italian and French. Unlike them, however, it has adopted words from neighbouring Balkan languages.

TURKISH belongs to the Turkic language family, not closely related to Indo-European. Its relatives include Azerbaijani, Kyrgyz, Uzbek and Uyghur. The only other Turkic language spoken in a marginal area to the Balkans is GAGAUZ (see on Moldova).

HUNGARIAN, spoken in parts of Transylvania and Vojvodina (see on Romania and Serbia respectively) belongs to yet another family, the Uralic, which includes Finnish and Estonian.

Some Balkan languages exist only as minority languages, in the sense that they are not the main or official language of any state. Below are some of the main examples.

AROMANIAN or VLACH is or was formerly spoken by communities in various regions, including parts of Albania, Bulgaria, Greece, Montenegro, North Macedonia and Serbia. It is a Latin-based (Romance) language, closely related to Romanian. In many places Aromanian was the language of stock-breeding communities, who practiced transhumance – that is, they migrated each spring with their flocks from the lowland winter pastures to the summer grasslands in the mountains. In many areas it is defunct or endangered, as Vlach families have settled in towns or villages and adopted the dominant language of the region. Aromanian is used in radio programmes in North Macedonia and Romania.

JUDEZMO or LADINO is the Spanish dialect spoken by Sephardic Jews in the Balkans, whose ancestors were expelled from Spain from 1492 on. Once widely spoken, especially in Istanbul, Thessaloniki and other cities, its speakers mostly perished in the World War II Holocaust. Emigration to Israel caused further reduction in the number of Balkan speakers. From over 50,000 Greek Jews before the War, Thessaloniki now has barely 1,000, all of whom speak Greek. However there has been a modest revival in Judezmo/Ladino in recent decades due partly to the popularity of songs in the language.

ROMANI, not to be confused with Romanian, is the language of the Roma (Gypsies), divided between several divergent varieties in various parts of Europe. Its origins were in the Indian subcontinent. Efforts have been made in recent times to standardize individual dialects. Romani is recognized as a minority language in Kosovo, North Macedonia, Romania and Serbia. In some countries it is used in radio broadcasts, while in Romania a standardized form is used in Roma community schools.

TIME-LINE OF MAIN EVENTS

1204 Sack of Constantinople by army of the First Crusade.

1204 on: Crusader leaders invade and occupy Greek lands, creating the Principality of Achaea (Peloponnese) and the Duchy of Athens.

Komnenos Doukas (Angelos) family establish Despotate of Epirus.

Laskaris dynasty established rule in western Asia Minor.

Empire of Trebizond (Pontus) independent under Komninos emperors.

1211–1645/69 Venetian rule in Crete.

1261 Byzantines under Michael Palaiologos regain Constantinople.

1262 Byzantines regain parts of southern Peloponnese, with capital at Mistra.

1331–53 Serbia under Stefan Dušan becomes dominant in the Balkans.

1358 The Ottoman emirate from Asia Minor captures Gallipoli, its first European outpost.

1362 Ottomans have now occupied Adrianoupolis (Edirne) and made it their capital.

1387 Ottomans capture Thessaloniki.

1389 Serbia defeated at Battle of Kosovo by Ottomans, who are now dominant in Balkans.

1453 Fall of Constantinople, which becomes capital of the Ottoman Empire.

1456 Ottoman conquest of Athens.

1460 Ottomans conquer most of the Peloponnese.

1461 Empire of Trebizond falls to the Ottomans.

1645 Ottomans invade Venetian-ruled Crete; the capital Candia (modern Heraklion) surrendered by the Venetians in 1669

1788-1820 Ali Pasha Tepelena gains de facto autonomy in Albania and much of Greece.

1789 French Revolution inspires thoughts of revolution among Balkan peoples.

1797 Fall of the Venetian Republic.

1797 Rigas Velestinlis (Pheraios) calls for a multi-ethnic "Hellenic Republic" in SE Europe.

1804 First Serbian Revolt.

1815–17 Second Serbian Revolt leads to autonomy under Ottoman overlordship.

1815 The United States of the Ionian Islands established as a British protectorate.

1821 Greek War of Independence begins.

1830 Greek independence established by the London Protocol.

1859 Wallachia and Moldavia united under one prince; renamed Romania in 1862.

1864 Ionian Islands ceded to Greece.

1867 Serbia gains full independence; established as a kingdom in 1882.

1878 After Russo-Turkish War, Bulgaria becomes autonomous under Ottoman overlordship. Bosnia and Herzegovina occupied by Austria-Hungary.

1881 Thessaly ceded to Greece.

1898 Crete becomes formally autonomous under Ottoman suzerainty.

1903 Ilinden uprising in Macedonia.

1908 Bulgaria declares independence from Ottoman Empire.

1912 Dodecanese islands (except Kastellorizo) occupied by Italy.

1912-13 Balkan Wars. Greece gains Crete, Epirus, Macedonia and Western Thrace.

1912 Albania declares independence from Ottoman Empire; established by treaty in 1913.

1914 A Serbian nationalist assassinates Austrian Archduke in Sarajevo, leading to Austrian invasion and hence to World War I.

1918 After World War I, the Austro-Hungarian empire is dissolved.

Former Austro-Hungarian territory of Transylvania is united with Romania.

Former Austro-Hungarian territories of Croatia, Slovenia and Bosnia and Herzegovina join Serbia to form the Kingdom of Serbs, Croats and Slovenes (renamed Yugoslavia in 1929).

1919–22 Greek-Turkish war.

1922 Defeat of Greek Army in Asia Minor. Asia Minor Greeks become refugees.

1923 Ottoman Empire abolished. Republic of Turkey established. Treaty of Lausanne enforces exchange of populations between Greece and Turkey.

Kastellorizo added to Italian-occupied Dodecanese.

1939–43 Albania occupied by Italy; from 1943 by Germany.

1939–45 World War II. Bulgaria joins German side, occupies much of northern Greece.

1941 Germany and allies occupy Yugoslavia and Greece.

1945 on: Albania, Bulgaria, Yugoslavia and Romania become single-party socialist states and part of the eastern European bloc of Soviet allies.

1946 New constitution establishes Federal People's Republic of Yugoslavia.

1946-49 Civil War in Greece ends with defeat of leftist forces.

1947 Dodecanese islands formally united with Greece.

1948 Yugoslavia ends its close alliance with the Soviet Union.

1953 on: After Stalin's death, Albania weakens ties with the Soviet Union and develops relations with China.

1967–74 Right-wing military regime in power in Greece.

1989 Socialist government overthrown in Romania.

1989 Campaign for political reform in Bulgaria leads to multi-party elections in 1990 and new constitution in 1991.

1990-91 Former Yugoslav federated states of Slovenia, Croatia, (Yugoslav) Macedonia and Bosnia–Herzegovina become independent; Yugoslavia now consists of Serbia and Montenegro only.

1991 Albania holds multi-party elections.

1992-95 Civil war in Bosnia – Herzegovina leads to formation of federal republic consisting of Republika Srpska and Croat-Muslim federation.

2006 Montenegro becomes independent, thereby ending the Yugoslav federation.

2006 Kosovo proclaims independence from Serbia.

2018 Former Yugoslav Macedonia recognized internationally under the name of North Macedonia.

List of Contributors

Billy Cotsis
Writer, director and documentary film producer.

Professor Nicholas Doumanis
Professor, Illinois Chair in Hellenic Studies, Department of History, University of Illinois-Chicago.

Dr Michael Karadjis
Lecturer, Political and International Relations, University of Western Sydney.

Professor Vrasidas Karalis
Sir Nicholas Laurantus Professor of Modern Greek, University of Sydney.

Eleni Elefterias Kostakidis
Teacher of Modern Greek, PhD candidate, songwriter and children's book author.

Mary Kostakidis
Journalist and former long-term news presenter at the Special Broadcasting Service, Sydney.

George Michelakakis
Artist, writer, radio and print journalist and social commentator.

Jorge Sotirios
Journalist, travel writer and researcher.

Dr Marian Ţuţui
Professor of Film Studies, Hyperion University, Bucharest, Romania.

Dr Helen Vatsikopoulos
Industry Fellow, School of Communication, University of Technology Sydney.

Costa Vertsayias
Solicitor and historian.

Dr Alfred Vincent
Honorary Associate, Modern Greek and Byzantine Studies, University of Sydney.

List of Illustrations, with Sources

1. Solon Lekkas, Lesvos, 1946-2022, singer and stoneworker (from Adela Media)
2. Tereza Kreshova Cingit, Albania, 1949- (from Adela Media)
3. Omer Pobrić, 1945-2021, the "accordian wizard", Sarajevo (from Adela Media)
4. The Balkans (Encyclopedia Britannica, with permission)
5. *Whose Is This Song* (dvd cover)
6. Adela Peeva (from Adela Media)
7. The Melody (Wikimedia Commons)
8. Anton Pann, songwriter, Sliven 1790s – Bucharest 1854 (Wikimedia Commons)
9. Poster for film *Kâtip* (1968) starring Zeki Müren (CineMaterial.com)
10. Draga Spasić as Koštana, 1914 (Wikimedia Commons)
11. The Manakia brothers, Ienache and Milton (Wikimedia Commons)
12. Lake Prespa, shared by Greece, Albania and North Macedonia (photo: Helen Vatsikopoulos)
13. *Graffiti over Marble* by Jorge Sotirios, front cover
14. Rigas Velestinlis (Pheraios), 1757-1798, by Damianos Kyriazis, Benaki Museum (Wikimedia Commons)
15. St George Rotunda church, Sofia (formerly Roman baths, 4th century), by teodor pk (Wikimedia Commons, Creative Commons Attribution 2.0 Generic license)

www.ingramcontent.com/pod-product-compliance
Lightning Source LLC
Chambersburg PA
CBHW042047290426
44109CB00006B/130